1 *and*

for

EVERYONE

OLD TESTAMENT FOR EVERYONE
John Goldingay

1 *and* 2 SAMUEL
for
EVERYONE

JOHN
GOLDINGAY

WESTMINSTER
JOHN KNOX PRESS
LOUISVILLE • KENTUCKY

First published in the United States of America in 2011 by
Westminster John Knox Press
100 Witherspoon Street
Louisville, KY 40202

First published in Great Britain in 2011 by
Society for Promoting Christian Knowledge
36 Causton Street
London SW1P 4ST

13 14 15 16 17 18 19 20—10 9 8 7 6 5 4 3

Unless otherwise indicated, Scripture quotations are the author's own translation.

Maps are © Karla Bohmbach and are used by permission.

Cover design by Lisa Buckley
Cover art: © istockphoto.com

Library of Congress Cataloging–in–Publication Data

Goldingay, John.
    1 and 2 Samuel for everyone : a theological commentary on the Bible /
John Goldingay.
        p. cm. — (The Old Testament for everyone)
    ISBN 978-0-664-23379-2 (alk. paper)
    1. Bible. O.T. Samuel—Commentaries.   I. Title.
    BS1325.53.G66   2011
    222'.4077—dc22

                                                    2010033597

⊗ The paper used in this publication meets the minimum requirements of the American National Standard for Information Sciences—Permanence of Paper for Printed Library Materials, ANSI Z39.48-1992.

Most Westminster John Knox Press books are available at special quantity discounts when purchased in bulk by corporations, organizations, and special-interest groups. For more information, please e-mail SpecialSales@wjkbooks.com.

CONTENTS

CONTENTS

CONTENTS

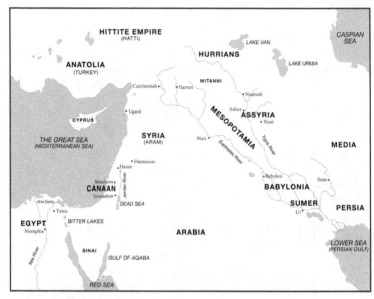

© *Karla Bohmbach*

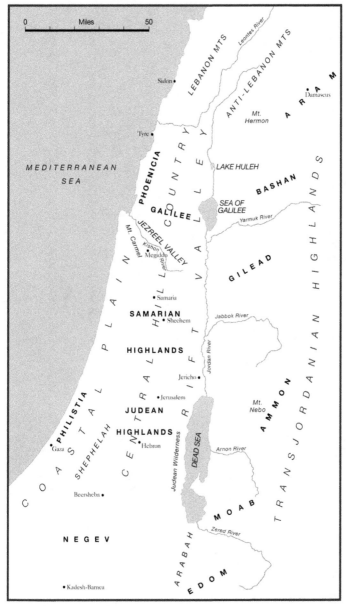

0   Miles   50

Leontes River

LEBANON MTS

ANTI-LEBANON MTS

Sidon •

Mt. Hermon

• Damascus

A R A M

Tyre •

PHOENICIA

MEDITERRANEAN SEA

LAKE HULEH

BASHAN

GALILEE

SEA OF GALILEE

Yarmuk River

Mt. Carmel

JEZREEL VALLEY

Kishon River

Megiddo

GILEAD

• Samaria

SAMARIAN

• Shechem

Jabbok River

HIGHLANDS

Jordan River

Jericho •

AMMON

• Jerusalem

Mt. Nebo

JUDEAN

HIGHLANDS

DEAD SEA

• Hebron

Judean Wilderness

Arnon River

PHILISTIA

SHEPHELAH

• Gaza

TRANSJORDANIAN HIGHLANDS

COASTAL PLAIN

CENTRAL HILL COUNTRY

RIFT VALLEY

Beersheba •

MOAB

NEGEV

ARABAH

Zered River

EDOM

• Kadesh-Barnea

© *Karla Bohmbach*

ix

ACKNOWLEDGMENTS

The translation at the beginning of each chapter (and in other biblical quotations) is my own. I have stuck closer to the Hebrew than modern translations often do when they are designed for reading in church so that you can see more precisely what the text says. Thus although I myself prefer to use gender-inclusive language, I have let the translation stay gendered if inclusivizing it would make it unclear whether the text was talking in the singular or plural—in other words, the translation often uses "he" where in my own writing I would say "they" or "he or she." Sometimes I have added words to make the meaning clear, and I have put these words in square brackets. Space confines do not allow for including the whole of the biblical text in this volume; where there is insufficient room for the entire text, I make some general comments on the material I have had to omit. At the end of the book is a glossary of some terms that recur in the text (such as geographical, historical, and theological expressions). In each chapter (though not in the introduction) these terms are highlighted in **bold** the first time they occur.

The stories that follow the translation often concern my friends as well as my family. While none are made up, they are sometimes heavily disguised in order to be fair to people. Sometimes I have disguised them so well that when I came to read the stories again, I was not sure at first who they were describing. My wife Ann appears in a number of them. A few months before I started writing this book, she died after negotiating with multiple sclerosis for forty-three years. Our shared dealings with her illness and disability over these years contribute to everything I write, in ways you will be able to see but also in ways that are less obvious. I thank God for her, and I am glad for her sake though not for mine that she can now sleep till resurrection day.

ACKNOWLEDGMENTS

I am grateful to Matt Sousa for reading through the manuscript and pointing out things I needed to correct or clarify and to Tom Bennett for checking the proofs.

INTRODUCTION

As far as Jesus and the New Testament writers were concerned, the Jewish Scriptures that Christians call the "Old Testament" *were* the Scriptures. In saying that, I cut corners a bit, as the New Testament never gives us a list of these Scriptures, but the body of writings that the Jewish people accept is as near as we can get to identifying the collection that Jesus and the New Testament writers would have worked with. The church also came to accept some extra books, the "Apocrypha" (see the glossary) or "deutero-canonical writings," but for the purposes of this series that seeks to expound the "Old Testament for Everyone," by the "Old Testament" we mean the Scriptures accepted by the Jewish community.

They were not "old" in the sense of antiquated or out-of-date; I sometimes like to refer to them as the First Testament rather than the Old Testament to make that point. For Jesus and the New Testament writers, they were a living resource for understanding God, God's ways in the world, and God's ways with us. They were "useful for teaching, for reproof, for correction, and for training in righteousness, so that the person who belongs to God can be proficient, equipped for every good work" (2 Timothy 3:16–17). They were for everyone, in fact. So it's strange that Christians don't read them very much. My aim in these volumes is to help you do that.

My hesitation is that you may read me instead of the Scriptures. Don't do that. I like the fact that this series includes much of the biblical text. Don't skip over it. In the end, that's the bit that matters.

An Outline of the Old Testament

The Jewish community often refers to these Scriptures as the Torah, the Prophets, and the Writings. While the Christian Old

Testament comprises the same books, it has them in a different order:

> Genesis to Kings: A story that runs from the creation of the world to the exile of Judahites to Babylon
>
> Chronicles to Esther: A second version of this story, continuing it into the years after the exile
>
> Job, Psalms, Proverbs, Ecclesiastes, Song of Songs: Some poetic books
>
> Isaiah to Malachi: The teaching of some prophets

Here is an outline of the history that lies at the background of the books (I give no dates for events in Genesis, which involves too much guesswork).

1200s	Moses, the exodus, Joshua
1100s	The "judges"
1000s	Saul, David
900s	Solomon; the nation splits into two, Ephraim and Judah
800s	Elijah, Elisha
700s	Amos, Hosea, Isaiah, Micah; Assyria the superpower; the fall of Ephraim
600s	Jeremiah, King Josiah; Babylon the superpower
500s	Ezekiel; the fall of Judah; Persia the superpower; Judahites free to return home
400s	Ezra, Nehemiah
300s	Greece the superpower
200s	Syria and Egypt, the regional powers pulling Judah one way or the other
100s	Judah's rebellion against Syrian power and gain of independence
000s	Rome the superpower

First and Second Samuel

These two books are thus part of the huge narrative that extends from Genesis to 1 and 2 Kings, and they bring that narrative to its second great climax. Its first climax is the Israelites' escape from Egypt, their time at Sinai, and their arrival in Canaan. Its second climax is the reign of David, during which Israel becomes not only a free people in its own land but a successful nation and a significant player on the international scene in its region. In between these two climaxes is the increasingly gloomy narrative of the book of Judges, which ends up with some horrifying stories that reflect how things are when all the people do what is right in their own eyes because there is no king in Israel (as Judges itself puts it). Judges thus prepares the way for the story of how Israel comes to have kings. The idyllic story of Ruth also prepares the way in another sense. As well as providing a welcome contrast to those stories in Judges it turns out to relate something of David's family history; Ruth is David's great-grandmother. By implication, having kings who can exercise some moral leadership makes it possible for the people to turn their backs on the social and moral chaos of the Judges period, and 1 and 2 Samuel tell no stories to rival the horrific nature of the ones in Judges. Yet their narrative does deconstruct, because in their own way the stories of the first two kings, Saul and David, portray them, too, as people who do what is right in their own eyes. Being the king makes it easier to do so. You could say that 1 and 2 Samuel are stories about men behaving badly. Saul and David are not the only men in the books who do so, but they take a lead in doing so.

First Samuel is the story of Saul's reign, and Second Samuel, the story of David's reign. The early chapters of 1 Samuel relate the background to Saul's becoming king, in which the prophet Samuel plays a key role (so he gives his name to the books). The middle chapters relate how Saul reached the position of king, had one or two great achievements, but then saw things immediately begin to fall apart. Soon God has David anointed as Saul's successor, and the latter chapters of the book relate the ongoing conflict between Saul and David as Saul tries to hold onto his throne and David tries to hold onto his life.

Second Samuel follows a similar plot line. The opening chapters relate how David becomes king, the central chapters tell of his great achievements and of God's covenantal commitment to him, but they too relate how things immediately begin to fall apart. The latter part of the book tells of the conflicts within his family, and it leaves us uncertain what will happen next. Like other "books" within Genesis to 2 Kings, the narrative as a whole thus reaches no conclusion but ends with a cliffhanger that makes the reader turn over the page into 1 Kings to find out what follows.

As part of the great narrative running from Genesis to 2 Kings, these two books must have come into existence after the last event they refer to, the fall of Jerusalem and the transportation of many people from Judah to Babylon in the sixth century BC. We don't have any unequivocal evidence to indicate whether they were written then or a bit later, in the Persian period. They incorporate older traditions and were hardly written from scratch at that stage, and the version that was incorporated in the Scriptures may be a kind of second edition of a narrative originally written decades earlier, but scholarly theories about this change. Really we simply lack the evidence to decide when the books were written, but this doesn't make a lot of difference to our being able to appreciate their story and see what God would have wanted Israel to learn from it.

Never again until Judah gained independence in the second century BC did the people have kings of their own. In the context of the decades and centuries after the fall of Jerusalem, other parts of the Old Testament suggest that people could be equivocal about the idea of having kings. On one hand, 1 and 2 Samuel tell of the way God was involved in appointing them and tell of God's making unequivocal covenant commitments to David and his successors. On the other, the books tell of how having kings also compromises the idea that God is Israel's king, and of how the actual kings are people characterized at least as much by human willfulness as by submission to God's expectations of us as human beings and as leaders. In the context of the exile and afterward, they both encourage Israel to expect that God will still fulfill the covenant commitment to David and also warn Israel (and anyone who might find himself on the throne in fulfillment of the promise) to recognize that kings always have feet of clay.

1 SAMUEL 1:1-8

How Not to Display Accurate Empathy I

[1]There was certain man from Ramathaim of the Zuphites from the mountains of Ephraim, named Elkanah, son of Tohu, son of Zuph, an Ephraimite. [2]He had two wives. The name of one was Hannah; the name of the other was Peninnah. Peninnah had children, but Hannah had no children. [3]This man used to go up from his city year by year to bow down and offer sacrifice to Yahweh Armies in Shiloh. The two sons of Eli, Hophni and Phinehas, were priests to Yahweh there. [4]On the day when Elkanah sacrificed, he would give portions to his wife Peninnah and all her sons and daughters, [5]and to Hannah he would give a double portion because he loved Hannah, whereas Yahweh had closed her womb. [6]Her rival would provoke her greatly to make her fret because Yahweh had closed up her womb. [7]So she would do, year after year. As often as she went up to Yahweh's house, she would provoke [Hannah] thus, and she would weep and not eat. [8]Her husband Elkanah said to her, "Hannah, why do you weep, why do you not eat, why is your spirit sad? Am I not better for you than ten sons?"

I don't very often shout out loud when I read an e-mail, but I did so a few weeks ago when a message came from a friend of mine who had returned to a country in Asia two or three years ago. She and her husband had been longing to have children, but she had been unable to conceive, and it had begun to seem that she never would. It seemed a shame not least because she is one of the most loving and caring people I know; I could imagine what a great mother she would be. I know more than one lovely loving couple who for different reasons don't want to have children but who (I suspect) will come to be loving parents if it happens, but they don't feel incomplete without having a baby. This other couple was very keen to do so. They had got a dog, which can sometimes be a way of making up a little for the spouse or baby that it seems you are not going to have. Then the e-mail came saying she was two months pregnant! So I shouted out loud. She is now four or five months along, so it looks as if it will all work out fine.

Hannah was more like this couple than those other two couples who have no great desire to have children. Deeply longing to have children is often thought to be a cultural thing. In a traditional culture, a woman's womanhood can seem to be tied to having children. If you don't have children, you are not complete as a woman. Yet a woman in the West can also be deeply grieved at not being able to conceive; it does correspond to an aspect of the way womanhood was created and to female physiology (I say "womanhood" to avoid giving the impression that every woman ought to have children).

It was probably really important to Elkanah, too. At one level that would be because he and Hannah need to have children to join with Elkanah in running the farm. Further, to whom is he going to pass on the family land if they have no children? But it need not be a merely practical issue. I know men who have felt incomplete because they do not have children either because they were infertile or because their wives were.

Quite likely a need and desire for children is the logic behind Elkanah's having two wives, as was the case when the infertile Sarah encouraged Abraham to take Hagar as a second wife (see Genesis 16). Elkanah will hope that Peninnah can bear children for Elkanah. Indeed she can. Actually she seems to drop them as easily as cooking lunch. Each year when the family goes to Shiloh for the festival, it seems that there is an extra baby to thank God for. Then what seemed to be a solution turns out also to be a problem. The situation again parallels the one that obtained with Abraham, Sarah, and Hagar. Encouraging Abraham to marry Hagar seemed a good idea in theory, but Sarah feels very different when Hagar is actually pregnant. Elkanah's taking Peninnah as a second wife might have seemed a good idea in theory, but Hannah feels different when Peninnah gives birth to baby after baby. In effect Hagar became a provocation to Sarah, and Peninnah becomes a provocation to Hannah. Maybe Peninnah did very little deliberately to provoke Hannah. Neither Hagar nor Peninnah would have needed to do anything to be provocative except be pregnant.

So Elkanah finds himself living with permanent tension in the household and with deep depression in the soul of the woman he loved first and best. The poor man does his best to handle the situation, but we guys are clueless about understanding women. "Am I not better to you than ten sons?" Actually,

Elkanah, no. Don't apply a Band-Aid to the wound. Get her to talk about it some more.

The order of the books in the Hebrew Bible is different from the order in the English Bible. In the Hebrew Bible, 1 Samuel follows directly on Judges (Ruth comes later). It's then suggestive to be reading this story as the beginning of the next stage in Israel's history following on Judges. When we finish reading Judges, we have a nasty taste in our mouths. The stories have become more and more troublesome as people are more and more doing "what is right in their own eyes," which isn't right in the eyes of any normal person. First Samuel starts by telling us about a particular family, as several of the stories in Judges do, and the family story it tells is one that begins with heartache and anguish, yet it will be a story with a happy ending and one that makes us want to read on rather than making us want to stop.

In particular, the sanctuary at Shiloh was the location of the last of the unsavory stories in Judges, whereas here Shiloh is the place where Hannah will get her prayers answered. Admittedly, it will transpire that Eli, Hophni, and Phinehas leave a lot to be desired as priests; but the birth of Hannah's son will also mean that God is onto that. Shiloh is located in the south of the mountains of **Ephraim** and thus relatively central for the clans who live on the main mountain chain of **Judah** and Ephraim. We will learn in chapter 2 that the **covenant chest** was at Shiloh at this time—it seems to have moved around from one place to another from time to time, for reasons we do not know. Its presence there would make Shiloh the natural place for one of the pilgrimage festivals that Israel held each year.

The **Torah** speaks of all Israel appearing before God three times a year for such festivals, but for most families it wouldn't be very practical to abandon the farm for two or three weeks and make the journey to the central sanctuary in that way. Elkanah's habit involves something more practical. Ramathaim (Arimathea in the New Testament, where the man who provided a tomb for Jesus was from) is in the lowlands not so far from Shiloh; the chapter later calls the location of the family home "Ramah," which rather suggests that *this* Ramathaim is another name for Ramah, even nearer Shiloh, only a day's journey south. So Elkanah took the family there once a year.

This would likely be the fall pilgrimage festival, the most practical time to leave the farm because the harvest was now over and the work of the new agricultural year had not yet begun. So people would be giving thanks for the past year (hopefully) and seeking God's blessing for the new year. In addition, they would be reminding themselves of the way **Yahweh Armies** had brought them out of Egypt and brought them to their own land, and they would be living in bivouacs for the festival (there were no motels), reliving how things had been on that journey from Egypt to **Canaan**; hence the name of the festival, Sukkot (bivouacs or shelters or booths or "tabernacles").

The sacrifices to which the story refers will be fellowship sacrifices, not burnt offerings (the whole of which were given to God) and not sacrifices designed to deal with offenses. When you offered a fellowship sacrifice, some went to God (that is, it got burnt up, as happened with the entirety of a burnt offering), but some was shared by the people who made the offering. So it was a barbecue in which God and the family shared. One of the priests would handle the technical side to the sacrifice, including the sprinkling of the animal's blood on the **altar** and the burning of the parts that went to God. Elkanah as the head of the family that brought the offering would then share round the cuts with all the members of the family and make sure everyone got their fair share. Except that he gave a double share to Hannah as a mark of his love for her, to make up a bit for the fact that she has no children. Maybe that might work with a guy, who can't get enough steak, but it doesn't work with Hannah.

We'll look at the idea of God's closing the womb when we come to verses 20–28.

1 SAMUEL 1:9–11

Sour Hour of Prayer

9After they had eaten and drunk at Shiloh, Hannah got up. The priest Eli was sitting on the seat by the doorpost of Yahweh's palace. 10[Hannah] was embittered in spirit. She made a plea to Yahweh and wept profusely, 11but made a promise. She said, "Yahweh Armies, if you actually look at the affliction of your

servant and are mindful of me, and do not put your servant
out of mind but give your servant a male offspring, I will give
him to Yahweh all the days of his life. No razor will come on
his head."

In his late seventies, my former colleague Lew Smedes wrote a
memoir of his life called *My God and I*, which reaches way back
into his childhood in Michigan in the 1920s and 1930s. The
family had come from the Netherlands and Lew's father died
when he was very small, leaving his mother with four children.
He was told that as the undertakers carried his father's body
out of the house, his mother moaned in her native Frisian, God
is "*zoo zuur* [so sour]." Subsequently, he says, what a hymn
calls "the sweet hour of prayer" was never sweet in their house.
He found himself weeping whenever they met with God as a
family for prayer. Meeting with God seemed to be a sadness
for his mother, too, whether at home or in the church prayer
meeting. He could not understand her prayers in the tongue
she had brought from Europe, but he could recognize the sobs
and tears and heaving. (Many years later, Lew asked her why
she had never married again. She explained that though she
was so tired and alone, she feared that another husband might
not care for her children as she did. He comments that he then
realized how profoundly he had found the love of his heavenly
Father tucked into the love of his earthly mother.)

For Hannah, too, the hour of prayer was initially sour,
though eventually sweet. Presumably she prayed when she was
at home in the village, as other Israelites did, but the occasion
when the family went to Shiloh would be a natural time for
special prayers. We have already seen how the annual festival
was designed to be an occasion of great joy and celebration as
people rejoiced in the harvest that God had given them and
also in the commemoration of God's giving them their freedom and their place in the land, but for Hannah it had become
consistently an occasion when her infertility was driven home
to her. This fact would give extra drive to her pressing her
agenda with God. Further, the sanctuary that is the focus of
the festival is, after all, God's this-worldly dwelling, an earthly
equivalent of God's dwelling in the heavens. It is God's palace;

Hebrew doesn't have a word for "temple" but uses either the word for "house" or the word for "palace," because the temple is the equivalent to a human being's home and thus in particular the equivalent to a king's palace. It is a portal; a place of contact, of interchange, and of movement between earth and heaven; a place from which prayers and praises can naturally reach the heavens and where messages from the heavens can reach the earth. It is thus the place where prayer is especially possible; and for Hannah the pain associated with this annual celebration makes it the place where prayer is necessary, too.

The festival is also an occasion for eating and drinking, and eating and drinking can get out of hand. Thus one reason why Eli would be sitting at the door of the sanctuary would be to guard against people approaching it when they are worse for wear. It was always part of the responsibility of a sanctuary's staff to act as doorkeepers who made sure no one and nothing came into the sanctuary that would defile it. One can imagine that this duty became a bit wearisome, and I get the impression Eli will be glad when all these pilgrims go home and he can get back to a regular routine.

Hannah comes there to the sanctuary bitter in spirit. In other words, she is in a similar state to that of Naomi, just a few pages ago in the English Bible. God let Naomi go through a series of tough experiences that she describes as "bitter"; God has let Hannah's lot be a tough one, and the storyteller knows that the bitterness has entered her own spirit. One might have thought that this would make her hesitant about praying. Maybe she would feel she had no wish to speak to the God who had closed her womb. Or maybe she would feel she needed to get her attitude together before she did so. Fortunately her desperation overcomes any such instincts. There is an old book titled *Prayer* by Ole Hallesby (Minneapolis: Augsburg, 1994; first published 1931) that talks about the way we can regard doubt or anger or bitterness as obstacles to prayer, when actually they are our way into prayer—they are the things we come to talk to God about. Hannah instinctively knew this was so.

She comes before God with a "plea." Like the English word, the Hebrew word has a legal background. In everyday speech it could suggest entering a plea to a court when you have been improperly treated and you want the court to do something about it. That is the nature of praying for oneself (or for someone else). You are assuming the right to come into the heavenly court and urge (demand is almost the word) that it take action on your behalf. That is what Hannah is doing. She has ways of backing up her plea. She addresses **Yahweh Armies**, the God they come to worship at the festival; the title implies that the sovereignty and power they acknowledge on that occasion is significant not just in the context of big military and political events but in the context of an ordinary person's needs. If God is Yahweh Armies, then this power ought to be applied to her life. She weeps profusely. It would be an expression of grief, but it would also be another way of getting God to take notice.

Hannah urges God to look at her. Color magazines at present are running a brave series of advertisements that portray children with cleft palates and such conditions; when you look at a lovely child with such an unfortunate ailment and you know you could meet its need by writing a check, how could you resist? If God looks at Hannah and at the dynamics of her family, how could God resist intervening in her life? She specifically urges God to be mindful of her and not to put her out of mind. The Hebrew words are usually translated *remember* and *forget* but they imply something more deliberate than those English words commonly suggest. In prayer people often ask God not only to look deliberately but to think deliberately, in the conviction that applying the mind to something leads to action, whereas putting something out of mind leads to continuing inaction.

Hannah appeals to her status as a servant. It may seem odd to refer to servanthood as a positive status, but this is the way the Old Testament sees it, especially in connection with prayer. The relationship between a servant and a human master is a mutual one. The servant is committed to the master, and the master, to the servant. I am your servant, Hannah says. Please will you behave in relation to me in the way a master should?

Furthermore she makes a promise. The rules in the **Torah**, the advice in Ecclesiastes, and some of the Old Testament's stories draw people's attention to the fact that making promises is a dangerous business, especially when God is the object of the promises. But Hannah takes the risk. In this case it is a

11

particularly costly promise. In effect Hannah is promising that Samuel will become a "Nazirite," a person dedicated to God whose dedication is expressed in letting his hair grow unusually long. What you do with your hair is a statement in many cultures; it was so for George Washington, John Adams, and Thomas Jefferson, long before it was so for 1960s' hippies. The other elements in such a commitment as these described in Numbers 6 are that you abstain from alcohol and that you avoid contact with anything "taboo" or unclean, as a priest does. The description of a Nazirite in Numbers 6 relates to someone making a temporary vow of this kind; the commitment Hannah is willing for her son to make will be lifelong. Presumably he would have the right to renegotiate it if he chose to; parents cannot impose things on their children in the Old Testament. As far as Hannah is concerned, she is willing to surrender to God the son she so wants.

This element in the story suggests another link with the latter part of Judges, which gives much space to the story of another infertile woman whom God enables to bears a child whom she will devote to God (see Judges 13–16). In that story, God lays down the expectation, whereas here it is Hannah's idea. On the other hand, Samson is not very good at fulfilling the vocation laid on him, which suggests another reason why this kind of promise is a risky business. In contrast, Hannah's child will fulfill the vocation laid on him.

Hannah's promise works.

1 SAMUEL 1:12–19a

How Not to Display Accurate Empathy II

¹²Because she kept on pleading before Yahweh, and Eli was watching her mouth ¹³and Hannah was speaking in her heart (only her lips were quivering, and her voice was not audible), Eli thought she was drunk. ¹⁴Eli said to her, "How long will you behave like a drunk? Put your wine away from you." ¹⁵Hannah replied, "No, sir, I am a tough-spirited woman and I have not drunk wine or liquor. I was pouring myself out before Yahweh. ¹⁶Do not take your servant for a worthless woman, because it

was out of my great tetchiness and provocation that I have been speaking all this time." [17]Eli replied, "Go in peace. The God of Israel: he will grant the request you have made of him." [18]She said, "May your servant find favor in your eyes." The woman went her way and ate, and her face was no longer [bitter]. [19a]They got up early in the morning, bowed down before Yahweh, and went back to their home in Ramah.

A little while ago a woman came to see me to talk about the way her husband was abusing her. It involved some physical abuse; he had hit her once or twice, but the background was not that he was an inherently violent person or a drunkard. The problem was more one of his negative, critical, dismissive attitude to her. The love he had once showed her seemed to have totally disappeared. So she came to ask what she should do. The trouble about the pastoral encounter was that I had in my head some of the things the New Testament says about wives submitting to their husbands and being willing to suffer as Jesus did, and I made two mistakes in my pastoral dealings with her. I failed to take into account the differences between the situation likely presupposed by those New Testament exhortations; and I failed actually to appreciate the dynamics and the pain of the woman's situation. (Fortunately, she was extraordinarily patient with me rather than dismissing me as another abusive man, so that even if the pastoral encounter did her no good, I learned a lot from it.)

You have to be a bit sympathetic with Eli. No doubt the festival gave him a number of occasions when he needed to exercise some discipline as people had rather too good a time in celebrating. Other parts of the Old Testament indicate that Israel knew about alcohol abuse, not least at festivals (Isaiah 5:11–12 is an example). This fact didn't make the Old Testament advocate abstinence, any more than the New Testament does, but it did make it aware of the dangers of alcohol. Eli simply assumes Hannah is guilty of drinking too much. He sees somebody muttering and shuddering but uttering no coherent words: he thinks he knows what her problem is. He doesn't need to ask. To him, coming in a drunken state to the very place where God lives marks out Hannah as obviously a "worthless woman." It is a frightening expression. The word for worthlessness is *belial*, which was later a term for the Devil. It doesn't have that significance in the Old Testament, but one can see why it comes to suggest this. It implies a marked degree of godlessness. It is the kind of word the Old Testament uses to describe people who lead others into worshiping other people's gods or who won't lend to the needy or who want to rape a guest. Ironically and grievously, 1 Samuel will soon use this word to describe Eli's own sons.

Like the woman I described, Hannah is more polite to Eli than he perhaps deserves. Her self-description as tough-spirited is surprising; translations usually assume that the expression means she is deeply troubled, but that is not what the expression usually means. Notwithstanding her sadness at her infertility, she has already presented herself as a tough person. Her embitteredness links with it; her being embittered doesn't mean she is a person you can put down. She has been standing up to the God who has closed her womb more courageously than we are often told it is proper to be to God. It is toughness rather than weakness of spirit that has made her pour herself out to God.

She makes the same point in different words when she describes herself as coming to pray out of her fretfulness as well as her provocation. She is under provocation from Peninnah (whether Peninnah intends it or not). Is she also under provocation from God, who has closed her womb? And she is tetchy. Again, translations usually describe her as anguished, but the Hebrew word usually means fretful in the sense of offended and angry. She is now illustrating how being angry or tetchy is not an obstacle to prayer. It doesn't make prayer impossible; it makes it possible and necessary, and it gives prayer energy and persistence ("all this time"). It means you don't just go through the motions of prayer, and you keep asking until you get a response.

Eli desperately tries to regroup and remember what they told him in seminary about dealing with distraught and angry women, and he manages to get his act together. Various stories in the Old Testament illustrate the dynamics of prayer in this connection, and this is an example. As the word *pleading* suggests, when the Old Testament refers to prayer it doesn't have in mind something like meditation or reflection, something designed to change us. Prayer is something more like the relationship of a child to its father or mother. When a child is hurt or scared, it comes to its parents to get them to do something about it, and (hopefully) they assure the child that they will. Eli knows that his job as a pastor in this connection is to bring God's response to Hannah's prayer. God's response to prayers in the Old Testament is not always positive, like the response of parents to their children's pleas. There will be occasions when Eli's initial response in which he rebukes Hannah is the right one. Now he sees that this is not such an occasion and brings God's true response.

We do not know how he perceived what the right response was. That it was the right response is indicated by what follows. Why it was the right response will also emerge in due course: while not every infertile woman who casts herself on God in the way Hannah is doing gets that response, God intends to do something special for Hannah that relates to doing something for Israel in connection with the fulfillment of God's ultimate purpose (even for you and me). Hannah is fortunate to be someone whose need will become part of the fulfillment of that purpose.

The right response on Eli's part begins, "Go in **peace**." Now, peace of heart is one thing Hannah does not have. She is torn apart by her infertility and its consequences in her relationships with her family and the wider community. But a declaration about peace in the Old Testament does not usually relate to peace of heart. Typically, the Old Testament deals with the same ideas as Christian faith does, but it often uses different words. When it wants to wish someone peace in our sense, it is inclined to say something like "Don't be afraid." Eli's words about peace have more far-reaching implications. *Peace* denotes well-being, fullness of life. For someone in Hannah's position, it is impossible to imagine well-being and fullness of life without that idea implying that she should be a mother. Eli's blessing implies that God will grant her prayer and not merely make her feel better about being childless. Further, maybe it's significant that Eli's expression is more literally "Go into peace." At the moment things are not going well in her life, but they are destined to do so.

The continuation of Eli's words makes that explicit: "The God of Israel: he will grant the request you have made of him." Eli emphasizes who the God is that he and Hannah are talking about. She had addressed God as **"Yahweh Armies."** While the second word points to the power of God, the first points to God's being the one revealed by name to Israel. Eli picks up that fact about Yahweh, who is "the God of Israel." It means God is committed to an Israelite like Hannah. The title will have further significance in light of what we will discover about the significance for Israel of the son she will bear. Translations usually have "The God of Israel: may he grant the request you have made of him." In other words, Eli can be understood either as making a declaration about what *will* happen or one about what *needs to* happen. If that latter way of understanding it is right, we should not infer that Eli is merely saying, "I hope he answers your prayer." That would be an anticlimax, and it would not make sense after encouraging Hannah to go in peace or into peace. In his wish he is rather identifying himself with what he perceives God intends.

It is also implicit in Hannah's reaction to Eli's words that she understands him to have spoken of something God will indeed do: she goes her way and eats with a face that is no longer downcast. In one sense the situation has not changed at all from what it was when she went to the sanctuary. She is no more pregnant than she was before. But she now knows she is going to get pregnant. Her experience and her reaction reflect the understanding of answers to prayer that appears in the Psalms. One might call these "answer-to-prayer stage one" and "answer-to-prayer stage two." Stage one is God saying, "Yes, I have heard; I will do that"; stage two is God actually doing it. Simply receiving the first stage of the answer transforms Hannah.

1 SAMUEL 1:19b–24

It Takes a Miracle

[19b]Elkanah slept with his wife Hannah, and Yahweh was mindful of her. [20]At the end of the year Hannah had gotten pregnant, and she gave birth to a son. She named him Samuel [and said], because "I asked for him from Yahweh." [21]The husband Elkanah and all his household went up to offer Yahweh the yearly sacrifice and [to fulfill] his promise, [22]but Hannah did not go up

"Because" [she said to her husband], "when the boy is weaned I will bring him. We will see Yahweh's face, and he will stay there permanently." ²³Her husband Elkanah said to her, "Do what seems good in your eyes; stay until you have weaned him. Only may Yahweh fulfill his word." So the wife stayed and nursed her son until she had weaned him, ²⁴and went up with him when she had weaned him, with a three-year-old bull, one measure of flour, and a skin of wine. She brought him to Yahweh's house at Shiloh when he was a boy.

In *Joshua, Judges, and Ruth for Everyone* I referred to one of my students who spent last year preparing to get married but also developed increasingly intense headaches. A month or so before her wedding date she had an MRI that suggested a brain tumor. The doctors wanted to operate on it as soon as possible, though it was not clear what the result would be; she might still end up disabled in some way. Her family and friends urged the couple to bring the wedding forward, prayed for her incessantly, and helped them make the wedding happen over just one week. As she went for the surgery, her mother commented, "There is so much prayer going on, this tumor hasn't a chance." It was a fine comment, but of course life doesn't work like that. Yet when the surgeons opened up her daughter's head, they could find no tumor, only a messy blob. So they removed that, and sewed her up, and started scratching their own heads (meanwhile, she stopped having headaches). Was it a miracle? Was it a weird infection? Was it a virus she caught when scuba diving in Africa? The next theory was that it was the result of a slight hole in her heart that she has had since she was a baby, but then they couldn't find much wrong with her heart. How does one think about the relationship between the way we understand things medically and the way we understand God's involvement when something extraordinary happens?

We have noted how it is suggestive that 1 Samuel follows on Judges in the Hebrew Bible, but that the order of books in the English Bible follows the order in the Greek translation of the Old Testament. Here it is suggestive that 1 Samuel follows on Ruth and thus that Hannah's story follows directly on Ruth's story. They are two women whose experience of marriage initially brings them pain: Ruth grieves the loss of her husband, and Hannah grieves her inability to have children. They are then two women who find healing and restoration.

A difference is that in Ruth's story both the loss and the healing come about without God's intervention; at least, her story does not say that God killed her husband, nor does it say that God provided her with her new husband. Naomi does in effect say both those things, and at some level God is responsible for both events because God is at some level responsible for everything; but the way the Old Testament speaks suggests the assumption that God bears more direct responsibility for some events than for others. Some events come about because God takes an initiative rather than simply letting things work out.

In contrast, 1 Samuel does say that God closed Hannah's womb, and it now links her being able to have a baby to God's being mindful of her in the way she asked (we looked at the idea of God being mindful in connection with 1:9–11). My guess is that if you were able to look empirically (scientifically) at what happens to the two women, you would hardly find a difference between their experiences. If you had Hannah's medical records, you would find that her inability to conceive had some physiological or anatomical reason and that her eventual conceiving was rather a surprise to the doctors. They would then say that sometimes "miracles" (by which they would mean inexplicable events) happen, as they might say about that student of mine.

There are some events in Scripture that require explanation in terms of divine intervention. If we had all the scientific evidence in the world, we would not be able to account for the creation of the world or the resurrection of Jesus (not merely his resuscitation but his beginning a transformed kind of renewed life). But the Scriptures recognize that most of the time life works out without divine intervention and that God works via processes of cause and effect. So Ruth's story tells of no interventions, yet it implies the assumption that God achieved something special by means of the series of ordinary events, coincidences, acts of human commitment, and withholding of human commitment that it relates. Hannah's story attributes her infertility to God, and it then attributes her pregnancy to God.

Well, Elkanah was involved, too. Presumably she told him what had happened between her and Eli; the later exchanges between Hannah and Elkanah imply she had done so. I can hardly begin to imagine what it was then like when they made love over the next weeks. The timescale is admittedly a bit unclear. The story refers to the end of the year. On the assumption that the festival is the one that takes place in the fall at the end of the agricultural year, the end of the year will mean a year after the visit to Shiloh. The obvious way to understand the story then suggests that it was a year before Hannah became pregnant. Again, what on earth would it have been like to live for a year with those words from Eli, to live for a year with the answer-to-prayer stage one but not to see stage two? A less obvious way to understand the story is to reckon that Samuel was actually born a year later, though in a way that makes little difference; Hannah still has to wait several months before she gets any evidence that stage two is happening.

When answer-to-prayer stage two does come, she names her son Samuel and associates it with the fact that she asked for him from God. Now, it is almost the rule rather than the exception that comments on people's names in the Old Testament don't relate to what we would have thought the name actually meant (for instance, "Abraham" doesn't actually mean "father of a multitude," as Genesis 17 might make you think). The comments the Old Testament offers often suggest linkages you could make if you exercised a bit of imagination. We don't actually know what (if anything) the name Samuel might "mean" to someone in Israel, though the last syllable would make you think it was something to do with God, because *el* is a Hebrew word for God. But the meaning of the actual name Samuel is unclear. What is clear is that it doesn't mean "asked of God." If there were a name that means "asked," it is the name Saul; this is exactly what the name Saul means. Maybe Israelites would notice this as they listened to the story, and maybe they would make a link with the fact that Samuel's ministry will be one that issues in the designation of Saul as Israel's first king, the process that opens up the possibility of moving on from the enormities that characterized the stories in Judges when "there was no king in Israel." In other words, Hannah's prayer is one whose answer results in Saul.

Presumably the year Elkanah went up for the festival and Hannah stayed at home was yet another year later, when Samuel was a year old. In the modern West that would be old enough for him to have been weaned, but weaning happens much later in traditional societies, so the time when Hannah takes Samuel to the festival will be when he is no longer a baby but a boy. We don't know what promise Elkanah was fulfilling at the festival that year, but the idea of promising to give something to God in the form of a sacrifice and then fulfilling it is a familiar one. It's one classic reason given in Leviticus 7 for offering the "fellowship sacrifices" referred to in the opening verses of 1 Samuel. In other words, maybe the implication is that every year there would be reason during the year for Elkanah, too, to be pleading with God about something and promising to express his thanks in this concrete, costly way if God answered, and each year he did so. It would not be surprising if Hannah's infertility and the conflict it generated in his own household was something he prayed quite a bit about and if his going up to the festival on the first occasion after Samuel's birth therefore gave him special cause for rejoicing and gratefulness.

The **Torah** speaks of the festivals as occasions when people go to "appear before" God, but Hannah uses a bolder expression. They are occasions when people go to "see God" (it's the same Hebrew verb, but a different form of it). No doubt she doesn't expect physically to see God; she is too wise a woman to reckon that God is bodily and visible. She will think of seeing God in not such a different way to the way Christians do when we speak of seeing God with the eyes of our hearts, as we might put it. Hannah knows that when you go to God's house, you really meet with God.

1 SAMUEL 1:25–2:10

On Giving Up Your Son

[25][Hannah] slaughtered the bull and brought the boy to Eli. [26]She said, "Excuse me, sir, as surely as you live, I am the woman who stood with you here to make my plea to Yahweh. [27]It was for this boy that I pleaded, and Yahweh gave me what I asked

of him. [28]I myself in turn hereby give him to Yahweh; for all the days that he lives he is given to Yahweh."
He bowed down there before Yahweh, [2:1]and Hannah prayed:

"My spirit exults in Yahweh, my horn lifts up high
   in Yahweh.
My mouth opens wide at my enemies, because I rejoice in
   your deliverance.
[2] There is no holy one like Yahweh, because there is no one
   apart from you; there is no crag like our God.
[3] Don't utter lofty speech, lofty speech, any more, [nor]
   should unrestrained speech come out of your mouth.
Because Yahweh is a God who knows; by him actions are
   weighed.
[4] The bows of warriors are broken, but people who were
   falling put on strength.
[5] People who were full hire themselves out for bread, but the
   hungry stop [being hungry].
The infertile woman bears seven, but the woman with
   many children is forlorn.
[6] Yahweh is one who puts to death and brings to life, sends
   down to Sheol and brings up.
[7] Yahweh is one who makes poor and makes rich, casts down
   and also lifts up.
[8] He is one who raises the poor from the dirt, lifts up the
   needy from the trash heap,
Seating them with the important people and allocating
   them seats of honor.
Because the pillars of the earth belong to Yahweh; he set the
   world upon them.
[9] He guards the feet of the people committed to him, but the
   faithless go silent into the darkness.
Because it is not by might that a person prevails;
   [10]Yahweh—his opponents will shatter.
He will thunder against them in the heavens; Yahweh will
   exercise authority over the ends of the earth.
He will give strength to his king, lift up the horn of
   his anointed."

As I write, two anniversaries have recently passed. Just over thirty years ago the Shah of Iran was ousted and the Ayatollah

Khomeini returned from exile to become the "Leader" of Iran, a more powerful position than that of the president. Eleven years later, Nelson Mandela was released from prison in South Africa on his way to becoming president of that country. Ayatollah Khomeini's return to Iran to assume his position under the new Iranian constitution was greeted by Christians as well as Muslims as a liberative event for the Iranian people; *Time* magazine named him man of the year. Thirty years later, the attitude of Westerners is rather different from what it was when it happened. The freeing of Nelson Mandela similarly seemed a profoundly liberative event for the people of South Africa, and still does so, notwithstanding the problems the country continues to face.

"Yahweh casts down and also lifts up." How far is that true? Did God elevate Khomeini and Mandela? As with closing and opening wombs in the context of family life, in the context of political life there must be a sense in which God has responsibility for all that happens. Yet the Bible also often attributes responsibility to God for particular events in a way that suggests a more direct involvement. God takes an initiative rather than simply letting things work out, and/or there are events that contribute to the fulfillment of God's ongoing purpose and other events that don't have that kind of significance.

In the context of Hannah's story, one initial question is why her song of praise in connection with the birth of her son opens up this issue for us. It is not surprising that she has some praise to offer in light of what God has been doing in her life over the preceding three or four years. One significance of her act of praise is that it brings to its proper closure the interaction between her and God over her infertility. When you have a need or a crisis, the way life with God works is that (a) you bring it to God and urge God to do something about it; you hope that (b) God makes a commitment to you in this connection in what I called "answer-to-prayer stage one," to which (c) you respond with trust and praise; and then (d) God does act, in what I called "answer-to-prayer stage two." That sequence doesn't actually reach completion and closure until (e) you come back to God to give thanks to God, and do so publicly in order that other people join in your praise and have their own trust in God and commitment to God built up. This is an important aspect of the significance of Hannah's visit to the sanctuary.

Her visit thus involves her personal thanksgiving and praise. What God has done for her makes it possible for her to reaffirm, "There is no one apart from you." Yet the vast bulk of her praise is not addressed to God. It speaks about God in the third person. It is addressed to other people (eventually to people like us who read her story). In its nature as address to God, it is thanksgiving, but in its nature as speaking about God, it is testimony. Gratitude for what God has done is not complete until one tells other people about what God has done. Hannah's opening words to Eli thus naturally take the form of words about God, not words to God, and they take the characteristic form of thanksgiving/testimony: they tell her story. "I am the woman who came here to plead with God; I pleaded for a son; and God gave me what I asked." When you have had a prayer answered, you thus recount what God has done. You also go on to point out its implications. You assume it was not just a one-time-only event that says nothing about God's character and characteristic way of acting. You assume it is an indication and confirmation of God's character and characteristic way of acting. This is why it is significant for other people's relationship with God. Paradoxically, it is especially significant for other people for whom God has not acted in the way God has acted for you. Hannah emboldens other infertile women to come to plead with God.

What is surprising in her thanksgiving/testimony is that her praise poem does not obviously relate at all in any direct way to her experience of God's opening her closed womb. It is a stretch even to make a connection via the opening verse about enemies (she has not exactly been **delivered** from Peninnah) or via the poetic line about the infertile woman bearing seven children (though Hannah does bear five more). Her praise relates to the political rather than to the personal and to her people rather than merely to Hannah herself.

The logic to this is that while Samuel's birth is significant for her, he is of much more significance. Samuel is going to be an important figure in Israel in connection with Israel's deliverance from oppression by the **Philistines** and then in the anointing

23

of the king whom God intends to use in the same connection (1 Samuel 7; 9). Hannah's song looks forward to these events. Indeed, it speaks of them as events that have already as good as happened, because Samuel has actually been born. They establish that **Yahweh** is the only one who really deserves the title "God," the crag, the creator, the guardian, the one with power over the entire world.

In other words, Hannah's song is also a prophecy, like Miriam's song in Exodus 15 with its anticipation of Israel's entering the land. Its being a prophecy becomes most explicit in the last line. Lifting up a horn in the way an animal such as a bull does is an image for forceful strength. God will lift up the horn of his anointed. In the context of the story, we don't yet know who Hannah might be referring to, but in a few chapters' time when Samuel has indeed anointed Saul, we will know his identity. When we know about David, the next anointed, and about his much greater achievements, we will realize how far Hannah's prophecy pointed. In speaking of her deliverance from her enemies, she speaks of deliverance from enemies she shares with her people. These enemies would be wise to give up exalting themselves as if they could maintain dominance over her people; they cannot. The economic pressure they put on her people will come to an end. Her people will flourish; its foes will decline.

If Hannah had the faintest clue that her son's birth was of such significance for Israel, it would make the sacrifice she makes at Shiloh more feasible. Her sacrifice involves not only the slaughter of a bull (a costly gift for a family) but the giving up of her son. We may be inclined to wonder how she could do this, but she knows that the meeting of her need relates not merely to her personally but to a much bigger purpose. So she can trust him to Eli and the sanctuary—or rather, to God. His bowing down to God is a sign of his acceptance of his vocation.

In the story that unfolds in 1 Samuel, Yahweh will indeed be the one who puts down kings and raises up kings. Alas, in the long run (as was the case with the elevation of Ayatollah Khomeini and Nelson Mandela) the significance of kings such as Saul and David will be more ambiguous. It will transpire that there is an interaction between divine initiative and human response. It is entirely possible to screw up the initiatives that God sets going. Fortunately God does not give up but thinks of another initiative.

1 SAMUEL 2:11–36

When Ministers Indulge Themselves

[11]So Elkanah went home to Ramah. The boy was ministering to Yahweh in the presence of the priest Eli. [12]But Eli's sons were worthless men; they did not recognize Yahweh. [13]The priests' practice with the people was that when each person offered a sacrifice, the priest's boy would come while the meat was boiling, with a three-pronged fork in his hand. [14]He would thrust it into the pan or kettle or cauldron or pot; all that the fork brought up, the priest would take with it. This is how they would act with all Israel who came there to Shiloh. [15]Further, before they turned the fat into smoke, the priest's boy would come and say to the person making the sacrifice, "Give [me] meat for the priest to roast; he will not accept boiled meat from you, only raw." [16]If the person said to him, "They should really turn the fat into smoke now, then you can take for yourself whatever you fancy," he would say, "No, give it now, or I am taking it by force." [17]The boys' wrongdoing in Yahweh's presence was very great, because these people treated Yahweh's offering with contempt.

[18]Now Samuel was ministering in the presence of Yahweh, a boy girded in a linen ephod. [19]His mother would make a little robe for him and bring it up each year when she went up with her husband to offer the annual sacrifice. [20]Eli would bless Elkanah and his wife and say, "May Yahweh give you offspring from this woman in place of the one she asked for from Yahweh," and they would go to their home. [21]Because Yahweh took note of Hannah, she got pregnant and had three sons and two daughters, but the boy Samuel grew up in Yahweh's presence.

[22]Now Eli was very old. He heard of all that his sons were doing to all Israel and how they were sleeping with the women who served at the entrance of the Meeting Tent. [23]He said to them, "Why do you do such things as these that I hear of, wicked things, from all these people? [24]Don't, my sons, because the account is not good that I hear Yahweh's people passing on. [25]If

25

someone does wrong against another person, God may plead for him, but if someone does wrong against Yahweh, who will enter in a plea for him?" But they would not listen to their father's voice because Yahweh wanted to put them to death. [26]But the boy Samuel was living and growing and making a good impression both with God and with people. [27]A man of God came to Eli and said to him, . . . [30]"Therefore (the oracle of Yahweh, God of Israel), I did say that your household and your father's household would go about [as priests] before me forever, but now (Yahweh's oracle), far be it from me, because the person who honors me I will honor, but the person who despises me will be disdained. . . . [34]This will be a sign for you that will come on your two sons, Hophni and Phinehas: on the same day, the two of them will die. [35]But I will raise up for myself a trustworthy priest. He will act in accordance with my mind and my spirit. I will build a trustworthy household for him. He will go about before my anointed forever. [36]Everyone who is left in your household will come to bow down to him for a payment in silver and a loaf of bread and will say, 'Will you appoint me to one of the priestly tasks so I have some food to eat?'"

Lent has just begun. Just beforehand, over dinner, the members of our Bible study group were wondering what Lenten discipline they might take on. I argued that discipline was better understood as a matter of doing something positive rather than as a matter of giving up something. Then on Ash Wednesday I took part in a symposium in the seminary on "Psychology of, with, and for the Poor," which challenged us all about our commitment to the poor and thus suggested angles on how discipline might involve a positive commitment. As far as I know, the fact that this symposium happened on Ash Wednesday was a coincidence, but it was a nice coincidence. Pastors, and a professor who is also a pastor, have to ask how far our ministry is self-indulgent. I guess most pastors get paid more than many members of their congregations, live in nicer homes, and have better health care.

It makes for uncomfortable reflection alongside the account of Eli's sons. Like kings and politicians, ministers were always a mixed blessing in Israel, as they have been in the church. As with kings, one cause is our human inclination to self-indulgence, which is combined with our being in a position to pander to that inclination. In the case of Eli's sons, there is no suggestion that they led people in worshiping false gods, but they were involved in what Paul will call making our stomach into our god (Philippians 3:19). In effect, then, they did not recognize **Yahweh**. With some irony, the story calls Eli's sons "worthless"; it was the description their father had applied to Hannah when he thought she had been indulging herself at the festival.

One cause of temptation was the fact that priests did receive a share from sacrifices as part of their support. Unlike other people, they could not give themselves to work on a farm so as to provide for themselves and their families, but one of the ways whereby God and the community provided for them was by their having a share in some of the sacrifices. There are rules in Leviticus that prescribe what happens to sacrifices (Leviticus itself did not exist in Eli's day, but there would have been some version of such rules). There were parts that went straight to God and were thus burned up and turned into smoke, as this story notes. There were parts that went to the priests. In the case of fellowship sacrifices of the kind that Elkanah and his family brought when they came to Shiloh, there were parts that were shared by the people who brought the sacrifice, so that they were occasions of fellowship between people and God. The Shiloh priests ignored all those conventions. They just wanted to make sure they got a good meal for themselves, and it was the job of their "boys" (their assistants) to make sure of this. So they treated Yahweh's offering with contempt.

We later learn that this was not all. It is said that there are three spiritual issues that men, and particularly pastors, have to deal with: money, sex, and power. Pastors are more likely to get into a mess in these areas than ordinary people, with more disastrous consequences for themselves and for other people. In a traditional society such as Israel there is no such thing as money, but there are the kind of things we would want to spend money on, things with which we can indulge ourselves, so Eli's sons' behavior in relation to the sacrifices already illustrates that they have a problem with the first and third of that unholy trinity of money, sex, and power. The allusion to their involvement with the women who serve at the sanctuary then

27

illustrates their problem with the second, and with the third again, because of the power differential between the priests and these women. (We don't know the form of the women's service, but there would be many practical duties to be fulfilled at the sanctuary in connection with its offerings.)

There are other scary aspects to the story. One is its ambiguous impression of Eli. He is a mixed-up person. Already we know he both did and did not know how to deal with a woman like Hannah at the sanctuary. He also did and did not know how to deal with his sons. Maybe he and his wife had done their best with them since they were boys, but he is incapable of doing anything with them now. His argument is a profound one: if you do wrong by another human being, God may mediate for you, but who is going to mediate for you if you do wrong by God? Alas, they are too far gone to listen.

That links with another scary aspect to the story. What is the relationship between divine commitment and human obligation? God had said that Eli's line would always be priests. There is no such precise promise in the Old Testament, but connecting some dots in Old Testament genealogies does suggest that Eli could trace his lineage back to Aaron, and the **Torah** does assume that God designated Aaron's descendants as the priestly line in perpetuity. The instructions in Exodus 28–29 for ordaining the first priests make the point; yet very shortly Aaron's two elder sons die for their wrongdoing (Leviticus 10). The promise about the priesthood's standing in perpetuity guarantees that God will not have a random change of mind about this question, but it does not mean our human response to God's promise is redundant. Eli's line is going the same way as Aaron's two elder sons. Further, as many Old Testament and New Testament passages presuppose, there are circumstances in which God gives up on people and determines that there is no alternative to judgment. To someone who repents, God would not say, "I won't forgive you," but sometimes (always?) repentance seems to be a gift God has to offer people, and God can decide to stop offering it and to leave people to the consequences of their actions. Eli will be replaced by a "trustworthy" priest. The next chapter will describe Samuel as "trustworthy," but trustworthy as prophet rather than priest, and in due course the trustworthy priest will be Zadok, senior priest in David's day. (The history of Israel's priesthood is impossible to trace, and one significance of this story may well be that it reflects rivalries over the priesthood and explains why one line lost and another line won.)

This is the context in which Samuel is brought up! Did Hannah know? What chance is there that he will grow up in the proper way, as a "boy" functioning among the other "boys" implicated in the abuses undertaken by Eli's sons? Fortunately Samuel is growing up "in Yahweh's presence" as well as "in Eli's presence."

1 SAMUEL 3:1–4:1a

A Summons, Not a Call

¹So Samuel as a boy was ministering to Yahweh in the presence of Eli, and Yahweh's word was rare at that time; there was no vision spreading about. ²One day Eli was lying down in his place. His eyes had begun to fail; he couldn't see. ³God's lamp had not yet gone out. Samuel was lying down in Yahweh's palace where Yahweh's chest was. ⁴Yahweh called to Samuel. He said, "I'm here," ⁵and ran to Eli and said, "I'm here, because you called me." [Eli] said, "I didn't call. Go back and lie down." So he went and lay down. ⁶Yahweh called yet again, "Samuel," and Samuel got up and went to Eli and said, "I'm here, because you called me." He said, "I didn't call you, son; go back and lie down." ⁷Now Samuel did not yet recognize Yahweh. Yahweh's word had not yet manifested itself to him. ⁸Yahweh again called Samuel, a third time, and he got up, went to Eli, and said, "I'm here, because you called me", and Eli perceived that Yahweh was calling to the boy. ⁹So Eli said to Samuel, "Go and lie down, but if he calls to you, say, 'Speak, Yahweh because your servant is listening.'" So Samuel went and lay down in his place.

¹⁰Yahweh came and stood there, and called as at the other times, "Samuel, Samuel." Samuel said, "Speak, because your servant is listening." ¹¹Yahweh said to Samuel, "Now. I am going to do something in Israel such that everyone who hears it—both his ears will tingle. ¹²That day I will confirm for Eli everything I spoke concerning his household, beginning to end, ¹³when I told him that I am judging his household forever

for the waywardness that he knew about, that his sons were disdaining God and he did not stop them. [14]Therefore I swear concerning Eli's household: if the waywardness of Eli's household ever finds expiation by sacrifice or by offering. . . ."

[15]Samuel lay down there until morning and opened the doors of Yahweh's house. Samuel was afraid to tell Eli the vision, [16]but Eli called Samuel and said, "Samuel, my son." He said, "I'm here." [17]He said, "What was the thing he spoke to you? You won't hide any of it from me. May God do so to you, and may he do more, if you hide from me anything of all that he said to you." [18]So Samuel told him everything and did not hide it from him. [Eli] said, "He is Yahweh. He will do what is good in his eyes."

[19]Samuel grew up. Yahweh was with him and did not allow any of his words to fall to the ground. [20]All Israel from Dan to Beersheba recognized that Samuel was trustworthy as a prophet belonging to Yahweh. [21]Yahweh again appeared at Shiloh, in that Yahweh revealed himself to Samuel with Yahweh's word, [4:1]and Samuel's word came to all Israel.

One of my friends is going through the "discernment process" whereby the Episcopal Church seeks to decide whether she is called to ordained ministry. It involves meetings with a group of people from your local church, with diocesan officials, and with the bishop. Initially, the priest in your own parish is the gatekeeper of the process; if you don't have his or her support, you won't be able to start. At the other end of the process, you may be required to attend a candidacy conference, and in the end, it is the bishop who ordains you who has the final yes or no. In Britain we have a process that works very differently but with the same aim. In both contexts, I have had friends who have gone through the process and been convinced that their priest, or their bishop, or some other people were like Eli. God was calling Samuel, but it took Eli three attempts to recognize that this was going on.

There are ways in which the pattern of Samuel's "call" indeed reappears when people are called to recognized ministry in the church, though the differences are so marked that they seem more significant than the similarities. To begin with, calling is something that applies to prophets rather than priests. In

Israel, you don't need a call to be a priest. It issues from the family you belong to. You could say that Samuel is more like a deacon than a priest in that he has a practical ministry in the sanctuary; he could have that ministry without belonging to the right family, but he still didn't need a vocation. Volunteers could be accepted.

Then there is something odd that has happened over the years to the way we talk in terms of calling and vocation in connection with ministry. Speaking with students often suggests to me that we think of ministry as something that enables us to find fulfillment, as it makes it possible for us to give expression to the gifts God has given us. Discernment thus begins as our seeking to perceive what our gifts are and how we may express them. There's none of this way of thinking in the Old Testament or the New Testament. Samuel is not called because this will be the way he finds fulfillment (neither is Paul). Given that the connotations of the word "call" have changed, we might do better to use the word "summons" rather than "call" to describe what happens to Samuel or Paul. Samuel gets the idea when he recognizes in the middle of the night that his boss has summoned him to do something, so he reports for duty; he just doesn't realize which boss it is. (Paul gets the idea when Jesus grabs him by the scruff of the neck and announces the intention to tell him what he is going to do.) I guess there is nothing wrong with people using their gifts to serve God (I hope I do that). It just has nothing to do with calling.

Samuel is presumably now somewhat older, though he can still be described as a "boy." As in 1:9, the sanctuary is described as **Yahweh's** palace; it is the place where the great King deigns to reside. Samuel sleeps there as a kind of guard until the light that burns there all night goes out at dawn, though maybe the idea of the light not having yet gone out also has a symbolic significance; in Israel and in the sanctuary the light is pretty dim. In the same way, Eli's failing eyesight affects not just his physical sight but his moral and religious insight. He evidently sleeps somewhere else nearby. The presence of the **covenant chest** highlights the importance of this sanctuary as the place that stands for God's covenant relationship with Israel, though it will turn out that this first reference to the chest also draws

31

attention to darkness that is about to fall in the next chapter, when the chest leaves Shiloh, never to return.

Samuel's summons is more or less the beginning of the story of the prophets in Israel. The story has some prehistory; the Old Testament has referred to several people as prophets or as prophesying, but before Samuel "Yahweh's word was rare; there was no vision spreading about." The expressions are a bit odd, but they make the point that prophecy was something occasional. You were not regularly hearing that someone had had a prophetic vision. This is about to change because of another change that is imminent, Israel's instituting a central government. Prophecy will be needed in association with that.

Specifically, God had not yet spoken a prophetic word to Samuel, and thus Samuel did not "recognize" Yahweh. Admittedly that is rather a chilling phrase, given the way it has been used of Eli's sons in 2:12, but Samuel has been growing up in God's presence (2:21), which implies that he has been growing up with a knowledge of God and in commitment to God, but God has not yet spoken to him in the audible way that now happens. An amusing scene thus unfolds. Perhaps Eli is no more to be faulted than Samuel for failing to realize what is going on, though the story may imply that the senior and experienced priest ought to have had more clue, so that his failure again suggests that his problems lie with his religious insight as well as his physical sight. Meanwhile, God waits patiently until the light goes on for Eli. When it does so, Eli at least knows how a person needs to respond after realizing that God is summoning.

As well as emphasizing divine sovereignty rather than human fulfillment, being summoned by God provides the backing for fulfilling an unpleasant task. Our instinct in reading 1 Samuel 3 is to stop after verse 10, "Speak, because your servant is listening," as our instinct in reading Isaiah 6 is to stop after reading "Lord, here am I, send me." In both chapters, it is nice to identify with the process whereby God's call comes, but we would rather not identify with the content of it. Samuel is not stupid when he lies awake all night after God appears to him. Poor Eli has tried to get a grip on his sons, at least recently, but has evidently not tried hard enough or not taken firm enough action when they take no notice of him. There would be things that could avert God's wrath, things such as the sons' changing their ways or Eli's disciplining them, but the Old Testament knows that in the absence of people changing their ways, sacrifices and offerings can't do that. Eli can submit to God's declaration with courage, and he does so, a little like Achan in Joshua 7, but it is too late to change the waywardness that makes God's action necessary.

So God turns Samuel from a bus boy in the sanctuary into someone through whom God speaks to Israel. There is nothing about Samuel that makes this happen. The master just decides that this is the servant he intends to use in this connection.

1 SAMUEL 4:1b–22

The Splendor Is Gone

[1b]Israel went out to meet the Philistines in battle, and camped at Help-stone, while the Philistines camped at Aphek. [2]The Philistines took up battle lines to meet Israel, and the battle spread, but Israel was defeated before the Philistines. They struck down some four thousand men in their lines in the field. [3]The company came to the camp and the Israelite elders said, "Why did Yahweh defeat us today before the Philistines? Let's get Yahweh's covenant chest from Shiloh for ourselves so he will come into our midst and deliver us from the hand of our enemies." [4]So the company sent and carried from there the covenant chest of Yahweh Armies Who Sits [Enthroned] on the Cherubs. Eli's two sons, Hophni and Phinehas, were with the chest there. [5]When Yahweh's covenant chest came into the camp, all Israel gave a great shout, and the earth resounded. [6]The Philistines heard the sound of the shout and said, "What is this sound of a great shout in the Hebrews' camp?" When they knew that Yahweh's chest had come into the camp, [7]the Philistines were afraid, because they said, "God has come into the camp." They said, "Alas for us! Who will rescue us, because nothing like this has happened to us before? [8]Alas for us! Who will rescue us from the hand of these mighty gods? These are the gods that struck down the Egyptians with every kind of blow in the wilderness. [9]Be strong, be men, Philistines, or you will serve the Hebrews as they served you. Be men! Fight!" [10]So

the Philistines fought and the Israelites were defeated and fled, every one, to their tents. The slaughter was very great. Of the Israelites, thirty thousand foot soldiers fell. [11]God's chest was taken, and Eli's two sons, Hophni and Phinehas, died.
[12]A Benjaminite ran from the lines and came to Shiloh that day. His clothes were torn and there was earth on his head. [13]When he came, there—Eli was sitting on a seat by the road, watching, because his spirit was anxious about God's chest. When the man came to tell the news in the city, the whole city cried out. [14]Eli heard the sound of the cry and said, "What is this sound of an uproar?" The man hurried to come and tell Eli. . . . [18]When he mentioned God's chest, [Eli] fell backward from on his seat by the side of the gate. His neck broke and he died, because the man was old and heavy (he had led Israel for forty years). [19]His daughter-in-law, Phinehas's wife, was pregnant and due to give birth. When she heard the report about God's chest being taken and Hophni and her husband being dead, she bowed and gave birth, because her labor pains came over her. [20]As she died, the women attending her spoke. "Don't be afraid, because you have had a son," but she did not answer. She did not pay attention. [21]But she called the boy "Where-is-the-splendor," saying, "The splendor has gone into exile from Israel," in connection with the taking of God's chest, and her father-in-law and her husband. [22]She said, "The splendor has gone into exile from Israel, because God's chest has been taken."

In his sermon yesterday, our rector (slightly apologetically) told us he had been watching a TV series about a psychopathic boy whom a police officer had adopted. The boy's stepfather gave him a "code": Don't kill innocent people; make sure you have the evidence that the person is guilty; prepare carefully; don't get caught. Our rector went on to tell us a story about his sister, who is a school principal in Watts in Los Angeles, the urban area where the 1965 race riots happened. The principal had been interviewing a student who had been selling marijuana in the school. He too had a "code": Don't get caught; don't ever reveal the identity of your source; don't fear a person such as your principal as much as you fear your suppliers.

The Israelites realize they need a code. Don't let other people control your destiny; make sure God is with you when you fight; therefore take the **covenant chest** with you into battle because that stands for God's presence. Unfortunately the **Philistines** also have a code, and unfortunately their code works better. Keep control of the peoples around; don't be put off when your opponents are jazzed; when their God is with them, fight harder.

The ironic aspect to the story lies in the theologies both sides work with. It's hard to decide whose theology is more mixed up. The Israelites are surely right that God wants them to be free of Philistine control and that God will likely expect them to fight for their independence. Yet these stories in 1 Samuel continue on from the stories in Judges. When the text says that Eli had "led" Israel for forty years, it uses the verb that describes the exercise of **authority** by the "judges" who were Israel's "leaders" in this period. Those stories suggest that Israel's **deliverance** from the domination of other peoples happens because God is involved in raising up leaders and giving them the dynamic energy to lead. In 1 Samuel 4 there is no such talk of God's raising up leaders. Israel's now having a prophet to mediate God's instructions to them highlights this fact. Because they assume they can make war when it seems a good idea, they will need a prophet to represent God's involvement and intervention in their life.

Even more obviously, Israel's reaction to its first reversal contrasts with its reaction on the occasion of the defeat at Ai in Joshua 7. They do begin by asking the right question ("Why has God let this happen?") but the question is really a rhetorical one. It is not actually addressed to God, and they do not wait for an answer. Instead they assume they can ensure God is with them simply by bringing the covenant chest into the camp. Then **Yahweh Armies** enthroned on the **cherubs** will be in their midst. For these Israelites, the chest has become the equivalent to an image of a god. An image is not identical with the god it represents, but it is a representation through which the god condescends to put in a real appearance among people. The army assumes that the chest likewise guarantees the presence and power of God in their midst. How could God not then give the army victory?

The Philistines' theology is more ironic. Like the Israelites, they think that bringing the covenant chest into the camp means bringing the deity into the camp. Further, the story portrays them as quite well-informed about the person and acts of Israel's God, like the people of Jericho and Gibeon when the Israelites crossed the Jordan and won their first victories. Yet their reaction is to determine to fight harder. And it works! It works, of course, because **Yahweh** is more concerned about the Israelites' misapprehensions than about those of the Philistines. Whereas the Israelites may think that Yahweh dare not let them be defeated when the covenant chest stands in their midst, actually Yahweh is quite prepared to risk seeming to be discredited. Indeed, being prepared to let Israel be defeated avoids being "credited" with being a different kind of deity from the kind Yahweh really is.

As the Benjaminite messenger drew near to Shiloh (he has run about eighteen miles), his appearance would already tell people that he has come bringing terrible news; he would already look like a person mourning some terrible event. The failing of his eyes means that Eli cannot see that, but in any case the road by which he is sitting is apparently not the one from outside the city that leads through the city gate; it is perhaps the street that leads to the sanctuary. He first simply hears the people's **cry;** then the messenger reaches him and tells him about the defeat and about his sons' death and about the fate of the covenant chest. It is this news that makes him drop dead.

The news also jolts his daughter-in-law into labor. Was it the loss of the covenant chest that was decisive for her, too? Remember, her husband had been bedding the women who served at the sanctuary, and presumably she knew. Indeed, according to her father-in-law in chapter 2, the whole city knew. So imagine the gossip as her pregnancy advanced. . . . Was she looking for a way out of a life that had become unlivable? Perhaps giving birth to a son meant little to her. Yet as she died, it gave her the opportunity to mark the significance of the day he was born, and perhaps to imply that the terror of the day was indeed the fate of the covenant chest, not the death of her husband. The precise meaning of the name she gave him, Ichabod, is not clear, but her comments make its implication clear enough. The covenant chest did indeed stand for the glorious presence of Yahweh in the sanctuary in the midst of Israel.

Ordinary people did not see the covenant chest or the cherubs, but they knew they were there and knew they stood for the invisible presence of Israel's glorious God. The loss of the covenant chest suggests the departure of the covenant God. It's as if God has gone into **exile**. It would be a telling verb for people who read this story during *the* exile. That event was the occasion of Israel's exile from its land. It was also the occasion when God abandoned the temple in Jerusalem, when God went into voluntary exile. This story is a kind of anticipation of that one.

1 SAMUEL 5:1–7:1

You Can't Mess with the Covenant Chest

¹When the Philistines took God's chest, they brought it from Help-stone to Ashdod. ²The Philistines took God's chest and brought it to Dagon's house and placed it by Dagon. ³The Ashdodites got up early next day and there: Dagon was lying face down on the ground in front of Yahweh's chest. So they took Dagon and put him back in his place. ⁴They got up early in the morning next day and there: Dagon was lying face down on the ground in front of Yahweh's chest, with Dagon's head and both his hands cut off, on the threshold. Only [the body of] Dagon remained to him. ⁵That is why Dagon's priests and all the people who come to Dagon's house do not tread on the threshold of Dagon in Ashdod. ⁶Yahweh's hand was heavy on the Ashdodites. He devastated them and struck them down with hemorrhoids. . . . ⁶:¹Yahweh's chest was in Philistine country for seven months. ²The Philistines summoned the priests and diviners and said, "What shall we do about Yahweh's chest? Tell us what we are going to send off with the chest of Israel's God to its place." ³They said, "If you are going to send off the chest of Israel's God, don't send if off on its own. Send a restitution offering back to him. Then you will find healing. He will cause himself to be acknowledged by you; his hand will certainly turn from you." ⁴They said, "What is the restitution offering that we should send back to him?" They said, "Five gold hemorrhoids and five gold rats, the number of the Philistine rulers, because the same epidemic has come to all of them—to your rulers, too. ⁵You are to make models of the hemorrhoids and of the rats that have been ravaging your country and give the God of Israel

honor. Perhaps he will ease his hand from upon you and your gods and your country."

[Verses 6–18 relate how they urge the Philistines not to follow the example of the Egyptians in resisting Yahweh. The Philistines duly send these models with the chest on a cart pulled by cows, who take it straight to Beth-shemesh.]

[19]But [Yahweh] struck down the men of Beth-shemesh because they looked in Yahweh's chest. He struck down seventy men (fifty thousand men) among the people. The people mourned because Yahweh had struck the people down with such a heavy blow. [20]The men of Beth-shemesh said, "Who can stand before Yahweh, this holy God? To whom might he go up from us?" [21]So they sent envoys to the inhabitants of Kiriath-jearim to say, "The Philistines have sent Yahweh's chest back. Come down; take it up to you." [7:1]The men of Kiriath-jearim came and took Yahweh's chest up and brought it into the house of Abinadab on the hill. They consecrated his son Eleazar to look after Yahweh's chest.

When I used to read Bible stories to my young sons, they would sometimes ask, "Did that really happen?" As far as I remember, they did not ask that question about big events like the Israelites' crossing of the Reed Sea (or Jesus' resurrection) but about stories like this one, and I think they were onto something. The stories of the Reed Sea or the resurrection involve much more marvelous—even miraculous—events, yet they are told in a quite matter-of-fact way. You may or may not believe them, but it's hard not to assume that the people who told the stories believed they were things that really happened.

The adventures of the **covenant chest** are related in a different way. The story is more like a cartoon or like one of Jesus' parables. It's larger than life in the way they are. It's formulaic; the same thing happens in Ashdod, then in Gath, then in Ekron (there are actually five Philistine cities, hence the five rulers the story goes on to refer to, but you often have three people or groups of people in a parable or a joke). It's humorous in the manner of a cartoon or a parable. It makes fun of the people of Ashdod, getting up early each morning to come and pray in Dagon's temple and finding Dagon humiliated. Its jokiness is juvenile and scatological: God sends judgment on the

Philistines by giving them boils on an uncomfortable part of their anatomy, and the Philistine religious experts get them to make amends to God by making models of hemorrhoids and rats. Excuse me?

Jesus' parables then have a way of kicking the listeners in the butt after they have gotten their attention and made them laugh, so that the listeners end up laughing on the other side of their faces. When the covenant chest gets back into Israelite territory at Beth-shemesh (the nearest Israelite city to Philistine territory), the Israelites are no more reverent or wise in the way they treat it (and thus treat God) than the Philistines, and they pay a more serious penalty. (The numbers are a puzzle, where seventy is followed by fifty thousand, but perhaps the reference to fifty thousand is there to make a comparison with the story we will read in 2 Samuel 24, when that number of people die in an act of chastisement on the whole people.) The Philistines found the chest a hot potato that they anxiously but futilely passed on from one city to another. The Israelites do the same.

One could argue that the Israelites show less insight than the Philistines. Indeed, even the cows pulling the cart show more insight than the men of Beth-shemesh. The Philistines' spiritual leaders who want to be rid of the chest at least recognize that it is unwise to mess with **Yahweh** because (like the men fighting the battle in chapter 4) they know about the way Yahweh dealt with the Egyptians. Once again, this is part of the cartoon or parable. Perhaps the Philistines would not actually know the story of the exodus. The point is to highlight what the Israelites fail to take account of.

The Philistines at least recognize that they need to send an offering that makes some restitution for the way they have slighted God. When you offend someone you try to make up for it in some way to show that your regret is not just words. The **Torah** lays down ways in which you can do this in relation to God by means of a restitution offering (the traditional English translation is "guilt offering"). The Philistines use the term that appears in the Torah in this connection. There are signs of repentance there. The people of Beth-shemesh react with words that are very appropriate: "Who can stand before Yahweh, this holy God?" They use the word "holy" in the proper

Old Testament way; it suggests the awesome transcendence of God, which means you have to take God really seriously. They have found, as the New Testament puts it, that "our God is a consuming fire" (Hebrews 12:29). But though their words are appropriate, they don't know where to go next with their awareness. They just want to get rid of the chest.

Why they chose Kiriath-jearim we don't know. It is a town up in the mountains (hence the people from there come *down* to Beth-shemesh and take the chest *up* to their city), half way to Jerusalem and just off the modern highway as it begins to draw near Jerusalem. The chest is thus nearer Israel's heartland and farther from its borders. Did the people of Beth-shemesh think the people of Kiriath-jearim were a bit slow on the uptake in being willing to welcome this dangerous object into their midst? If so, the joke is on them. The people of this city know how to look after the chest with more reverence, though solemnly we will read in 2 Samuel 6 (which picks up the story of the chest) that there is further trouble to follow from looking after it.

1 SAMUEL 7:2–14

As Far as This Yahweh Has Helped Us

[2]From the day the chest settled at Kiriath-jearim a long time passed, twenty years. Then the whole people of Israel mourned after Yahweh, [3]and Samuel said to the whole household of Israel, "If with all your soul you are returning to Yahweh, remove the foreign gods and Ashtorets from your midst and direct your soul to Yahweh. Serve him alone. He will rescue you from the hand of the Philistines." [4]So the Israelites removed the Masters and the Ashtorets and served Yahweh alone. [5]Samuel said, "Gather all Israel at Mizpah and I will plead with Yahweh on your behalf." [6]They gathered at Mizpah and drew water and poured it out before Yahweh. They fasted that day and said there, "We have done wrong against Yahweh."

So Samuel led the Israelites at Mizpah, [7]and the Philistines heard that the Israelites had gathered at Mizpah. The rulers of the Philistines went up against Israel, and the Israelites heard and were afraid of the Philistines. [8]The Israelites said to Sam-

40

uel, "Do not be deaf to us by not crying out to Yahweh our God so that he may deliver us from the hand of the Philistines." [9]So Samuel got a suckling lamb and sacrificed it as a burnt offering to Yahweh. Samuel cried out to Yahweh on behalf of Israel, and Yahweh answered him. [10]As Samuel was sacrificing the burnt offering, the Philistines were drawing near for battle against Israel, but Yahweh thundered with a loud voice that day against the Philistines and threw them into confusion, and they were defeated before Israel. [11]The men of Israel went out from Mizpah and pursued the Philistines, and struck them down as far as below Beth-car.

[12]Samuel took a stone and put it between Mizpah and Shen, and named it Help-stone; he said, "As far as this Yahweh has helped us." [13]The Philistines subjected themselves and did not anymore come into Israel's territory. Yahweh's hand was against the Philistines all the days of Samuel. [14]The cities the Philistines had taken from Israel returned to Israel, from Ekron to Gath; Israel rescued all [the cities'] territory from the hand of the Philistines, and there was peace between Israel and the Amorites.

"Helping" can have a variety of connotations. On one occasion a tire came off my wife's wheelchair when we were on our way to church. As I was bending down trying to get the tire back on, with Ann still in the chair, a car driver stopped and "helped" me get it back on. His lending me a hand was a great help and maybe prevented us from being late for church, but if he hadn't stopped, I would eventually have managed to get the tire back on; at least, on other occasions I did so. But two people could do the job more easily. On the other hand, on occasions when Ann had pneumonia and couldn't breathe properly, so that I had to take her to Urgent Care, our need for help was quite different. It was a life-and-death matter, and without medical professionals I was helpless.

The Old Testament can use its word for "help" in the same two ways, but when it talks about God's helping, the second connotation regularly applies. "Helping" is then not so different from **delivering**. It is something God does when you cannot help yourself. When Samuel gives the name "Help-stone" to the place where God delivers Israel from the **Philistines**, that's the kind of help he is referring to. Before the calamitous defeat in chapter 4, the Israelite army had its base at Help-stone; maybe this Help-stone is the same place or maybe a different one with the same name, but either way it draws attention to the difference in the two events. There was an irony about the name of that place in chapter 4. If it's the same place, maybe it always had this name, and Samuel is now drawing attention to a new significance that the name now has. That is often the case with Old Testament names. Either way, formerly it was not a place where Israel experienced God's help, either when they didn't seek it or when they thought they could manipulate it.

Help-stone has now lived up to its name. It's no coincidence that this happens when Israel has moved on in its relationship with God, though the people have apparently needed time to do so. Evidently the Philistines' return of the **covenant chest** did not imply a resolution of tensions between the Philistines and the Israelites. The Philistines are still controlling considerable territory on the coastal plain that counts as part of "the promised land." So Israel "mourns" after God; it grieves over its position.

Now Samuel regularly shows himself capable of being a tough guy. A mere show of weeping gets no one anywhere with him. Never mind the tears: what about your stance in relation to **Yahweh** and in relation to the Masters and the Ashtorets?

The Hebrew word for Master is *baal*, an ordinary Hebrew word for a master, lord, or owner but also a word used to describe a **Canaanite** god. The use of it is thus parallel to the use of the word *Lord* to describe Yahweh. So like *Lord*, in effect *Master* can be a proper name. The Old Testament generally uses *Master* for a Canaanite god and *Lord* for the real God, Yahweh, to make the difference clear. Like other ancient peoples, the Canaanites acknowledged a number of gods, and, strictly speaking, the Master was simply one of them (though one of the most prominent), but here as elsewhere the Old Testament uses the plural *Masters* to refer to Canaanite gods in general. In a similar way, Ashtoret or Ashtarte was a particular goddess, but the name came to be used in the plural as a general term for a goddess. So the Masters and the Ashtorets denote Canaanite deities, male and female, in general. (Ashtoret is probably not the real pronunciation of the name but a bowdlerized version that combines the consonants of the actual name and the vowels of *boshet*, the Hebrew word for "shame." It thus suggests that worshiping these deities is something utterly shameful. We will come across other names, such as Ish-bosheth and Mephibosheth, that are more obviously bowdlerized names.)

Perhaps the opening of the story implies that the defeat related in chapter 4 had led to the Israelites' abandoning Yahweh to see if serving other gods would work out better. If so, some years have passed, and it has not done so. They are now "mourning after Yahweh," but not in such a way as to give up their recourse to other gods. Samuel challenges them to do so. So first they remove these alien gods, then they gather for Samuel to **cry out** and plead for them with Yahweh. First there has to be the action that indicates "turning" or "returning" to Yahweh; second there has to be the expression of sorrow in the context of worship, in words and in symbolic ways. All these are aspects of repentance. The water-pouring rite does not appear elsewhere in the Old Testament, but it could naturally suggest a way to seek cleansing.

The Philistines rightly perceive that the Israelites' gathering in this way portends trouble, but (like the Israelites themselves in chapter 4) they don't draw the right conclusions. Instead of making them withdraw, it makes them attack. The Israelites in turn panic, not believing Samuel's promise about God delivering them. Fortunately this doesn't make God simply despair and go off, and fortunately they also again turn to Samuel in a way they did not turn to Eli in chapter 4. One implication and result is that the significance of Samuel grows by leaps and bounds. He started off as a sanctuary janitor. Then God turned him into a prophet. In this chapter he has become someone "leading" Israel or exercising **authority**, the term that described the "judges" and was also used of Eli. Samuel also functions here as a priest. While his effective adoption by Eli might mean he counted as belonging to the priestly line, the other unique features of stories such as this one suggest that the rules in the Torah were not operative in his day. Further, he prays on the people's behalf, which he might do both as prophet and as priest. His burnt offering is an accompaniment to his prayer, so that the people's committing themselves to God is again not merely a matter of words. As with the water pouring, the Old Testament does not otherwise refer to offering a suckling lamb (another indication that the rules in Samuel's day were different from the ones in the Torah). God's answer to his prayer comes not in words but in action, in a thundering that reduces the Philistines to confusion, so the Israelites do not have to fight them but just mop them up. There could hardly be a sharper contrast with the story in chapter 4. Yes, God "helps" them in that second sense.

In the hymn "Come Thou Fount of Every Blessing" we declare, "Here I raise my Ebenezer." *Ebenezer* is the Hebrew for Help-stone. The hymn expresses a sense of being not quite at home in this world and looking forward to heaven, and in connection with this line it expresses the conviction that God has been with us so far in our lives, to get us to where we are, and will certainly not abandon us before we indeed reach our heavenly home. For the Israelites, the battle meant God had been an extraordinary and decisive help to them "as far as this" in making it possible for them to reach their destiny as a people. They were not all the way there yet, but they were well on the way, and experiencing God acting powerfully on such an occasion had the capacity to embolden them about the certainty that God would take them to that destiny. During the narrative that will unfold through the story of Saul and into the early years of David, God will do so.

1 SAMUEL 7:15–8:20

Appoint Us a King

7:15Samuel exercised authority for Israel all the days of his life. 16He went each year and traveled around to Bethel, Gilgal, and Mizpah and exercised authority for Israel in all these places, 17then made his return to Ramah because his home was there. He exercised authority for Israel there and built an altar to Yahweh there. 8:1When Samuel got old, he made his sons the people who exercised authority for Israel. 2The name of his elder son was Joel, and the name of his second son Abijah; they were authorities in Beersheba. 3But his sons did not walk in his ways but turned after profit and accepted presents, and overturned the exercise of authority. ⁴So all the elders of Israel gathered and came to Samuel at Ramah, ⁵and said to him, "Right. You are elderly and your sons have not walked in your ways. Now appoint us a king to exercise authority like all other nations." ⁶The thing was displeasing in Samuel's eyes when they said, "Give us a king to exercise authority for us," and Samuel prayed to Yahweh. ⁷Yahweh said to Samuel, "Listen to the people's voice in everything they say to you, because it is not you they have rejected, because it is me they have rejected from being king over them. ⁸In accordance with all the deeds they have done from the day I brought them out of Egypt even until this day, they have forsaken me and served other gods; so they are doing also to you. ⁹So now listen to their voice. But testify against them solemnly and tell them about the authority of the king who will reign over them."

¹⁰Samuel spoke all Yahweh's words to the people who were asking him for a king. ¹¹He said, "This will be the authority of the king who will reign over you. Your sons he will take and make into charioteers and horsemen for himself. They will run in front of his chariot. ¹²He will make them commanders of thousands and of fifties. They will plow his fields. They will reap his harvest. They will make his battle equipment and his chariot equipment. ¹³Your daughters he will take as perfumers, cooks, and bakers. ¹⁴Your best fields, vineyards, and olive groves he will take and give to his servants. ¹⁵Your seed and your vineyards he will tithe and give to his commanders and his servants. ¹⁶Your male and female servants, your best young men and your asses, he will take and make his work force. ¹⁷Your flocks he will tithe, and you yourselves will become his servants. ¹⁸You will cry out on that day on account of your king whom you have chosen for yourselves, but Yahweh will not answer you on that day."

[Verses 19–22 relate how the people still insist on having a king to rule over them and fight their battles.]

Almost every day, television and the newspapers report the cost that ordinary people pay for their government. Sometimes the cost lies in expenditure that may be inevitable. Representatives have to be paid salaries and expenses and need buildings to meet in, and perhaps these meeting places need to be reasonably impressive lest the state or the central government look unimpressive. A fundamental task of government is maintaining the country's independence and thus maintaining an army. The desire to attract able people into government means paying them salaries higher than ordinary people earn. Further, legitimate expenditure shades into more questionable luxury, and legitimate expenses shade into cheating on expense accounts. The problem is not only a financial one. As I write, the news is full of reports of a governor's aide's involvement in a sexual assault and of the governor's crossing a line in the way he sought to protect his aide. It is hard to face the reality that these phenomena are not mere isolated exceptions. They are endemic to the way politics works.

That is Samuel's point in his warning about the way a king will exercise leadership or **authority**. The problem is endemic in giving authority to people, whether the authority lies in a monarchy or an elected body. Depressingly, you do not avoid problems by not having a central government. When "there was no king in Israel" and "people did what was right in their own eyes," Israel experienced moral and social chaos. The grievous opening to 1 Samuel 8 underlines the point in reporting that, like Eli, Samuel did not manage to bring up his sons in his own ways.

The circuit Samuel traveled to exercise authority covered only a small area in the center of the country. We do not know what his activity involved. Maybe it was largely judicial and he functioned as a kind of appeal judge, deciding difficult cases; and/or maybe he taught the people in a city, and particularly the elders. Building an **altar** in his home city suggests he stands in the tradition of Abraham, Moses, and Joshua. His sons' activity in Beersheba places them far south of his circuit, at Israel's southernmost city, so perhaps this was their earlier responsibility before they took over more generally from their father in his old age.

They then exposed their waywardness in a way that anticipates a problem familiar in the modern world. Pressure groups or individuals can influence decision makers by gifts or sweeteners: "Enjoy a couple of weeks in my condo in Hawaii; no one else is using it." It is easy to justify accepting such gifts. As a politician you get paid more than many people but possibly less than you would get paid in the private sector. Samuel could resist that temptation, but his sons could not. They had not had the experience of God's waking them up in the night to turn them into prophets.

Another weird feature of political life in the modern world is that we always think a change of government will improve the situation in the country, bringing more freedom or justice or jobs. Perpetually our hopes are disappointed, and we assume yet another change of government will make all the difference, and so on forever. In effect Samuel points out that being governed by kings rather than by people like Samuel's sons will make no difference. For the most part his realistic account of what it will be like to have a stable, fixed form of central government does not imply that this government will be characterized by gross abuse. Kings and presidents have to have a staff, and the staff has to be paid. People sometimes seem to think that governments have magical, mysterious sources of funds, but they do not. "There's no one but you to foot the bill."

Before he comes to this point, Samuel is bidden to look at the situation theologically, not merely pragmatically. The story does not tell us why the people's request displeases Samuel. Perhaps God's subsequent words imply that Samuel feels rejected by them. While this would not be an unreasonable reaction on his part, more profoundly they have rejected God as king. Gideon's people once proposed that he should "rule" over them (they use the word "rule" rather than "reign as king," so their idea is a less radical one than the people in Samuel's day), but Gideon declared, "I will not rule over you, nor will my son rule over you. **Yahweh** is the one who will rule over you."

When the people now say they want a human king and thus implicitly reject God as king, one might have expected God to tell Samuel, "So do not yield to their request. Tell them I intend to reign over them." Yet one of the terrible aspects of the way God runs the world is sometimes to give us what we ask for. To put it the way Paul does in Romans 1, God gives us up to the desires of our hearts, to a debased mind. So as an act of judgment God says, "Okay, give them what they ask for." Their request is not a strange aberration. It is in keeping with the way they have related to God since they came out of Egypt. So this is a moment at which God says, "That's it. That's the last straw. No more long-suffering. I'm outta here."

Yet whenever God says this, it never needs to be the last word. It is after saying this that God bids Samuel point out to the Israelites what it will be like to have a central government and to **cry out** as a result. Because it's never over till it's over. Maybe they will see sense and withdraw the request. But no.

In reaffirming their desire, they reexpress it. They want a king to go out ahead of them and fight their battles. In one sense, this simply restates what it means to have a king. One theory about the very idea of central government is that its single, indispensible job is to defend the nation's existence and freedom, its integrity and its borders, in relation to other nations that imperil these. The Israelites' experience of God's kingship in this connection has been mixed. Sometimes God has given them amazing victories. Sometimes God has let them experience notable losses. In a story such as that in 1 Samuel 4, of course, God had good reason for doing so, but how can they function as a people if they are subject to God's whim about what happens between them and their enemies? They want the freedom to safeguard their own destiny. Okay, says God.

1 SAMUEL 8:21–9:27

How Saul Lost Some Donkeys and Found More than He Bargained For

²¹When Samuel heard all the people's words, he recounted them in Yahweh's ears. ²²Yahweh said to Samuel, "Listen to their voice. Make a king for them." Samuel said to the Israelites, "Each of you, go to his city."
^{9:1}There was a man from Benjamin whose name was Kish son of Abiel son of Zeror son of Becorath son of Aphiah, a Benjaminite, a man of substance. ²He had a son named Saul, a fine, handsome man. There was none handsomer among the Israelites than he; from his shoulders up, he was taller than all the people. ³The donkeys belonging to Kish, Saul's father, got lost,

and Kish said to his son Saul, "Will you take one of the boys with you and set off and go look for the donkeys."

[In verses 4–5 they spend some time looking, and Saul is inclined to give up.]

⁶But [the boy] said to him, "Now, though, there is a man of God in this city. The man is honorable. Everything he says truly comes about. Let's go there now. Perhaps he will tell us about the journey we have come upon."

[In verses 7–10 Saul objects that he has nothing to give the man, but the boy has a quarter.]

¹¹When they were going up the ascent to the city, they met some girls coming out to draw water, and said to them, "Is the seer here?" ¹²They replied to them, "He is. There, in front of you. Hurry now, because today he has come to the city because the people have a sacrifice at the high place today." . . . ¹⁵Now Yahweh had opened Samuel's ear the day before Saul came, saying, ¹⁶"This time tomorrow I will send you a man from the country of Benjamin. You are to anoint him ruler over my people Israel and he will deliver my people from the hand of the Philistines, because I have seen my people, because their cry has come to me." ¹⁷When Samuel saw Saul, Yahweh declared to him, "There: the man I said to you. This man is to control my people."

[In verses 18–21 Samuel tells Saul the donkeys are safe but that he has something else to talk to him about.]

²²Samuel took Saul and his boy, brought them into the hall, and gave them a place at the head of the guests (they numbered thirty people). . . . ²⁴ᵇSo Saul ate with Samuel that day, ²⁵and when they came down from the high place to the city, he spoke with Saul on the roof. ²⁶Early in the morning, at break of day, Samuel called Saul on the roof, "Get up, and I will send you off." Saul got up, and the two of them, he and Samuel, went outside. ²⁷As they were going down to the edge of the city Samuel said to Saul, "Tell the boy to pass on ahead of us" (and he did so) "but you stop here now and I will let you hear the word of God."

A friend of mine begins his church ministry tomorrow, fifteen years after he first had a sense that he might be called to the ministry. Of course he has been involved in ministry in different senses through most of those fifteen years, but he has now been officially appointed to a church (and it is going to pay him a salary!). Last night we were comparing notes about calls to the ministry and found overlaps and differences. For us both, the story went back to our midteens, the time when we first took Christian faith seriously. He had wondered about ministry then because he somehow thought it was the only way to take Christian faith seriously. Eventually he came to see that there was a sense in which this was true but also a sense in which it was false, and only later did a pastor suggest to him that his gifts might indeed indicate he was called to ministry in the more technical sense. Although I got interested in theology as a teenager, I somehow knew that a call to the ministry was a different matter, and I knew I didn't have such a call. But subconsciously I was probably looking for something—not lost donkeys, but an idea about what to do with my life. One day I got caught in the rain and sheltered in a doorway, and out of the blue (or out of the rain) suddenly came a conviction: God wants me in the ministry.

Saul was looking for donkeys, and it was a very important task, because donkeys fulfill the role of trucks in a traditional society (just this week I read an article about the way mules do so for U.S. forces in Afghanistan, where the mountains make trucks impractical). The farm could not function without its donkeys. The buildup that the story gives for Saul implies he has a star future as the manager of the family farm, as the husband of a beautiful wife, and as an upstanding member of the local community. He has no need to look for a vocation, only for donkeys, but we noted in connection with Samuel's own call or summons that when God issues a vocation, it's not for the sake of the person. It's for the sake of the purpose God is pursuing. Further, there is something scary about the back story to Saul's vocation. He is about to be summoned to do a job that God doesn't want to have done. That fact will hang over Saul's entire story.

Admittedly, alongside the picture of Saul as the good-looking son of a famous father there is a hint that he is not so quick on the uptake, which also hints at a motif that will recur in his story. When they can't find the donkeys, Saul wants to give up and go home; it is his boy who points out that there is a man of God living in the nearby town (which was perhaps Samuel's own home town, Ramah). When Saul points out that they have nothing to give the man of God, it is his boy who produces his credit card. In the Old Testament, the phrase "a man of God" has different implications than it has in Christian parlance, where it suggests someone marked by a deep spirituality. In the Old Testament, a man of God is someone with mysterious powers and capacities. In this chapter he is a "seer," someone who can see things invisible to other people, and a "prophet," someone who can hear things inaudible to other people. He is not just concerned with big issues and religious questions but with the everyday issues in people's lives, like losing your truck. The boy knows that a prophet or a priest can help you deal with such questions. But like any other full-time minister, a man of God or prophet or seer needs financial support in order to be able to focus on that ministry; Samuel is not involved in looking after the family farm in Ramah. So when you need his services, you give him something for them.

Already, coincidence and human initiative have entered into the story, as they do with many Old Testament stories. Saul and the boy just happen to be near a town where you can often find Samuel; Samuel happens to be here today; they happen to meet some girls who can tell them where to find him; an event at the sanctuary happens to be imminent; as they enter the town they happen to meet Samuel; they ask someone where they can find the seer, and it is Samuel himself that they happen to ask. The Old Testament does not say that God orchestrates things so that they work out this way, but it portrays God as being able to make coincidence and human initiative serve the divine purpose. The way it gives this portrait is underlined by its reference to the actual initiative that God takes. It does not say God made all these coincidences happen; it does say that God had spoken to Samuel the previous day, which shows how the coincidences serve God's purpose.

51

The "high place" will be the sanctuary in the town, which is located at its highest point and/or is elevated by means of a platform. The Old Testament will later disapprove of the high places because they were associated with worship of other gods, or with worship of **Yahweh** as if Yahweh were like one of the gods indigenous to the country, but evidently there could be proper worship of Yahweh offered at the high places. Here it rather looks as if the event at the sanctuary is something like a fellowship sacrifice for one of the kin groups in the city (it seems that the girls are not involved, which will then be because they belong to a different kin group). Perhaps someone has had a baby, and they are all gathering to celebrate and give thanks to God. Whatever it is, the family never discovers that something is happening that has nothing to do with their celebration; the scene is a bit like that at the wedding at Cana where Jesus changes water into wine. Samuel invites two total strangers to the celebration and treats them like honored guests. One wonders if some time later people commented, "The man who has become king, doesn't he remind you of that guy who showed up at our party?" Indeed, the meal becomes something like a secret coronation banquet. Saul and his boy are presumably bemused as they get drawn into the event and have to stay the night in Samuel's house. They have been reassured about the donkeys but have been told that Samuel has something else to discuss with them. The flat roof is where the guest room would be located.

It transpires that God's words to Samuel had indicated another aspect to God's feelings about the people's desire for a king. They reflect the inbuilt ambiguity about having kings. The people have cried out in the way they did in Egypt and in the period of the "judges," and their **cry** has reached God, as that earlier cry did. Yet God cannot quite bring himself to talk about appointing someone as "king" so that he will "reign." God rather talks about a "ruler" who will "control" the people. This is the only passage that describes the king as designed to "control" or "restrain" the people, though we can see that they sure need some control or restraint.

1 SAMUEL 10:1–16

Is Saul among the Prophets, Too?

¹Samuel got a flask of oil and poured it on [Saul's] head and hugged him, and said, "Yahweh has indeed anointed you as ruler over his own people. ²When you go from me today, you will come across two men by Rachel's tomb in the territory of Benjamin at Selsah. They will say to you, 'The donkeys that you went to look for have shown up. Now. Your father has given up talking about the donkeys and is anxious about you, saying, "What shall I do about my son?"' ³You will pass on from there and come to the oak at Tabor. Three men will meet you there, coming up to God to Bethel, one carrying three kid goats, one carrying three loaves, and one carrying a skin of wine. ⁴They will ask you if you are doing well, and they will give you two loaves. You are to accept them from their hand. ⁵After this you will come to God's Hill, where the Philistine outpost is. When you come into the city there, you will encounter a group of prophets coming down from the high place, with banjos, tambourines, pipes, and guitars in front of them. They will be prophesying. ⁶Yahweh's spirit will erupt on you and you will prophesy with them; you will turn into another man. ⁷When these signs have come about for you, do what your hand finds to do, because God will be with you. ⁸You are to go down ahead of me to Gilgal. There: I will be going down to you to offer up burnt offerings and to sacrifice fellowship offerings. You are to wait seven days until I come to you and make known to you what you are to do." ⁹As he turned round to leave Samuel, God changed [Saul's] spirit. All these signs came about that day. . . . ¹¹ᵇThe people said to one another, "What is this that has happened to the son of Kish? Is Saul among the prophets, too?" ¹²One person from there answered, "And who is their father?" Thus it became a saying, "Is Saul among the prophets, too?" ¹³When he finished prophesying, he came to the high place.

¹⁴Saul's uncle said to him and to the boy, "Where did you go?" He said, "To look for the donkeys. When we saw they were not there, we went to Samuel." ¹⁵Saul's uncle said, "Do tell me what he said to you." ¹⁶Saul said to his uncle, "He simply told us that the donkeys had shown up." As for the matter of the kingship, he did not tell him what Samuel said.

For most of church history, visions and prophecies and miraculous healings have been uncommon events in the mainline churches, but during the time when I was teaching in England, they came to be more common once more, and we used to have prayer for healing in seminary chapel. On one occasion I was praying for one of the students who was part of my pastoral care group, and I had an image come into my mind, of a boy walking through a shopping mall with his father. I thought to myself, "If I was the sort of person who had visions or pictures, that would be one. But I'm not, so it obviously isn't." Nevertheless I incorporated the image in my prayer, and after the service the student came to see me, very excited, because that image had been such a help to him; it was the thing that had brought him some emotional healing. I realized I had become someone who did have pictures or visions. There was a sense in which I had become a different person.

For me and for Saul, an experience of that kind comes not in order to give us a spiritual experience but because of something God wants to do for other people. The day before Saul showed up, God had told Samuel he was to anoint Saul as ruler over Israel. In the Old Testament, anointing is a rite that involves smearing olive oil on the head of someone or on an object when the person or the object is dedicated to God or commissioned to a new function. Most often in the Old Testament it is priests who are anointed, but here it happens to the person designated as king, and the term "anointed one" most often refers to the king. Yet because anointing can be applied to other people, it would not be immediately obvious what it signified; hence Samuel makes explicit that Saul is anointed as "ruler." As is the case with other observances, such as baptism or a wedding, both symbolic action and words play a part. The physical action is necessary because we are physical people; the words are necessary because without them the action would be opaque in meaning.

God graciously grants Saul not only the ceremonial act but also some other "signs." He will meet some people who will tell him the donkeys have shown up and some other people who will give him some bread (Saul and the boy will need some sustaining on the journey home). The fulfillment of these prophecies would be impressive in itself. The third sign is more telling. It will take place near the location of the **Philistine** outpost. (In passing, this note reveals the justification in the people's desire to find **deliverance** from the Philistines; here in the heart of the mountain country is a Philistine outpost.) There Saul will meet a group of prophets who have been at a local sanctuary, a little like Samuel in the previous chapter; perhaps they have been there for a community celebration like the one Saul got caught up in. If so, presumably they were making music and prophesying when they were at the celebration, and they are continuing to do so as they go home. Their celebration was not confined to the occasion of worship.

Our picture of prophets is shaped by the accounts of individuals such as Isaiah and Jeremiah, but the Old Testament refers to various other sorts of prophets. If these prophets were the kind of people who could bring a word from God to a person, as Samuel did, it is not what they are doing here. Prophesying is something more like speaking in tongues (I also thought I was not the kind of person who spoke in tongues, but in due course I found I sometimes did). Perhaps the reference to musical instruments implies it is something more like "singing in the Spirit," as sometimes happens in churches today when people sing together in unplanned and extempore fashion. Or perhaps that reference to music reflects the way the use of music can open people to supernatural influence.

Modern translations sometimes use expressions such as "speaking in ecstasy" instead of "prophesying," which makes clear that they are not prophesying in what is for us the classic sense, though the disadvantage is that it implies they are out of control, which is not the case, at least when someone speaks in tongues. It does involve God's **spirit** "erupting" on them. Something extraordinary happens that invites a supernatural explanation. It is not just ordinary human speech. There can be something contagious about it. Saul indeed catches their spirit and is turned into another man, a different kind of person from what he was and what he would ever have envisaged being. God changes his spirit—more literally his heart, his inner person. Everybody can see that Saul is behaving in a way that belies what they thought about him. "Is Saul among the prophets, too?" evidently became a familiar saying, and this story is one setting where the question is appropriate; it will recur in another setting in 1 Samuel 19. "And who is their father?" is a more obscure question. Maybe it links with the way a group of prophets can be called "the sons of the prophets," which might imply that their leader could be seen as their "father." That might in turn imply that Saul is being seen as the prophet par excellence and that the saying expresses even more astonishment that this has come about, with Saul of all people.

The point about the experience is to give Saul evidence that God is with him, and not simply so that he can be grateful for a nice experience. It is because there are things he is going to find himself doing or challenged to do, and he could be tempted to think, "I couldn't do that." Indeed, he had said to Samuel, "I'm just a member of the smallest of the twelve clans" (that was certainly true), "and I am a member of the smallest kin group within Benjamin" (we can't check on whether that was false modesty). God's granting him this experience is designed to forestall such talk. "God will be with you" or "God is with you" is the classic Old Testament promise that God gives people when placing some impossible prospect or task in front of them. What you are is irrelevant. The fact that God is with you (of which this experience gives evidence) is what counts.

Meanwhile, Saul is to wait for Samuel at Gilgal, down in the Jordan Valley and thus off to the east, as far away as you can get from the Philistine center of power on the Mediterranean to the west. There Samuel will fulfill his priestly role of praying for the army, making the offerings that accompany such prayers and mediating God's instructions about a battle, before Saul fulfills his more kingly role of actually leading the army in the battle. This division of responsibilities is important but will be tricky for Saul and future kings to maintain.

1 SAMUEL 10:17–11:13

How Not to Evade the Draft

[17]Samuel called the people to Yahweh at Mizpah. [18]He said to the Israelites, "Yahweh the God of Israel has said this: 'I brought

Israel up from Egypt and rescued you from the hand of the Egyptians and of all the kingdoms that oppressed you, ¹⁹but today you have rejected your God who was a deliverer for you from all your troubles and pressures. You said, 'No: you are to set a king over us.' So now, take your stand before Yahweh by your clans and groups." ²⁰Samuel presented all the Israelite clans, and the clan of Benjamin emerged [in the drawing of lots]. ²¹He presented the clan of Benjamin by its kin groups, and the kin group of the Matrites emerged. Then Saul son of Kish emerged, and they looked for him but they couldn't find him. ²²They asked Yahweh again, "Has anyone else come here?" Yahweh said, "There, he is hiding with the stuff." ²³They ran and got him from there, and he took his stand in the midst of the people. He was taller than all the people, from his shoulders up. ²⁴Samuel said to all the people, "Have you seen the one Yahweh has chosen, that there is no one like him among all the people?" All the people shouted and said, "Long live the king." ²⁵Samuel described to the people the authority of the monarchy, wrote it in a scroll and deposited it before Yahweh, and Samuel sent all the people each to his home. ²⁶Saul also went to his house in Gibeah, and the fighting force whose spirit God had touched went with him. ²⁷When some worthless men said, "How can this man deliver us?" and despised him and did not bring him a gift, he was silent.

¹¹:¹Nahash the Ammonite came up and camped against Jabesh-gilead. All the men of Jabesh said to Nahash, "Seal a covenant to us and we will serve you." ²Nahash the Ammonite said to them, "On this basis I will covenant to you, on the basis of gouging out the right eye of every one of you; I will make it a disgrace to all Israel." ³The elders of Jabesh said to him, "Let us alone for seven days and we will send envoys through all Israel's territory. If there is no one who will deliver us, we will come out to you." ⁴The envoys came to Gibeah of Saul and reported these things in the people's ears, and the entire people raised their voice and wept. ⁵So. Saul was coming from the open country, behind the oxen. Saul said, "What's wrong with the people, that they are weeping?" They told him the words of the men from Jabesh. ⁶God's spirit erupted on Saul when he heard these words and his anger flared right up. ⁷He got a pair of oxen and cut them up and sent them around the entire territory of Israel by the hand of envoys, saying, "If there is any one of you who

does not come out after Saul and Samuel: so it will be done to his oxen." Awe from Yahweh fell on the people, and they came out as one person.

[In verses 8–11 Saul defeats the Ammonites and thus rescues the people of Jabesh.]

[12]The people said to Samuel, "Who was it said, 'Saul is to reign over us?' Give us the people and we will put them to death." [13]But Saul said, "No one is to be put to death this day, because today Yahweh has brought about deliverance in Israel."

I am sometimes asked why I am so involved with the Old Testament, and I have various answers. I may talk about two great Old Testament teachers I had, one at university and one at seminary. I may refer to the fact that I had learned Greek before I came to study theology, so I was freer to focus on Hebrew than most students. I may talk about the way the Old Testament keeps talking about God's involvement in life as it really is. All those are true. In a similar way, I am sometimes asked how I came to be teaching in the United States, and again I have various answers. I may talk about a meeting with the previous president of Fuller Seminary. I may say that the dean of the School of Theology kept e-mailing me, and it was the only way to get him off my back. I may say I wanted to get out of running a seminary, to get back into being just an ordinary professor. All those are true, too. As a consequence, it might be hard for someone to piece together the actual stories about how these things happened.

It is hard to piece together the precise story of how Saul became king. Was it because Samuel anointed him? Was it because the people drew lots? Was it because he took that heroic action to rescue the men of Jabesh-gilead? When God inspired the composing of 1 Samuel, the people God used as compilers apparently went about the task by simply placing end to end various stories; neither God nor they were too worried about the way the stories link with one another in narrative terms. They believed that all the stories relate something significant about the process whereby Saul became king, and they were not worried about lacking a continuity person to make sure the stories dovetailed neatly.

We have noted that the account of the donkeys and the anointing makes clear the interweaving of God's initiative, human actions, and coincidence. It portrays Saul as having the physical characteristics appropriate to a king (like David) and the reticence appropriate when one is drafted by God (like Moses or Gideon), though also as being a bit slow on the uptake. That account also relates God's ability to turn him into a new person.

The story about the gathering at Mizpah reaffirms that the very idea of having a king is something God looks at with disfavor; this augurs ill for Saul's fulfilling his role. He will turn out to be a not-very-suitable candidate to do a job God doesn't really want done. Yet once again the story emphasizes God's involvement in the choice of Saul, indicated by the use of the lot. Although having a king is the people's idea, he is not to be democratically elected because he is to be the means of God's ruling, not the means whereby the people fulfill their own wishes. Samuel's laying down the way the monarchy is to work goes along with that. On the other hand, Saul is democratically recognized. God's approval is further signaled when he is supported by an impressive potential fighting force of people whose spirit God has touched, while the people who ask questions about his appointment are characterized as worthless men. The story again notes how Saul has the reticence appropriate to someone God is going to use. God doesn't believe in people volunteering for service any more than God believes in democratic elections. Saul is not a person of ambition. (Of course this expression of reticence seems odd in light of what had happened between him and Samuel in the first story; but that is an instance of the way we need not seek to tidy up the relations between the stories.) Nor is he someone who reacts negatively to people who are not impressed by him.

The segue into the third story is again untidy and also puzzling if we have modern expectations about narrative logic. If Saul has been designated king, what is he doing plowing?! Once more the story about Jabesh-gilead as much parallels the previous ones as standing in linear sequence with them. It is another account of how he was shown to be the right person to be king. Initially, it incidentally reveals how the Israelites are under pressure on more than one front. From the west they are under pressure from the **Philistines**, whose center of power is in the coastal plain but who have an outpost in the mountains, indicating that they are advancing there too. You could infer that in the struggle for control of **Canaan**, the Philistines are winning. In addition, from the east the Ammonites are applying their own pressure. Gilead is the area immediately east of the Jordan. It had been settled by two and one half of the Israelite clans who liked the look of that territory and asked to settle there after they had stood with the other clans in occupying the main part of the promised land. The problem east of the Jordan paralleled the problem west of the Jordan. These neighbors of the Israelites' to the east were interested in expanding their territory into the former Amorite territory now occupied by Israel, and they have a vicious way of seeking to assert control, involving a **covenant** no one would want to sign.

Once again God demonstrates a sovereign involvement in the process whereby Saul becomes king. As in the first story it involves God's **spirit** erupting on him and making him act in a way that would not come naturally. Common to these stories is a portrait of Saul as a person who by nature does not take initiatives. He likes to sit in the back row and keep quiet. So God takes hold of him rather than some man who thrusts himself forward. God inspires a monumental anger in him; anger is an appropriate reaction to the enormity of the way the Ammonites propose to treat the men of Jabesh. Anger is here a fruit of the Spirit, because it energizes a mild man into being someone who takes the kind of action that is needed in the situation. The dismembering of the oxen is a symbolic act suggesting that "this is what God will do to you if you do not come and join in doing what needs doing." God's involvement appears not only in inspiring anger in Saul but in inspiring awe or panic on the part of the people who receive these frightening parcels, and then in bringing about "**deliverance** in Israel" through Saul's action.

The magnanimous way Saul responds to people's desire to lynch the men who questioned his suitability to be king once again marks him as someone full of God's spirit.

1 SAMUEL 11:14–12:25

Far Be It from Me to Sin by Not Praying for You

¹⁴Samuel said to the people, "Come, we should go to Gilgal and renew the kingship there." ¹⁵So all the people went to Gilgal and made Saul king there before Yahweh at Gilgal. They offered fellowship sacrifices there before Yahweh. Saul and all the Israelites had a great celebration there.

^{12:1}Samuel said to all Israel, "Right. I have listened to your voice with regard to all that you said to me and I have made a king reign over you. ²So now, there is your king walking about before you. I myself am old and gray, though my sons—there they are, with you. I myself have walked about before you from my youth until this day. ³Here I am. Testify against me in the presence of Yahweh and of his anointed. Whose ox have I taken? Whose donkey have I taken? Whom have I defrauded? Whom have I crushed? From whose hand have I taken a ransom so that I might close my eyes to someone? I will return it to you." ⁴They said, "You have not defrauded us, you have not crushed us, you have not taken anything from anyone." ⁵He said to them, "Yahweh is witness against you and his anointed is witness against you this day that you have not found anything in my hand." They said, "He is witness."

[In verses 6–15 Samuel reminds them of the story of God's acts over the years and then of their insisting on having a king, and challenges them to revere Yahweh.]

¹⁶"Now then. Take your stand and see this great thing that Yahweh is going to do before your eyes. ¹⁷It's the wheat harvest today, isn't it? I will call to Yahweh and he will give thunder and rain. You will acknowledge and see that you did a great wrong in Yahweh's eyes in asking for a king for yourselves." ¹⁸Samuel called to Yahweh, and Yahweh gave thunder and rain that day. All the people were very afraid of Yahweh and Samuel. ¹⁹All the people said to Samuel, "Plead on behalf of your servants to Yahweh your God so that we do not die, because we have added to all our offenses the wrong of asking for a king for ourselves." ²⁰Samuel said to the people, "Don't be afraid. You yourselves have done all this wrong. Nevertheless do not turn away from following Yahweh. Serve Yahweh with all your heart. ²¹You shall not turn away, because [it would be] after something

61

empty, things that are no use and cannot rescue, because they are empty. [22]Because Yahweh will not abandon his people, for the sake of his great name, because Yahweh undertook to make you into his people. [23]As for me, far be it from me to sin against Yahweh by failing to pray for you, and I will teach you in the way that is good and upright. [24]Nevertheless, revere Yahweh and serve him truthfully with all your heart, because you can see the great things he has done for you. [25]But if you do act wrongly, both you and your king—you will be swept away."

The day of my wife's memorial service was also the day I received the page proofs for a writing project. Someone who was reading those proofs, when he heard that Ann had died after living with multiple sclerosis for many years, wondered whether she had committed herself to staying with me to the completion of the project but now felt able to say her *Nunc Dimittis*: "Now, Lord, you let your servant go in peace." There had been four or five times when Ann had had pneumonia and I had been assured that she was about to die, but she had declined to do so. This time she did. Another friend commented more generally on the way people who are seriously ill and unable to speak (even facing death), as Ann was, can have the capacity (along with God) to determine that "now is not the time." It is as if there is a job to be done, and they stay to do it.

The Old Testament tells the story of people such as Moses, Joshua, and now Samuel in such a way as to imply that this is so. Admittedly its way of telling Samuel's story in this connection is somewhat paradoxical. Back in chapter 8 he was already old; now he is old and gray, yet he will continue to play a vital part in the story for quite a while; his death will come only in chapter 25. Yet perhaps that underscores the point. He is old and in one sense his job is done; yet he has a lot more to do, and he will not be able to go until his work is done (indeed, even then he will not be able to rest, we will discover from chapter 28).

When Paul similarly comes toward the end of his life, we are invited to picture him looking back and claiming he has fought the good fight and lived a life characterized by patience, love, and endurance (2 Timothy 4). Samuel looks back in a similar way and claims he has behaved with total integrity.

Many priests, prophets, and pastors could make no such claim. Samuel is a tough and forthright guy, and he will become more prickly rather than more laidback the older he gets, but he can look the community in the eye and submit himself to scrutiny. His toughness is expressed in yet another condemnation of the rebelliousness expressed in the people's insistence on having a king. The recurrent condemnation parallels the recurrent accounts of the way Saul became king and once again reflects the way the book has been put together. The opening verses of this section again illustrate how the book as a whole isn't too worried about continuity; the account of the way God's spirit inspires Saul to deliver the people of Jabesh closes with the people making Saul king, which we thought had happened once or twice already. The book's compilers didn't want to abandon any single good story. The upside to the book's jerkiness means each of the individual stories about how Saul became king can be read on its own (it's possible to harmonize them by stressing that this is a moment when the people *renew* Saul's kingship).

It would have been a shame to abandon this particular account of Samuel's condemning the people's desire for a king because of where the account then leads. It portrays the people recognizing they have done wrong and asking Samuel to pray for them. One significance of that request is the recognition that it is part of a prophet's or a priest's task to pray for the people. One can see an equivalent in the way Paul emphasizes his commitment to praying for the congregations for which he has some responsibility (I'm not sure how far pastors see praying for their people as integral to their ministry). We often think of prophets as people who bring God's word to the people, and we think of priests as people who bring the people's offerings to God. But prophets are involved in a two-way mediation; being a prophet means taking part in the meetings of the heavenly cabinet, and this involves a responsibility to represent your people in those meetings as well as a responsibility to tell the people about the decisions it has taken. Priests are also involved in a two-way mediation. As the story of Hannah and Eli shows, they bring God's word to people as well as bringing their offerings to God, but in bringing people's offerings priests

63

also bring the prayers and praises of which the offerings are an outward expression.

Of course the story of Hannah and Eli also shows that people knew they didn't need a priest's mediation in order to pray; anyone can come to God and pray. But Paul's letters again emphasize the importance of prayer for one another, which increases the number of people taking part in the cabinet's discussions about what should happen. Some people in some situations are hesitant to speak up for themselves and feel the need for other people to do so. This is one of those occasions. The people recognize they have done the wrong thing, and they are justifiably hesitant to look God or the other members of the cabinet in the face. They will feel better about Samuel's doing so on their behalf.

That may be especially so given the content of what they want said. If they have now recognized that they have done wrong, then surely they should be saying, "Okay then, we'd better go back on the idea of having a king. It's great that Saul sorted out the Ammonites but let's get him to turn in his crown now." Such action might seem to be required if they are really now repenting of their wrongdoing. The story is indeed talking about repentance, though it does not use the word. Elsewhere, there are two Hebrew words that get translated "repent," one meaning "be sorry," the other meaning "turn" or "turn back." One is a feelings word; the other, an action word. The prophets are characteristically interested in the second kind of repentance, but here the people are offering only the first kind (as we often do). They just want to avoid the punishment that might follow on the request that they now recognize was wrong. The extraordinary thing is that Samuel settles for this form of repentance. Prophets (and God) often have to settle for what they can get. Indeed, in some situations it is too late for turning. We may be unable to undo the effect of our actions, and we and God may have to settle for our being sorry and pleading for mercy. The people evidently assume it is too late to undo the introduction of a monarchy. What they can do is commit themselves to walking God's way in this style of life that is actually in inherent tension with walking in God's way. Samuel knows that it is indeed possible to make such a commitment in a wholehearted fashion and that God will then be with them as they walk in a way that was not the way God wanted. He knows how extraordinarily merciful God's grace is in meeting us where we are, even when we should be somewhere else, and how fortunate we are that God's own reputation has become bound up with us.

1 SAMUEL 13:1–22

When the King Has to Take Decisive Action

[The first verse of the chapter seems designed to give a chronology for Saul's reign, but the figures are incomplete.]

²Saul chose for himself three thousand men from Israel; two thousand were with Saul at Michmas and in the mountains at Bethel, and a thousand were with Jonathan at Gibeah in Benjamin. The rest of the company he sent off, each one, to its tents. ³Then Jonathan struck down the Philistine outpost at Geba, and the Philistines heard. When Saul sounded the horn throughout the country, saying, "The Hebrews are to hear!" ⁴and all Israel heard that "Saul has struck down the Philistine outpost, and now Israel has become intolerable to the Philistines," the people let themselves be summoned behind Saul at Gilgal, ⁵while the Philistines gathered for battle with Israel: thirty thousand chariots, six thousand cavalry, and a company like the sand on the seashore in number. They went up and camped at Michmas, east of Beth-aven. ⁶When the men of Israel saw that the situation was tough for them and the company was hard-pressed, the company hid in caves, in thickets, in rocks, in pits, and in cisterns; ⁷while Hebrews crossed the Jordan to the country of Gad and Gilead, Saul was still at Gilgal, and the whole company was terrified under his command.

⁸He waited seven days for the appointed time that Samuel [set], but Samuel did not come to Gilgal, and the company was scattering from him. ⁹So Saul said, "Bring me the burnt offering and the fellowship offerings," and he offered up the burnt offering. ¹⁰As he finished offering up the burnt offering, there—Samuel came. Saul went out to meet him, to greet him. ¹¹Samuel said, "What have you done?" Saul said, "I saw that the company was scattering from me, and you had not come by the appointed time in days, and the Philistines were gathering at

Michmas. ¹²I said, 'The Philistines will now come down to me at Gilgal, and I have not entreated Yahweh's favor.' So I forced myself and offered up the burnt offering." ¹³Samuel said to Saul, "You have been stupid. You have not observed the command of Yahweh your God, which he issued to you. Because Yahweh would now have established your kingship over Israel in perpetuity, ¹⁴but now your kingship will not stand. Yahweh has sought for himself a man he has decided on. Yahweh has declared him to be ruler over his people, because you did not observe what Yahweh commanded you." ¹⁵And Samuel set off and went up from Gilgal to Gibeah in Benjamin.

Saul mustered the company of those that were present with him, some six hundred men. ¹⁶Saul and his son Jonathan and the company that was present with them were staying at Geba in Benjamin, and the Philistines were camped at Michmas. ¹⁷A raiding party came out from the Philistine camp in three columns. One column would head for the Ophrah road, toward the region of Shual. ¹⁸One column would head for the Beth-horon road. One column would head for the border road overlooking the Valley of Hyenas, toward the wilderness.

[Verses 19–22 note that at this time the Israelites had no iron tools (they had to go down to Philistine territory to get their implements sharpened), and only Saul and Jonathan had iron weapons.]

Twice in the course of our marriage I dared to take my wife to see a Western movie despite knowing that she hated Westerns. The first was *Butch Cassidy and the Sundance Kid*. As we walked through the parking lot to the movie theater one dark evening (I can still remember that the ground was wet after rain), she asked what sort of movie it was, and I told her it was a kind of Western. She stopped in her tracks and said, "I'm not going to see a Western." "I think it's a different kind of Western," I said defensively. It became one of her favorite movies. The second was *Unforgiven*, a movie that deconstructed the genre more profoundly. One of the ways both movies did so was in portraying people having less control of the decisions they make than we would like to believe we have. It's nice to think we are in control of our lives and make free decisions, though realistically our decisions are often constrained.

Sometimes they are constrained by decisions we have ourselves made in the past. Sometimes they are constrained by other people.

That's how it is for Saul. The movement between the stories in these chapters is once more puzzling until you realize that the narrative is again not trying to give you a linear account of Saul's life. Here we move almost straight from Saul's confirmation as king to his rejection as king, and as there is more than one account of his becoming king, there is more than one account of his rejection as king. The thing that really matters about Saul is that he was David's predecessor, so a focus of the account of Saul is how he lost his position as king, and the first announcement of his rejection comes right at the beginning of the account of his reign. This way of telling the story thus compares with Luke's way of telling Jesus' story when he puts the account of Jesus' rejection at Nazareth at the beginning of the account of Jesus' ministry, whereas the other Gospels put it much later. Luke recognizes that it will help us read the story correctly if he tells us at the beginning where it is headed. The arrangement of Saul's story has the same effect.

You might well be sympathetic with the position Saul is put in. Jonathan has taken some action that provokes the **Philistines** to a more serious confrontation with Israel and will eventually lead to a great victory for Israel. The Philistines' center of power lies to the west, in the coastal plain. In response to Jonathan's action, they march their army eastward to the top of the mountain ridge where the center of Israelite power lies, and where the story initially locates the Israelite forces under Saul and Jonathan. Saul musters his army down the other side of the ridge at Gilgal by the river Jordan. The Israelites in general are understandably in a state of panic about the threat of a huge Philistine force, and they start disappearing in all directions. Saul as the army commander-in-chief needs to take some decisive action. What is he to do? Wait for the Philistines to come down the mountains to attack and neglect to seek God's help? Take the initiative and go into battle without seeking God's help? Seek God's help as if he were a priest who could take the lead in offering sacrifice? Or wait for Samuel to show up and risk his army dissipating until there is virtually nothing left and the force that is left gets slaughtered? What would you or I do?

There is no ideal course of action. Saul makes the decision that he thinks circumstances require; after all, Samuel talked about waiting seven days, and Saul has done so. Then he gets into trouble for it. By implication, he should have waited longer, but what exactly is the divine command that he has disobeyed? Samuel sees his delay as test of obedience, though that seems a bit tough; he had not said what Saul was to do after seven days elapsed. Perhaps it is also a test of trust; a number of stories in Judges and the books of Samuel tell of God's rescuing people though they get into desperate situations and of God's giving Israel victory when their numbers have become very small.

So Saul's monarchy is rejected. This rejection does not mean that at this stage he himself is to be dethroned as king. Samuel's point is that whereas a monarchy is usually hereditary and after a king's death he is succeeded by his son, in Saul's case God will not allow this to happen. It is apparently too late to go back on the idea of having kings, but Saul will not be succeeded by his son as one might have expected. Someone else will succeed. (There is an irony here, as Saul's son Jonathan looks to be an ideal candidate, except perhaps that he is too nice and not very interested in power.)

God will seek for himself "a man he has decided on." Translations conventionally have "a man after God's own heart," which is entirely accurate but is inclined to mislead readers. The English expression sounds as if it implies someone who has the kind of character that pleases God, even someone whose own heart matches God's heart. Actually it needs to mean only someone whom God's heart is set on, someone God chooses. Indeed, Saul had been such a person; God had decided on him. God is now going to decide on someone else. The man after God's own heart is of course David, and he will indeed be someone who will keep a steadfast commitment to **Yahweh** rather than to other gods, unlike many of his successors; but he will hardly be "a man after God's own heart" in the sense of someone who in other respects lives the kind of life God looks for or who has a heart like God's.

1 SAMUEL 13:23–14:52

The Fog of War

²³So the Philistine outpost had gone out to the pass at Michmas. ¹⁴:¹That day Jonathan, Saul's son, had said to the boy who was his arms bearer, "Come on, let's cross over to the Philistine outpost on the other side.... ⁶ᵇPerhaps Yahweh will act on our behalf, because Yahweh has no difficulty delivering by many or by few...." ⁸Jonathan said, "Right. We are going to cross over to the men and we will let them see us. ⁹If they say this to us, 'Stay still until we reach you,' we will stay where we are and not go up to them. ¹⁰But if they say this, 'Come up to us,' we will go up, because Yahweh will have given them into our hand. This will be a sign for us...." ¹²So the men of the outpost affirmed to Jonathan and his arms bearer, "Come up to us and we'll teach you something," and Jonathan said to his arms bearer, "Come up after me, because Yahweh has given them into the hand of Israel." ¹³Jonathan went up on his hands and feet with his arms bearer behind him, and they fell before Jonathan.... ¹⁸Saul said to Ahijah, "Bring God's chest here" (because God's chest was at that time with the Israelites). ¹⁹But while Saul spoke to the priest, the turmoil in the Philistine camp continued to go on and increase, so Saul said to the priest, "Take away your hand," ²⁰and Saul and the entire company with him summoned themselves together and went into battle.... ²³Thus Yahweh delivered Israel that day.

When the fighting passed beyond Beth-aven ²⁴the Israelite men were hard-pressed that day. Saul had laid an oath on the company, "Cursed is the man who eats food before evening when I have gotten redress from my enemies," and the entire company tasted no food.... ²⁷But Jonathan had not heard his father make the company swear, and he put out the end of the cane in his hand into a honeycomb and brought it back to his mouth, and his eyes brightened....

³¹They struck down the Philistines that day from Michmas to Aijalon, and the company was very faint. ³²So the company pounced on the plunder, got sheep, cattle, and calves, and slaughtered them on the ground. The company ate with the blood. ³³Saul was told, "Now. The company are doing wrong in relation to Yahweh by eating with the blood." He said, "You have acted faithlessly. Roll a big stone to me now."

³⁴Saul said, "Spread out among the company and tell them, "Bring to me everyone his ox or sheep and slaughter it here, then eat. . . .""

³⁷Saul asked God, "Shall I go down after the Philistines? Will you give them into Israel's hand?" But he did not answer him.

[In verses 38–43 further inquiry establishes that the reason is Jonathan's disobeying Saul's oath.]

⁴⁴Saul said, "May God do thus and more [to me] if you do not indeed die, Jonathan." ⁴⁵But the company said to Saul, "Is Jonathan to die when he brought about this great deliverance for Israel? Certainly not. As Yahweh lives, not a hair of his head is to fall to the ground, because he brought [it] about this day with God." So the company redeemed Jonathan. He did not die.

[Verses 46–52 summarize the story of Saul's victories and his family.]

I recently watched a British movie called *In the Loop*, a Monty Pythonesque version of how we came to invade Iraq. It was a cynical, fictionalized account of how the implications of intelligence from the Middle East got turned upside down to justify an invasion that some people in government were determined to bring about one way or another. It reminded me of the expression "the fog of war," which summarizes a point made by the Prussian soldier and military thinker Carl von Clausewitz. He noted the problems caused by the great uncertainty of all data in war. Every action you take has to be planned in a kind of twilight. Further, that twilight often has the effect of a fog or moonshine. It gives things exaggerated dimensions and an unnatural appearance. *The Fog of War* became the title of another movie, about Robert McNamara, U.S. Defense Secretary during the Vietnam War, who analyzed eleven mistakes the United States made in Vietnam.

Saul marches around in fog as he fights the **Philistines**. The story starts from the same point as the previous chapter, with Jonathan's victory over the Philistine outpost in the mountains whose presence suggests Philistine aspirations to control

Israel's heartland, and tells of what happens from a different angle. It provides another perspective on why it was inevitable that Saul's monarchy would fail, raising the question whether God chose the wrong man as king unless God wanted the monarchy not to work. Paradoxically, it begins to show how by nature Jonathan looks like a much more promising candidate for leadership. Saul was capable of taking a spectacularly brave initiative when God's spirit burst on him, but he was not this kind of person by nature. In contrast, it is in Jonathan's genes to behave this way.

Jonathan's not experiencing God's spirit bursting onto him doesn't mean God is not involved with Jonathan or that Jonathan is not open to God. While Jonathan doesn't wait for God's prompting before he takes some action, he knows there can be a difference between a merely harebrained idea and a stratagem that God will bless. Hence his "perhaps." You cannot take for granted that God will bless your harebrained schemes. Further, the fog of war means that on your own you may not be able to discern the difference between a great stratagem and a harebrained scheme. The reality of the fog of war is one piece of background to his magnificent awareness that God has no difficulty giving Israel **deliverance** by means of a large army unit or just a couple of guys. Gideon's story in Judges 6–7 shows as much. Strange things happen in war, and you can sometimes see God behind the way they work out.

So Jonathan sets up the possibility of God's giving him a sign, as Gideon once did. Jonathan's approach may be a little like tossing a coin and trusting God for the result, though the way he sets up the question may not be random. An army unit that is prepared to come out to fight looks like a more courageous outfit than one that simply sits in its outpost believing its secure position protects it.

We know from the beginning of chapter 13 that Saul and Jonathan have two separate bases with separate groups of men, and Saul is probably not to be faulted for being unaware of what Jonathan is doing. When he hears the commotion from across the valley, his first instinct is to consult God about what is going on and about what he should do. He has with him a priest called Ahitub, whose father had died in the catastrophe related in chapter 4, and Ahitub has the **ephod** with him. It is a sign of Saul's awareness that when you are fighting God's battles, you need to take God's servants with you so that you can check out that you are taking the action to which God directs you. At one level Saul knows as well as Jonathan does that you do not fight as if war is a purely secular enterprise. So Saul gets Ahitub to consult God, but before the process is over he concludes that he cannot afford to wait. He again needs to take decisive action. The chapter tells the same story as unfolded at Gilgal in chapter 13. The negative implication about Saul is clear. Yet his action does not stop God from giving Israel victory. You can rarely second-guess God or know when mercy will triumph over what we deserve.

Unfortunately Saul takes another false step that compromises the extent of the triumph. In the Old Testament, promises designed to encourage God to give victory are inclined to rebound; here, Saul's action reminds us of the story of Jephthah in Judges 11. First Saul's oath tempts his troops into gorging themselves when they at last have the chance to eat after they have become famished. As an act of respect to God, you do not eat an animal's blood but let it drain out, because blood stands for life; when blood flows out, life flows out. The men are too hungry to be able to bother with such niceties. At least Saul takes appropriate action in that connection, building a makeshift **altar** so that they can kill the animals properly as a kind of sacrifice before satisfying their hunger.

Then Jonathan unwittingly infringes Saul's promise in the way he finds some refreshment ("his eyes brightened"). In connection with this event, relations between Saul and his men are reversed. Whereas Saul thinks the same way as Jephthah (a promise is a promise is a promise), even Saul's ordinary soldiers know that God is not a legalist and that it's possible to raise with God the question whether circumstances make it feasible to renegotiate a promise. Some kind of offering can be made to God that can take the place of the life that was promised. So Jonathan's life is saved, but the victory fails to be the extensive one that it might have been.

1 SAMUEL 15:1–33

When the King Isn't Tough Enough

¹Samuel said to Saul, "It was I that Yahweh sent to anoint you as king over his people, over Israel. So listen now to the words Yahweh has to say. ²Yahweh has said this: 'I am attending to what Amalek did to Israel when [Amalek] set [himself] against them on the way, when they were coming up from Egypt. ³Now go and strike Amalek down and devote everything he has. You will not spare him. Kill men and women, young people and babies, oxen and sheep, camels and donkeys.'" ⁴Saul summoned the company and mustered them at Telaim, two hundred thousand infantry, and ten thousand men from Judah. ⁵Saul came to the city of Amalek and lay in wait in the wash. ⁶Saul said to the Kenites, "Go, get away, come down from among the Amalekites, so that I do not gather you up with them, given that you showed commitment with all the Israelites when they came up from Egypt." So the Kenites got away from among Amalek. ⁷Saul struck down Amalek from Havilah until one comes to Shur, which is over against Egypt. ⁸He captured Agag the king of Amalek alive, but the entire company he devoted to the edge of the sword. ⁹Saul and the company spared Agag and the best of the sheep, the cattle, and the second-born, and the lambs, everything that was good. They were not willing to devote them. But everything that was despised and emaciated—they devoted it.

¹⁰Yahweh's word came to Samuel: ¹¹"I regret that I made Saul reign as king, because he has turned from following me and has not fulfilled my words." Samuel was vexed and cried out to Yahweh all night. ¹²Next morning Samuel got up early to meet Saul. Samuel was told, "Saul has been to Carmel. There: he set up a monument for himself. He left and passed on, and went down to Gilgal." ¹³When Samuel came to Saul, Saul said to him, "Blessed are you by Yahweh! I have fulfilled Yahweh's command." ¹⁴So Samuel said, "So what is this sound of sheep in my ears, and the sound of cattle that I hear?" ¹⁵Saul said, "They were brought from the Amalekites, because the company spared the best of the sheep and cattle to sacrifice to Yahweh your God. The rest we devoted." ¹⁶Samuel said to Saul, "Stop. I will tell you what Yahweh said to me last night." [Saul] said to him, "Speak." ¹⁷Samuel said, "Though you were small in your eyes, you are

actually head of the Israelite clans. Yahweh anointed you as king over Israel [18]and Yahweh sent you on a journey and said to you, 'Go and devote the wrongdoers, the Amalekites. Do battle against them until you have finished them off.' [19]Why did you not listen to Yahweh's voice but swoop on the plunder and do what was wrong in Yahweh's eyes? . . . [22]Are burnt offerings and sacrifices as pleasing to Yahweh as listening to Yahweh's voice? There: listening is better than sacrificing, heeding [is better] than the fat of rams. [23]Because rebellion [is as bad as] the wickedness of divination; arrogance [is as bad as] the waywardness of effigies."

[Verses 24–32 recount how Samuel continues to rebuke Saul, Saul admits he did wrong, and Samuel kills Agag.]

According to news reports, at U.S. bases in Guantanamo Bay in Cuba in the first decade of the twenty-first century we were engaged in the torture of people suspected of terrorist acts. This involved keeping people in constrained positions for long periods, beating them, subjecting them to sexual degradation and sexual assault, burning them with cigarettes or cutting them with barbed wire or glass, and imposing loud noise or extreme temperatures on them for long periods. A distinctive technique we used at Guantanamo Bay was waterboarding, putting people on their backs with their heads downward and pouring water over them in such a way as to make them go through an experience that resembles drowning and can lead to brain damage or death. There is some dispute over whether this counts as torture, as is also the case with the sleep deprivation we impose on people that makes it impossible for them to sleep for days on end; it has been described by someone who has experienced it as wearying the spirit to death.

The Amalekites would have been good at torture. According to Genesis, Amalek was a descendant of Abraham and Sarah and of Isaac and Rebekah, so the Amalekites were distant relatives of the Israelites, but Exodus 17 relates how they attacked the Israelites when they were on their way from Egypt toward Sinai. Deuteronomy 25 adds that the Israelites were in a weary and worn-out state and that the Amalekites acted by attacking the people at the back of the Israelite wagon train, the people who were lagging behind. The Amalekites thus become a symbol for people with no human instincts or reverence for God, and they are the only people the Israelites are expected to eliminate outside the context of the Israelites' conquest of the **Canaanites**. Maybe their symbolic significance links with the way they keep reappearing in the Old Testament after they have been annihilated, like monsters in a sci-fi movie. The last descendant of Agag in the Old Testament is the Persian Haman, who seeks to appropriate the power of the great empire of the day to eliminate the Jewish people. The Amalekites stand for opposition to God's purpose that is designed to bring about the redemption of the world, and for unprincipled violence toward weak people, and their story stands for God's implacable commitment to punishing the kind of wickedness they embody. Metaphorically, Adolf Hitler has been described as a descendant of Agag, and the president of Israel referred to 1 Samuel 15 in declining to support pleas for clemency toward the Nazi war criminal Adolf Eichmann.

The problem with Saul is that he didn't take seriously enough this commitment of God's. He was supposed to "**devote**" the Amalekites and everything that belonged to them. In other words, he had to give them wholly over to God by destroying them. This practice means there is no danger of making war because of what you may gain from it; you gain nothing. Saul fails to devote everything, and he has a rationale for his action, but Samuel sees it as merely a rationalization. To put it another way, Saul did not take seriously enough the fact that he was **Yahweh's** "anointed." He had been taken hold of and designated by God to do what God wanted done, to act as God's representative. There are things that happen in the world that so incense God that they make it essential for God to take action against them, and such are the deeds of the Amalekites. They are a symbol of human resistance to God and God's purposes in the world and of human inhumanity toward other human beings. As God's anointed, Saul is God's means of taking this action against them.

We do well to worry about the idea that God would tell Saul to slaughter a whole people. Admittedly, the fact that apart from the story in Joshua this is the only occasion when God requires such action means that we cannot generalize from it. Yet in another sense, it is important that we should generalize from it. It affirms God's implacable opposition to the ill-treatment of weak people by powerful people and God's intention to put down powerful people who act in that way. History provides example after example of the way powerful empires get put down, and the Scriptures invite us to see God's activity behind their downfall.

So we are right to be scared of this story. It reminds us of what God might decide to do to us, insofar as we are Amalek. The question raised for us is whether our life as a nation is characterized by ill-treatment of weak people rather than by commitment to them. It is hard for us to accept responsibility for what we as a nation do in Guantanamo Bay, but we elected the government that authorizes the use of force, whose protection we enjoy. We cannot evade responsibility for what happens, and the story recognizes our dilemma. Saul knows God wishes to punish only the people actually responsible for that atrocity at the time of the exodus. The Kenites were another group among the wider Abrahamic family living in the area between Egypt and Canaan and now living among the Amalekites. They had shown a **commitment** to Israel that contrasted with the Amalekites' ruthlessness. So Saul gives them chance to escape. If we want to escape God's taking redress on the nation we live in, we would be wise to find a way of dissociating ourselves from its Amalek-like lifestyle.

Saul's reluctance to do what God says causes God to "regret" making him king, and in light of what has emerged about Saul's character, God has a change of plan. The Old Testament often refers to God's having a change of plan or a change of mind. It thus reflects the real nature of God's relationship with us. God does not just decide things ahead of time and implement them regardless of what happens. How God relates to us interacts with our decisions and our lives. Saul's unwillingness to do what God said about Amalek is just as bad as if he had been involved in divination by means of **effigies**.

In contrast, at the end of this story Samuel warns Saul that God will not have a change of mind or a change of plan in such a way as to decide that after all Saul can continue as king. That declaration reminds us that while God does act in interaction with us, God is not fickle or arbitrary. We don't have to be afraid of God's having a change of plan, as if that is a threat to us when we are walking in God's way. Indeed, most references to God's having a change of plan refer to God's giving up the idea of bringing trouble to someone. If Saul really had turned back to God, even he could have been restored.

1 SAMUEL 15:34–16:23

Yahweh's Good Spirit and Yahweh's Bad Spirit

³⁴Samuel went to Ramah, and Saul went up to his home at Gibeah of Saul. ³⁵Samuel did not see Saul again until the day of his death, because Samuel lamented for Saul, while Yahweh had regretted that he had made Saul king over Israel. ¹⁶:¹But Yahweh said to Samuel, "How long are you going to lament for Saul, when I myself have rejected him as king over Israel? Fill your horn with oil and go: I will send you to Jesse the Bethlehemite because I have seen a king for myself among his sons." ²Samuel said, "How can I go? When Saul hears, he will slay me." Yahweh said, "If you take a heifer with you, you can say 'It is to sacrifice to Yahweh that I have come,' ³and invite Jesse to the sacrifice. I myself will let you know what you are to do. You will anoint for me the one I say to you." ⁴Samuel did as Yahweh spoke. When he came to Bethlehem, the city elders were alarmed to meet him and said, "Does your coming mean things are well?" ⁵He said, "Things are well. It is to sacrifice to Yahweh that I have come. Sanctify yourselves and come with me to the sacrifice." He sanctified Jesse and his sons and invited them to the sacrifice. ⁶When they came, he saw Eliab and said, "Surely Yahweh's anointed is before him!" ⁷But Yahweh said to Samuel, "Don't pay attention to his appearance or how tall he stands, because I have rejected him, because it is not what a human being sees, because a human being sees what is visible, but Yahweh sees the inner person."

[In verses 8–10 Yahweh goes on to reject six more of Jesse's sons.]

¹¹Samuel said to Jesse, "Are these all the boys?" He said, "The youngest is still left. Now. He is tending the flock." Samuel said to Jesse, "Send and get him, because we will not sit down until

he comes here." [12]So he sent and brought him. He was tanned, handsome in appearance, good-looking. Yahweh said, "Go on, anoint him, because this is the one." [13]Samuel got the horn of oil and anointed him in the midst of his brothers. Yahweh's spirit erupted on David from that day onward. Samuel set out and went to Ramah.

[14]Now Yahweh's spirit had left Saul, and a bad spirit from Yahweh had assailed him. [15]Saul's servants said to him, "Okay, now. A bad spirit from God is assailing you. [16]Our lord might like to say that your servants who are before you should seek for someone who knows how to play the guitar. When the bad spirit from God is upon you, he would play and it would be good for you." [17]Saul said to his servants, "Will you look for someone who plays well for me, and bring him to me." [18]One of the servants declared, "Right. I have seen a son of Jesse the Bethlehemite who knows how to play. He is a strong guy and a fighter, but skilled in words and good-looking, and Yahweh is with him." . . . [21]So David came to Saul and attended on him, and [Saul] liked him a lot and he became an arms bearer for him. . . . [23]When the spirit from God came to Saul, David would get the guitar and play, and there would be relief for Saul. It was good for him. The bad spirit would leave him.

I was recently reading a profile of Clint Eastwood; it was this profile that made me think about his movie *Unforgiven* in connection with 1 Samuel 13. In that and other later movies he is both actor and director, but he started off simply as an actor, and I had not realized till reading this profile that he was a hunk. No one meeting him in his twenties would have thought he was any more than a good-looking, tanned Californian who liked beer, women, cars, and music. Yet as an actor he became a kind of mythic hero and redemption figure like John Wayne, and then as a director he came to explore the ambiguity of the violence he once embodied, to explore lostness and vulnerability, guilt and self-destruction, and to face how our past decisions and acts and experiences shape us in a way we cannot escape. Being good-looking and being thoughtful turn out not to be incompatible.

That assumption underlies the ambiguity with which 1 Samuel speaks about good looks. Saul was the prettiest and tallest guy in town, which endears him to the community. While God hardly chose him for his looks, it seems that God was pleased to be able to choose a man who has the looks for the part. God likes beautiful things. Yet mere good looks can obviously become too important, both to their possessor and to other people, and Saul's story in effect implies that he has the outward qualifications to be king but not the inward ones.

One might then think that God would decide to ignore looks next time around, and the story of how Samuel comes to identify David as God's replacement for Saul at first gives the impression that this is what will happen. There are some humorous notes in the story, such as God's willingness to collude with Samuel in being economical with the truth about the reason for his visit to Bethlehem and the alarm of the city elders who know that the arrival of a prophet is usually bad news: literally they ask, "Is your coming **peace**?" When Samuel is introduced to Jesse's eldest, he is told to take no account of his appearance or height, because God looks at the inner person. We then eventually meet Jesse's youngest, and we expect that he will be a little weed, but he too is tanned from spending his life out in the open and thus good-looking. The story of his introduction to Saul adds to that account. He is strong and handsome, and a fighter, and also good with words and music.

We are told nothing about the inner person that God can see. David will manifest character flaws at least as great as Saul's, but he has one great strength that will stand out as the subsequent Old Testament story looks back on him and compares him with his successors. Those successors often failed to give **Yahweh** the exclusive commitment Yahweh looked for. For all his faults, at least David never looked to other deities. There was something God could see about him.

The story is not explicit about how we are to relate what God could see and how God deals with David. The story of his designation comes to an end with God's **spirit** bursting on him. It seems a formulaic statement. It is the expression that was used of Samson and Saul, and after God's spirit burst on them they did things like tear a lion apart with their bare hands, kill thirty people, speak in tongues, and rescue a city besieged by a foreign army. After God's spirit bursts on David he does . . .

nothing. Indeed, 1 and 2 Samuel will never speak of the activity of God's spirit on David. No doubt God's spirit was involved with him, and this comment at his anointing asserts as much, but God will work much more through what he could "naturally" do. Perhaps talk of God's spirit bursting on him through his life is another way of expressing the point that one of Saul's servants makes when he says, "Yahweh is with him." It's the expression Genesis used of Joseph when it went on to comment that as a consequence (in William Tyndale's sixteenth-century translation) "He was a lucky fellow." Joseph was a handsome guy who found that his looks could get him into trouble, but God was with him, and he was successful against the odds, not because God kept doing miracles for him but because things just worked out that way. This is how things are when God is with you. You fall on your feet. David will do that. Sometimes.

David will thus be the antithesis to poor Saul. Saul has made his mistakes, put his wrong foot forward, acted stupidly, failed to listen carefully enough to what God told him, and through the rest of 1 Samuel he is going to carry on doing such things, falling over every small stone instead of landing on his feet. So the story juxtaposes God's spirit erupting on David with God's spirit leaving Saul, and (worse) a bad spirit from God attacking him. We need to be careful what we read into this statement. The Gospels talk about evil spirits attacking people, and translations of 1 Samuel use phrases such as "evil spirit" in connection with Saul. Yet the Old Testament does not talk about evil spirits in the way the Gospels do, which raises questions about whether the idea of evil spirits is intended here. Furthermore, the Hebrew word in this story is more like the English word *bad* than the English word *wicked*. While it can suggest something morally bad, it can also suggest that the thing we experience is bad, something that brings trouble or suffering to us.

If we think of God's sending Saul a bad spirit, even a bad temper, we will probably get the right idea. It is exactly a bad spirit or a bad temper that afflicts him through the chapters that will now unfold. As a supplement to the music therapy David gives him, I expect another therapist would in theory be able to help him see how his bad spirit is a natural reaction to the way his life is unraveling, but Saul doesn't appear to be the kind of person who would be able to generate the insight to face this. Seeing that God is involved in sending Saul this bad spirit suggests an awareness that this natural process is God's way of rebuking and chastising Saul. It does not rule out the possibility of Saul changing. The question is how he deals with his experience. The story that unfolds will suggest that he lacks the capacity or the willingness to change. Neither Saul nor David is the kind of person who grows in his human awareness as he grows older, in the way the profile I read suggests Clint Eastwood has done. Maybe the temptation of power is what makes the difference. Saul and David's problem was the fact that they were kings. "All power corrupts; absolute power corrupts absolutely."

1 SAMUEL 17:1–54

How to Recycle Your Killer Instinct

¹The Philistines gathered their forces for battle. They gathered at Socoh belonging to Judah and camped between Socoh and Azekah, at Ephes-dammim. ²Saul and the Israelites gathered and camped in the Elah Valley and drew up their battle line to meet the Philistines. ³The Philistines were standing on one mountain and Israel was standing on another mountain with the ravine between them. ⁴A representative came out from the Philistine forces; his name was Goliath, from Gath. His height was six cubits and a span. . . . ⁸He stood and called to the ranks of Israel and said to them, "Why should you come out and line up for battle? I am indeed the Philistine and you are Saul's servants. Choose yourselves someone to come down against me. ⁹If he can do battle with me and strike me down, we will become your servants. If I can overcome him and strike him down, you will become our servants and serve us."

[In verses 10–25 Goliath issues his challenge for forty days, but no Israelite volunteers to take him on. On one occasion, David arrives with provisions for his big brothers.]

²⁶David said to the men standing by him, "What will be done for the man who strikes down that Philistine and removes reproach from Israel? Because who is this uncircumcised Philistine that

he has reproached the ranks of the living God?" . . . ³¹The things David said were heard and were told to Saul, and he got hold of him. ³²David said to Saul, "A person's heart should not fail him. Your servant will go and fight with this Philistine." ³³Saul said to David, "You cannot go to this Philistine and fight with him, because you are a boy and he has been a warrior from his boyhood." ³⁴David said to Saul, "Your servant has been shepherding the flocks for his father. When a lion or a bear comes and carries off a sheep from the flock, ³⁵I go out after it and strike it down and rescue [the sheep] from its mouth. If it rises up against me, I seize it by the beard and strike it down and kill it. ³⁶Both lion and bear your servant has struck down. This uncircumcised Philistine will be like one of them, because he has reproached the ranks of the living God." ³⁷David said, "Yahweh who rescued me from the hand of lion and bear: he will rescue me from the hand of this Philistine."

[In verses 38–44 Saul gets David to put on his armor, but it is too big. David advances on Goliath with his cane, five stones from the wash, and his sling.]

⁴⁵David said to the Philistine, "You come to me with sword, spear, and javelin, but I come to you in the name of Yahweh Armies, God of the ranks of Israel whom you have reproached. ⁴⁶This day Yahweh will deliver you into my hand and I will strike you down and cut off your head."

[Verses 47–54 relate how David fells Goliath with a stone from his sling and cuts off his head. The Philistines run, and the Israelites give chase.]

It was the Oscars last weekend (I went to a great jazz concert two blocks away, though I was nearly late because of the road closures in Hollywood), and against the odds, *The Hurt Locker* beat *Avatar* (which grossed fifty times as much). How did David beat Goliath? the press asked. Last night, Merrimack College played Boston University at hockey (I went to a jazz concert three thousand miles away), and Merrimack's coach said it was like David playing Goliath (David took an early lead, but eventually lost). Another reporter comments that nearly all sports movies adopt the David-and-Goliath trajectory, but it then carries over into politics, such as those of an upcoming

British election; while in Florida, a senatorial candidate yesterday agreed that his campaign could make people think of David against Goliath, and he reminded them that David won. In the U.K., the most popular technology story of this week was the "David and Goliath battle between Microsoft and i4i" (I'm not really clear what that means, but I suspect that David and Goliath come in the wrong order for the metaphor to work). Traveling around Silicon Valley last week, another reporter tells us that he heard the David versus Goliath story over and over again.

We clearly have a powerful story line here, so it's worth noting what the original version does with it. First, the **Philistines** have a really sensible idea about how to wage war. In traditional societies, war is generally waged by the entirety of the (adult male) community, as was in effect the case in modern societies in (for instance) the 1939–1945 war, though in tension with this, just-war theory maintains a distinction between combatants and civilians, while a war such as that in Iraq was fought by a professional army. The Philistines work with the idea that the battle should be decided by one guy from each side fighting each other. Whichever side's champion wins, they will now be top dog and henceforth will be in charge; the side whose champion loses will obey their orders. It would be even more sensible if the decision could be taken on the basis of (say) a game of chess or soccer, or a knitting competition. Of course the Philistines are convinced that they cannot lose (Goliath is ten feet tall), and it is perhaps not surprising that when their champion loses, they forget the sensible rule they proposed.

What bothers David is the reproach Goliath brings on Israel. At one level it is not much of an argument. Yet when a team loses a game or an army loses a battle, it is ashamed. It crawls back home, and it wants to hide in disgrace. This is illogical, but real. David cares about Israel's honor. On the other hand, there is more to his concern than this. His concern is that Goliath is bringing reproach and shame on the army of the living God. When a church does something shameful (as if!), this brings discredit on God. When Israel quakes in fear before the Philistines and their champion, this brings discredit on God. It is a price God pays for setting up an association with a people.

83

David knows this and is passionately concerned to do something about it.

David holds together his confidence in himself and his confidence in God, seeing the two as interwoven. He is not a mere shepherd boy who has no experience of fighting. He has fought lions and bears and lived to tell the tale. Those battles will already have demonstrated to him that the outcome of a fight can be decided not by how big you are but by how clever and/or how brave you are. Yet David also knows that he might not have escaped from the lion or the bear unless God had also been involved. Though he may not know how these two considerations interweave, he knows that they do. No courage and shrewdness, and he dies. No involvement of God, and he dies. He has needed both and will need both again. Maybe it's also significant that in his argument with Saul his experience of successful fighting has the first word, but his conviction that God will rescue him has the last word.

The basis for that conviction is that God is **Yahweh Armies**. David knows that God really does have all power in the heavens and on the earth, and he knows that God is prepared to use it. God is not merely sovereign in people's religious and personal lives but in the world's political and military life. God has the power and is prepared to use it, but God characteristically uses it on behalf of someone like David, not on behalf of someone like Goliath, who hardly needs it (in theory). What God delights to do is turn odds upside down. When God acts (as Hannah put it near the beginning of 1 Samuel), the bows of warriors are broken and people who were falling gain strength, because it is not by might that a person prevails. David's story is good news for little people.

In a way, David's entire character comes out in this story. I suggested that being "a man after God's heart" needn't mean what we think it means; it simply indicates that David was someone God chose. But you can see why David would become "a man after God's heart" in that other sense. David manifests a commitment to Yahweh and a trust in Yahweh the like of which we have hardly seen before in the Old Testament. It is a shame that (as is the case with Saul) David's first moments are also his best moments.

1 SAMUEL 17:55–18:16
How to Be a Dysfunctional Royal Family

[55]When Saul saw David going out to meet the Philistine, he said to Abner, the army commander, "Whose son is the boy, Abner?" Abner said, "By your life, your majesty, I don't know." [56]King Saul said, "You ask whose son the young man is." [57]When David came back from striking down the Philistine, Abner got him and brought him before Saul, with the Philistine's head in his hand. [58]Saul said to him, "Whose son are you, my boy?" David said, "The son of your servant Jesse the Bethlehemite." [18:1]When he had finished speaking to Saul, Jonathan's very self became bound to David's self. Jonathan became as loyal to him as he was to himself. [2]Saul took [David] that day and did not let him go back to his father's household. [3]Jonathan and David sealed a covenant because [Jonathan] was as loyal to him as to his own self. [4]Jonathan took off the coat he had on and gave it to David, and his shirt, along with his sword, his bow, and his belt.

[5]On all [the missions] Saul sent him, [David] would succeed, and Saul set him over the men of war. This was good in the eyes of the whole company, and also in the eyes of Saul's servants. [6]When the men came [home] and David got back from striking down the Philistine, the women came out from all the cities in Israel to sing and dance when they met King Saul, with tambourines, with festivity, and with guitars. [7]The women proclaimed as they played, and said, "Saul struck down his thousands; David his ten thousands." [8]But it vexed Saul very much; this thing was bad in his eyes. He said, "They have given David ten thousands and given me thousands. Only the kingship will now be his." [9]Saul was watching David from that day on. [10]Next day a bad spirit from God erupted on Saul and he prophesied inside the house while David was playing, as he did each day. There was a spear in Saul's hand. [11]Saul threw the spear. He said, "I will pin David to the wall." But David eluded him twice. [12]Saul was afraid of David because Yahweh was with him and had moved away from Saul. [13]Saul removed him from his presence and made him head of a thousand, so he went out and came in before the company. [14]David was successful in all his ventures; Yahweh was with him. [15]Saul saw that he was very successful and he was terrified of him, [16]but all Israel and Judah were loyal to David, because he went out and came in before them.

Queen Elizabeth II declared 1992 her annus horribilis, her "horrible year." The phrase is a riff on the expression annus mirabilis, "miracle year," the phrase devised by the poet John Dryden to describe 1666, the year when the English navy defeated the Dutch navy (apologies to any Dutch readers) and when the City of London escaped the much greater devastation it might have experienced from the Great Fire of London (Dryden ignored the Great Plague of 1665–1666, but maybe he took plagues for granted the way we take it for granted that thousands of people die in traffic accidents every month). For the Queen, 1992 was the year Windsor Castle caught fire and the year the marriages of two of her sons broke up.

Saul has had his annus mirabilis; indeed he has had two of them. The first was the year he rescued the men of Jabesh-gilead; the second was the year David killed Goliath and thus set the Philistines on the run. He now has his annus horribilis; indeed, that is the only kind of year he will have until the end of his life.

His problems as king and his problems as father interweave. Perhaps they always do; this will certainly be a motif in David's story, too. First there is his son, who becomes David's best friend at the same time as Saul comes to view David as his chief enemy, and for overlapping reasons. Saul is not exactly wrong in his view of David. David actually is the person who is going to replace him as king. It ought to be Jonathan, as Jonathan presumably knows, but Jonathan doesn't care. Saul didn't need to be a leader and tried to avoid it, but once he got into that position he became attached to it. It defines who he is. Maybe Jonathan has watched that and knows he doesn't want to go the same way. We have noted that his attack on the Philistine garrison in chapter 14 suggests that he has more inbuilt leadership instinct than Saul; he doesn't need God's **spirit** to come on him to make him take a crazy initiative. He is in fact like David, the killer of lions and bears; it looks as if this is what drew Jonathan to David. They were both archetypal male heroes. Jonathan could see himself in David. You couldn't simply say they were Type A males (one reason is that the whole Type A–Type B typology is probably a myth). If anything it's Saul who looks Type A. Jonathan lacks the inner need to be a leader. He would have made a better king than Saul or David, but he's not bothered, and Israel's system (like ours) means you end up having as leaders people who want to be leaders, which is a really bad idea.

Jonathan and David have overlapping characteristics, though not identical ones. As well as having no need to be in a leadership position, Jonathan knew how to be someone's friend. He knows about personal relationships. David is clueless about personal relationships; this is key to understanding his story. There is a sense in which the friendship is quite one-sided. Jonathan becomes committed to David. In speaking of Jonathan's loyalty, the story uses the Hebrew word that suggests love, but that translation can be misleading, and I have thus avoided it. One reason is that the Hebrew words for love and hatred suggest at least as much a moral and political loyalty as an emotion (as when Jesus says disciples have to hate their parents). Middle Eastern political documents talk about underlings loving the superior powers. So Jonathan is making a political **commitment** to David as well as a personal one. In effect he is yielding to David the position of Saul's potential successor. The same point emerges from the way the two young men make a **covenant**, because the Hebrew word for a covenant is also the word for a treaty, a political commitment. The relationship between them has a bit of both about it.

Jonathan is not the only one who is smitten with David. To start with, all the women in Israel are. You would have to be a big man to cope with their enthusiasm for one of your junior officers, and Saul is not a big man. With some irony, this time the story speaks of the bad spirit from God "erupting" on Saul, the word it had used of God's spirit bursting on him when Samuel anointed him, and when it inspired him to take action to rescue the men of Jabesh-gilead, and when Samuel anointed David. It even has the result of making him "prophesy," as he did at the beginning. He behaves in some way that makes it clear that something supernatural is going on. Nothing has changed from when he was anointed, but everything has changed. There was a sense in which it was a bad spirit that came on him when it inspired him to fight against the Ammonites. It was a bad spirit as far as they were concerned, a spirit that aroused energy and meant trouble for them. Now it's a bad spirit in the sense that it arouses energy and threatens trouble for David, but David has a charmed life. You could say that God protected David, but the story just says that David evaded Saul. David knows how to watch his back. On the other hand, when Saul sends David on risky missions in the hope that he will get killed, instead he succeeds on the missions (he "goes out," and he also "comes back" at the head of the military unit), and that happens because "Yahweh was with him." You could say that he knew how to look after himself, but in this connection the narrative reminds us that there are these two ways of looking at what happens. Human courage and sharpness are involved, and things would not have turned out the way they do without these. Divine protection is involved, and things would not have turned out the way they do without this.

You may have been puzzled about why Saul needs to ask his army commander who David is when we have already been told that David has been the court's resident singer-songwriter for quite a while. It is another indication of the way the narrative about Saul and David has been compiled from a series of independent, overlapping stories that have been put together to give us a composite picture of Saul and David, without the stories being open to being turned into a neat linear picture. It fits with this that 2 Samuel 21:19 attributes the killing of Goliath to a man called Elhanan. There are a number of ways of explaining this, but the one that seems most plausible to me is that the process is similar to the one whereby stories get attached to well-known figures such as Robin Hood, or the way stained-glass windows glorify biblical heroes. A heroic figure like Robin Hood was a real person who undertook spectacular acts, so telling stories about him that historically concerned someone else isn't exactly wrong. The stories enable us to understand the person's true significance. Likewise, if it wasn't David who killed Goliath but someone else, attaching the story to David fills out the picture of David in a way that gives us a true impression of his significance. If this is the kind of thing that happened, it explains why the stories don't form a neat jigsaw. If you think it is inconceivable that God should have colluded with that way of bringing the Scriptures into being, you are free to take one of the other explanations (such as that

Elhanan is another name for David; lots of people in the Bible do have more than one name). Either way, we need to read each story in its own right rather than fretting too much about the continuity issues they raise.

1 SAMUEL 18:17–19:24

Everyone Is against Me

[17]Saul said to David, "Here is my oldest daughter Merab. I will give her to you as wife. . . ." [19]Then at the time for giving Saul's daughter Merab to David, she was given to Adriel the Meholathite. [20]But Saul's daughter Michal loved David. Saul was told, and it was pleasing in his eyes. [21]Saul said, "I will give her to him and she will be a trap for him so that the hand of the Philistines may be against him. . . ." [25]Saul said, "Say this to David: 'The king has no desire of a marriage gift except the foreskins of a hundred Philistines, to take redress on the king's enemies. . . .'" [27]David set off and went, he and his men, and struck down two hundred Philistines. David brought their foreskins and they counted out their full number to the king so that he might become the king's son-in-law, and Saul gave him his daughter Michal as wife. [28]Saul saw and recognized that Yahweh was with David and that Saul's daughter Michal was loyal to him, [29]and Saul grew more afraid of David. . . .

[19:1]Saul told his son Jonathan and all his servants to kill David, but Saul's son Jonathan favored David, [2]so Jonathan told David. . . . [4]Jonathan spoke well of David to his father Saul . . . , [6]and Saul listened to Jonathan's voice. Saul swore, "As Yahweh lives, he will not be killed. . . ." [9]Then a bad spirit from Yahweh came on Saul. . . . [11]Saul sent aides to David's house to keep watch over him and kill him in the morning, but his wife Michal told David, "If you don't run for your life tonight, you'll be killed tomorrow." [12]Michal let David down through the window. He went and escaped and fled. [13]Michal took the effigies and put them in the bed and put a goat's hair quilt at its head and covered it with clothes. [14]When Saul sent the aides to take David, she said, "He is sick," [15]but Saul sent the aides to see David: "Bring him up to me on the bed, to kill him." [16]So the aides came and there—it was the effigies in the bed and the goat's hair quilt at its head. [17]Saul said to Michal, "Why did you

deceive me like that and help my enemy get away so that he escaped?" Michal said to Saul, "He himself said to me, 'Help me get away. Why should I kill you?'"
[18]When David fled and escaped, he came to Samuel at Ramah. . . . [20]Saul sent aides to take David. They saw a group of prophets prophesying, with Samuel standing presiding over them. Yahweh's spirit came on Saul's aides and they too prophesied. [21]Saul was told, so he sent more aides, but they prophesied, too. Saul again sent, the third aides, and they prophesied, too. [22]So he went to Ramah, too . . . [23]and on him, too, God's spirit came, so that he walked on and prophesied until he came to Naioth in Ramah. [24]Then he also stripped off his clothes and he too prophesied in front of Samuel. He fell down naked all that day and all night. That is why they say, "Is Saul among the prophets, too?"

Last night I watched a Jordanian Oscar-nominated movie called *Captain Abu Raed*, whose central figure is an airport janitor at Amman Airport (just up the street from Jabesh-gilead, actually). In a subordinate plot point, he gets to know a woman called Nour who actually is a pilot. She is a successful woman in her thirties, but she has to endure her well-to-do father's periodic attempts to marry her off to implausible suitors. Now, many people who had their marriages arranged by their parents comment on how well the system works. Indian author Farahad Zama describes how he met his wife only for forty-five minutes over tea; they fell in love after the wedding. But he would have had the chance to say no on the basis of the forty-five minutes, which is what Nour in the movie does in rather less than that time. The trouble is, the more important your father is, the more likely it is that the matches he devises will be driven by politics, and they will then take some resisting. While this does not entirely explain the problems of the British royal family we noted in the previous chapter, it is a contributory factor.

It is evidently also the problem for Saul's daughters. First there is Merab; we do not get the impression that she has any say in whether she is given to (a) David or (b) Adriel. While Saul's change of mind may simply suggest his fickleness, the way the story unfolds may imply that David could not raise a marriage gift of appropriate value to enable him to marry Merab. Translations sometimes refer to this as a bride price, but the term is misleading if it implies that a groom buys his bride from her father and thus that a wife is her husband's property—except in the sense that she is "his wife" and he is "her husband." Rather, the exchange of gifts at a marriage (the marriage gift and the woman's dowry) is part of the social convention whereby a marriage is sealed by the giving of goods, as happens in Western culture. It is also a recognition that marriage means a man gains something of great economic value.

When he hears that Michal has taken a shine to David (like most all the other women in Israel), Saul has a vested interest in overcoming David's financial embarrassment, because he sees he can use this as a means of getting David out of the way. The story incorporates a number of notes of humor, mostly at Saul's expense, and the first is a note of coarse humor, of which the Bible is fond. The Israelites were scornful of the **Philistines** as uncultured Europeans who do not practice circumcision like civilized people (male circumcision was a regular practice among Middle Eastern peoples, though it usually happened at puberty, and it was given distinctive significance within Israel in connection with the **covenant**). So let David circumcise a few of these wild men. Of course they will not submit to this voluntarily: "Excuse me, do you mind if I just circumcise a hundred of you; I need the foreskins." "You'll have to kill us first." Saul's overt logic is that this will be a means of teaching the Philistines a lesson, a means of pursuing his task of asserting Israelite sovereignty over land that it sees as its own, though he also has that other motivation. It's win-win for Saul: he hopes David fails, but if he wins, that will also be useful in its way. David of course succeeds and doubles the number for good measure, and the story invites us to imagine David counting them out one by one. All to gain a wife. Who is this man? A man who wants to be king!

Saul can never see beyond the end of his nose. That is true in a profoundly religious connection. He can see that God is with David, and his appropriate reaction is to become more afraid of David. He is right that David is a serious threat to him. One might have thought that anyone with an ounce of good sense

would see that there was no point fighting God, but this awareness just makes Saul fight harder. Then he fails to see the further implications of the fact that Michal loves David. We have
noted an ambiguity about that word *love*. It suggests commitment and loyalty as well as feelings. Michal's feelings for David
are something Saul can use to try to get David killed: she wants
to marry him, but with luck David will get killed in fulfilling
Saul's condition. He doesn't. But Michal's love also means she
is committed to David (*love* is the same Hebrew word that I
translate *loyal* in 18:28). Like Jonathan's love/loyalty to David,
her love/loyalty to David is something with practical, political
implications. Marriage means you leave your father and stick to
your husband. Falling for David means she takes David's side
against Saul, and she will deceive and lie in order to save him
from death. Agreeing to let Michal marry David was the action
Saul took that he thought would give him a way to dispose of
David, but it turns out to be something that keeps David alive.
Poor Saul! The irony is underlined by the story of the **effigies**.
It does raise the question how David's wife comes to have these
effigies, and the incidental reference to them draws our attention to something that archaeological discoveries also make
clear, that everyday religious life in Israel was very different
from what the **Torah** prescribes.

Of course Jonathan is also no use to his father in connection
with getting rid of David. Jonathan "favors David" rather than
Saul; it is another way of describing his loyalty. The expression
is one Saul had told his courtiers to use in telling David of his
own attitude to him, which led him to offer him Merab. The
irony is that he didn't really mean it, whereas it actually is his
own son's attitude to David, and it leads Jonathan to spill the
beans to David as well as to talk Saul out of his intentions. This
works only for a while, because Saul has a bigger problem than
his son's being against him and his daughter's being against him
and his own stupidity's being against him: God is against him.
The final note of divine ruthlessness and humor comes in the
story of how once again Saul ends up prophesying. Once, way
back at the beginning, this had been a sign that God really was
with Saul. Now it is a sign that God really has abandoned him.
(Perhaps the fact that this meeting is an expression of judgment

is why Samuel is prepared to behave differently from what he said in 15:35.) Yet Saul still will not see sense and turn back.

1 SAMUEL 20:1–21:16

Friendship

[First Samuel 20:1–13a tells how David asks Jonathan to find out whether his father will continue to try to kill him, and Jonathan agrees to do so.]

¹³ᵇ"If it seems good to my father [to do] wrong to you, I will disclose it to you and send you off, and you will go to safety, and may Yahweh be with you as he was with my father. ¹⁴While I am still alive you are not to fail to keep Yahweh's commitment with me. Nor when I die ¹⁵are you to cut off your commitment with my household, ever, even when Yahweh has cut off David's enemies, each one, from the face of the ground. ¹⁶Jonathan has covenanted with David's household. Yahweh will require it from the hand of David's enemies." ¹⁷So Jonathan again swore to David by his loyalty to him, because he was as loyal to him as he was to himself . . . : ²³"The word that we have spoken, you and I: there, Yahweh is between you and me forever."

²⁴David hid in the countryside. It was the new moon and the king sat down for dinner, to eat. ²⁵The king sat in his seat as usual, the seat by the wall. Jonathan got up and Abner sat at Saul's side, but David's place was empty. ²⁶Saul made no comment that day because he said [to himself], "Something has happened so that he is not pure. . . ." ²⁷Then the day after the new moon, the second day, David's place was empty, so Saul said to his son Jonathan, "Why didn't Jesse's son come to dinner either yesterday or today?" ²⁸Jonathan answered Saul, "David asked urgently of me [if he could go] to Bethlehem. ²⁹He said, 'Do let me go, because we have a family sacrifice in the city and my brother has ordered me to it. So now, if I have found favor in your eyes, may I get away and see my brothers?' That is why he has not come to the king's table." ³⁰Saul's anger flared up at Jonathan and he said to him, "Son of a perverse, rebellious woman! I know very well that you are choosing Jesse's son, to your shame and the shame of your mother's nakedness! ³¹Because all the days that Jesse's son is alive on the earth, you

and your kingship will not be secure. So now, send and get him for me, because he is destined to die." [*Jonathan protests, Saul throws his spear at Jonathan, and Jonathan storms out and goes to tell David.*] ⁴¹ᵇ[David] fell on his face to the ground and bowed low three times, and they hugged each other and wept with each other, until David [did so] greatly. ⁴²Jonathan said to David, "Go to safety, because the two of us have sworn in Yahweh's name, 'Yahweh be between you and me and between your offspring and mine forever.'" ²¹﹕¹So David set off and went. While Jonathan came to the city, David came to Nob, to the priest Ahimelech. . . . ⁸But one of Saul's servants was there that day, detained before Yahweh. His name was Doeg the Edomite, chief herdsman to Saul.

[*Verses 9–16 relate how, having brought no weapons, David acquires Goliath's sword from Ahimelech, as well as provisions, and goes on to Gath, where he takes refuge with King Achish.*]

I know someone now in her eighties who lived for forty or fifty years with a friend. They had separate jobs, but in the rest of life they were inseparable, involved together in church and social life and spending their holidays together. The friend had a stroke a few years ago, and the woman I know took early retirement in order to be able to look after her and to make it possible for them to continue as full a life as possible together, still going off on adventurous holidays, and she went through grim bereavement when her friend eventually died, the kind of bereavement someone goes through when his or her spouse dies. There was the kind of relationship of mutual commitment between them that you might call covenantal. I used to ponder the likelihood that it would be much harder nowadays for two women or two men to make that kind of semipublic mutual commitment in the kind of conservative Christian circles to which they belonged because it would be broadly suspected that the relationship was in effect a same-sex marriage, and they would be horrified at that idea. In the modern West we have gotten into such a mess about same-sex relationships that the very idea of same-sex friendship has become imperiled.

It affects the way people read the relationship between David and Jonathan. Both straight people and gay people have asked whether it was a physically homosexual relationship. Of course the story never says, "Oh, by the way, they weren't gay." Its framework for describing the relationship between them is friendship and mutual **commitment**, though this mutuality doesn't mean the relationship meant the same to both men. The relationship's energy comes from Jonathan. He "loves" David, cares about him, is loyal to him rather than to his father, cares about him as much as he cares about himself. He bound himself to David. It was his care and loyalty that led to the making of a **covenant** between them.

In the West in recent years we have come to assume that a person's spouse is also his or her best friend. That worked for my wife and me, but it's an idiosyncratic assumption. There's no indication in the Bible that marriage is supposed to work that way, and it puts extra pressure on a relationship that has all the other demands that apply to it. A relationship of friendship and mutual commitment with another person of the same sex avoids some of that complication. Maybe a relationship of friendship and mutual commitment with a person of the opposite sex can do that, though that kind of relationship also carries the risks of getting sexually entangled. Then, of course, if one or both of the people involved is someone who is attracted to people of the same sex, this fact reshapes all those considerations.

The presuppositions of the story about Saul's dinner are that the beginning of the month is a special occasion celebrated before God, with a special dinner eaten in God's presence. But then, various things such as having sex or having contact with a dead body can make it inappropriate to rush into God's presence, because sex and death are alien to God's own character. Such considerations could make it appropriate to miss the first day of this celebration, but such taboos do not take long to wear off, so Saul could reasonably expect David to show up the next day. His failure to do so puts Saul on the track of the fact that something odd is going on. Related considerations surface in the story of David's emergency visit to Ahimelech, where he has to assure the priest that his men have not had sex lately before Ahimelech is willing to let them eat provisions from the sanctuary. His willingness to do so was still irregular. In Mark

95

2 Jesus refers back to this story as an example of how the Old Testament is not legalistic in the way it treats the **Torah**, so that there is similarly no need to be legalistic about the Sabbath. The point about the note concerning Doeg will emerge in the next chapter.

As usual, in reading this story it is worth asking why someone wrote it and what function it fulfilled. The connected narrative as a whole belongs at least to the time when David had become king, and one function it would fulfill is to assure its readers that the process whereby David came to the throne was entirely honorable. After all, Jonathan is the person you would expect to succeed his father as king. Why did he not do so? At one level the answer is that God determined otherwise, but people would know that David was capable of being a sharp political operator, at least until he lost his groove in the middle of his reign. Did he maneuver Jonathan out of his "rightful" place as Saul's successor? No, the story says, Jonathan was so enthusiastic about David (like everyone else apart from Saul) that he maneuvered himself out of his rightful place. Whether he realized it or not, to put it theologically Jonathan was happy to go along with God's intention to put David on the throne. "May Yahweh be with you as he was with my father," he says. Both halves of the sentence are worth pondering. The first is a wish that God may prosper and advance David, never mind if Jonathan loses. In the second, the grievous feature is the past-tense verb. God used to be with Saul, which meant that things went well for him. Now God is not, and they do not.

The story also acknowledges expectations that would apply to David as king. He is to keep commitment to Jonathan not only during his lifetime but after his death. The two men are of similar age so you might not expect that Jonathan would die before David, but actually he will do so. So what will happen to Jonathan's family? For all David's popularity in his own circles, there will be many people still loyal to Saul who will assume that someone from Saul's family should succeed Saul. Such considerations mean that after a coup, a new ruler is tempted to make a point of eliminating potential rivals to the throne, and these include Jonathan's sons. Second Samuel 9 and 21 will tell us how David made a point of honoring his promises to Jonathan in the way he arranges to care for Jonathan's handicapped son Mephibosheth and to arrange for Jonathan's burial.

1 SAMUEL 22:1–23:24

David on the Run

¹David went from there and escaped to a cave at Adullam. His brothers and all his father's household heard, and went down to him there. ²Everyone who was in trouble or who had a creditor or who was discontented in spirit gathered together with him, and he became their leader. There were some four hundred men with him. ³David went from there to Mizpeh in Moab and said to the king of Moab, "May my father and mother come out to be with you until I know what God will do for me." ⁴So he led them into the presence of the king of Moab and they stayed with him all the time David was at the stronghold. ⁵But the prophet Gad said to David, "You shall not stay in the stronghold. Go, take yourself to Judah." So David went, and came to the Hereth Forest.

⁶Saul heard that David and the men with him had been discovered. Saul was sitting under the tamarisk at Gibeah on the height, with his spear in his hand and all his servants standing with him. ⁷Saul said to his servants standing with him, "Do listen, Benjaminites. To all of you will Jesse's son give fields and vineyards? Will he make all of you commanders of thousands or commanders of hundreds? ⁸Because all of you have conspired against me. There is no one who informs me when my son covenants with Jesse's son. There is none of you who cares about me or informs me when my son has made my servant into someone lying in wait for me this very day." ⁹Doeg the Edomite, who was standing with Saul's servants, declared, "I saw Jesse's son come to Nob to Ahimelek son of Ahitub. ¹⁰[Ahimelek] inquired of Yahweh for him, and gave him provisions, and gave him the sword of Goliath the Philistine." ¹¹So the king sent to summon Ahimelek son of Ahitub, the priest, and all his father's household, the priests at Nob. All of them came to the king. ¹²Saul said, "Do listen, son of Ahitub." He said, "Here I am, my lord." ¹³Saul said to him, "Why have you and Jesse's son conspired against me, in giving him food and

a sword, and inquiring of God for him, so that he can arise and lie in wait for me this very day?" [14]Ahimelek answered the king, "But who among all your servants is as trustworthy as David, the king's son-in-law, commander of your bodyguard, and honorable in your household?" ... [17]But the king said to the runners standing with him, "Turn and kill Yahweh's priests, because their hand is also with David. They knew he was fleeing and they did not inform me." But the king's servants were not willing to raise their hand to strike Yahweh's priests, [18]so the king said to Doeg, "You turn and strike the priests." Doeg the Edomite turned, and he was the one who struck the priests and killed them that day, eighty-five men wearing the linen ephod. [19]He struck down Nob, the priests' city, with the edge of the sword—men and women, children and babies, oxen, donkeys, and sheep, with the edge of the sword.

[Verses 22:20–23:29 relate how Abiathar, Ahimelek's son, escapes to David, who realizes the massacre came about because of him. David attacks the Philistines who are raiding the Judahite city of Keilah and escapes an attempt by Saul to capture him there, and escapes subsequent attempts in the Ziph Wilderness.]

The other day, a student was discussing his future plans with me. He believed God was telling him that he should stay at the seminary for another year to do further courses to improve his chances of getting into a doctoral program, that he should then apply to our seminary for doctoral study, and that in order to focus on his study he should give up his current job and take on something more part-time. I nodded sagely, but inside I rolled my eyes. What gives people the impression that God guides them over such matters? The Bible does not say so. If I ask them this question, as I sometimes do, they reply that surely God is a loving Father who is interested in the details of our lives. And I respond by affirming that surely our Father is indeed passionately interested in the details of our lives, as I am passionately interested in the details of my sons' lives. But my interest doesn't mean I want to tell my sons what decisions to make. I want them to live like adults, and they have to live with the consequences of their decisions; they need to make them. Because God is a loving Father, he wants us to live like adults, and generally leaves us to make our own decisions. There are exceptions; I have occasionally believed God was giving me guidance of that kind, and for all I know that student may be right in thinking that God was giving him guidance about the details of his life (which is another reason for me to keep my eye-rolling inside my head).

The story of David's escapes, which I summarized at the end of the scriptural translation above, shows how there can be exceptions to that rule. David hears that the pesky **Philistines** are raiding Keilah and plundering its harvest. Keilah was one of the places in the borderlands between Israelite territory and Philistine territory, the borderlands between the mountains and the plain that extends inland from the Mediterranean; nowadays, Keilah is thus on the border of the West Bank and Israel proper. So it's a **Judahite** city in a vulnerable location. Now, the one priest who had escaped the massacre at Nob had brought the **ephod** with him. Ahimelek and Abiathar were descendants of Eli, the priest at Shiloh (see chapter 1–4); if they were based at Nob (not far from Shiloh) and the ephod was there, evidently Nob had replaced Shiloh as the key sanctuary in the area. The Old Testament elsewhere refers to the sanctuary at Shiloh being destroyed, so maybe this had happened in the course of the conflict between the Israelites and the Philistines, though 1 Samuel doesn't tell us about how that happened.

Abiathar's bringing the ephod means David can ask God whether he is to go and attack the Philistines who are troubling Keilah, and God's answer is affirmative. His men point out that this is a dangerous proposal, so David consults God again, and God confirms that things will work out okay. They do; the people of Keilah are presumably grateful, and David and his men settle there for a while, being glad of somewhere friendly where they can get a burger and a shower. Saul hears about this and comments, "God has delivered David into my hands" because a city with gates and the other kind of bars is easy to besiege, but his pronouncements about what God intends come simply from his own calculations. David hears that Saul is planning to come and again consults God about whether Saul will actually come ("Yes") and whether that will lead the people of Keilah to panic and surrender David ("Yes"), so he gets out of there.

So sometimes God does guide people about the details of what they should do. How does God decide when to do so? How do you know when to ask God what you should do? The story suggests two insights. One is that there is something special about David. He is the man after God's heart—that is, the man God has chosen. He has a distinctive place in God's purpose as the person God intends to use as king, which is significant for you and me because what God is doing in Israel relates to the fulfillment of God's purpose for you and me. It is in that connection that God deals with him in ways that may not apply to me or you. We might be tempted to be jealous and resentful; why doesn't God use me and thus relate to me as God did with David? We might be wise to be glad that this is so, because (like Saul) having a place in God's purpose is a mixed blessing. David is not a happy man, and he will get unhappier. I'm glad I'm not David. The encouragement in the story is that if ever God needs to guide you in order for you to fulfill your place in God's purpose, God will do so.

The other insight is that even David doesn't ask God what to do every five minutes. Usually he makes his own decisions, takes responsibility for his own (and his men's) destiny. After escaping from Keilah, he runs for the hills, once again without showers or burgers or bars. God is protecting David, but there is no reference to supernatural guidance in this bit of the story. David just uses his human acumen. Admittedly that can bring other problems, as the massacre at Nob shows. David knows the massacre issued from his action. We make decisions, and we sometimes can't see their implications.

Two other things work in David's favor. One is a visit from Jonathan, which was presumably risky on the part of the man whose father had just now thrown a javelin at him for taking David's side. Jonathan "strengthens his hand by Yahweh," reaffirming that things are going to work out, that God will protect him, that he will end up as king. The other is that when Saul goes looking for him, "God did not give David into his hands"—contrary to what Saul thought. At one point David and his men are going along one side of a mountain, and Saul and his men are going along the other side, about to close in on David, but messengers come to Saul to tell him about another

Philistine raid, and he has to give up his pursuit. David could not have manipulated Jonathan's friendship and loyalty or a Philistine invasion at the right moment, but "chance" events in which God was not directly involved work in David's favor, and one can imagine that God is glad.

1 SAMUEL 24:1–25:44

Fool by Name and Fool by Nature

[First Samuel 24:1–25:1 relates how David declines a chance to kill Saul, and then tells of Samuel's death.]

²There was a man in Maon whose business was in Carmel. The man was very wealthy; he had flocks of three thousand and a thousand goats. He was shearing his flocks in Carmel. ³The man's name was Nabal; his wife's name was Abigail. The woman was intelligent and beautiful. The man was hard and an evildoer. He was a Calebite.

[In verses 4–9 David sends some of his heavies to Nabal with the hint that he might offer some protection money.]

¹⁰But Nabal answered David's servants, "Who is David, who is Jesse's son? There are many servants running away from their masters today. ¹¹Shall I take my bread and water and the meat I have slaughtered for my shearers and give them to men who are from I don't know where?"

[In verses 12–17, in response David assembles a posse, and someone tells Abigail what is going on.]

¹⁸Abigail hurried to get two hundred loaves, two skins of wine, five dressed sheep, five measures of roasted grain, a hundred blocks of raisins, and two hundred blocks of figs, put them on donkeys, ¹⁹and said to her boys, "Go on ahead of me. There. I am coming after you." She did not tell her husband Nabal. . . . ²³When Abigail saw David, she hurried to get down from the donkey and fell on her face before David, and bowed to the ground. ²⁴When she fell at his feet, she said, "The waywardness is my own, my lord. May your servant speak to you. Listen to your servant's words. ²⁵My lord should please not give

his attention to this worthless man, to Nabal, because he is the same as his name. "Stupid" is his name and stupidity goes with him. . . . [28]Do bear with your servant's presumption, because Yahweh will definitely make for my lord an enduring household, because my lord is fighting Yahweh's battles, and wrong will not be found in you as long as you live. [29]When someone arises to pursue you and seek your life, my lord's life will be bound up in the bundle of the living with Yahweh your God, but the life of your enemies he will hurl away [as if it is] in the midst of a sling's hollow. . . ." [32]David said to Abigail, "Yahweh the God of Israel be praised, who sent you this day to meet me. [33]Blessed be your good judgment and blessed be you yourself, who restrained me this day from coming to bloodshed and achieving deliverance for myself by my own hand. . . ." [36]When Abigail came to Nabal, there, he was having a feast in his house, a feast like that of a king. So Nabal was in a good mood and was very drunk, and she did not tell him anything small or great until morning dawned. [37]In the morning, when [the effect of] the wine had left Nabal, his wife told him these things, and his heart died inside him. He turned to stone. [38]Some ten days later Yahweh struck Nabal and he died.

[Verses 39–44 relate how David marries Abigail; he had also married Ahinoam, but Saul had given Michal to someone else.]

You sometimes wonder how on earth a certain woman ended up marrying a certain man, but sometimes you can see that a couple are a good match. My office is located between the offices of two of my married colleagues; I joke that my job is to keep them apart during work hours. They met as students at the seminary, went off to do graduate work together elsewhere, then both came back to teach. They are terrific people and a great match. Yet I don't know what their parents thought about their marrying. When my wife's parents discovered who I was, they didn't think much of the match; she was going to be a doctor, and I was a mere pastor. When my parents discovered who my sister wanted to marry, they didn't think much of that match either, and he did abandon her (pregnant) after two or three years.

It looks as if Nabal was a good catch in economic terms, but that was all. His name says everything. *Nabal* is one of the

Hebrew words that means *fool*. When the Old Testament talks about fools and folly, it does not refer merely to low scores on SATs. Folly lies in refusing to live in the real world, failing to pay attention to reality, reality that includes God and God's expectations of humanity. Nabal was a fool by name and a fool by nature. Admittedly there are several Hebrew words that could lie behind the name Nabal; one of them is the word for a guitar. I imagine that it was not *nabal = fool* that his parents had in mind when they named him; perhaps his father was a good guitarist, and they hoped Nabal would be. But the name turned out to be curiously apt, because it had this other meaning. In some sense Nabal must have been shrewd, otherwise he would not have done so well as a sheep farmer, but perhaps he was unscrupulous. Israelite life was not designed to work in such a way that some people ended up as big sheepfarmers who controlled the destiny of ordinary families, but one way or another Nabal had managed to evade the constraints of the **Torah**. Maybe that fact links with the comment on his being a Calebite. Caleb is himself a hero in the Old Testament story, but he was not by birth an Israelite, so maybe it is inappropriate to assume that he was bound by the Torah. Given the description of Nabal as hard and an evildoer and morally stupid, there might be another implication in the description of him as a Calebite, because the name Caleb is also similar to the Hebrew word for a dog.

Abigail had another sort of intelligence. She knew how to relate to an outlaw like David. She recognized that you don't mess with a guy like David who is prepared to take desperate and ruthless measures in order that he and his gang can survive when they have to live outside the law. Further, she has the religious insight that her husband lacks. If they belong on the margins of Israel, then she joins people such as Rahab and Caleb, who were not Israelites but came to recognize and submit to Yahweh's action more clearly than some Israelites one could name (such as Saul).

So David and Abigail make a marvelous if potentially fiery match, both of them good-looking, shrewd, insightful about what God is doing, and capable of seeing what is in their interest and going for it. There is no suggestion of a love match; David is never said to love a woman, and the chapter closes by telling us about some of David's other marriages. For David, there was no link between love and marriage, and neither is there any suggestion of such a link for Abigail. Whereas we have been told that Michal loved David (but then she lost him), we are not told that Abigail loved him any more than she loved Nabal (but then she did get David, or at least part of him). She can see how events in Israel are developing; she can see that God is involved; and she does have her eye to what is in her interests.

All through this story of human shrewdness, calculation, and stupidity, God is again at work bringing about the fulfillment of the intention to keep David safe so that he can eventually be king. We can see that process in what happens to Nabal. The story declares that God struck Nabal so that he died; this makes one wonder why God didn't strike Saul so that he died, which would make it possible for the story to cut to the chase. Yet the story also implies that the post mortem would have revealed nothing odd about Nabal's death. He was a hard worker, a hard eater, and a hard drinker (another of those words that his name could remind you of is the word for a skin of wine, which also features in the story). Then he had a major fright, and it was all too much for his heart. God used that collocation of facts and events as God used Abigail's shrewdness. In addition, David is able to point out with some heartlessness that God has thereby gotten rid of someone who insulted David (!) while also restraining David from getting blood on his own hands in doing so. Scripture gives the impression that God sometimes intervenes and does things that would have the coroner wondering why that happened, but once more we see how God also works through ordinary human processes, decisions, and chances.

1 SAMUEL 26:1–28:2

Who Can Lay Hands on Yahweh's Anointed and Get Away with It?

[First Samuel 26:1–5 relates how the Ziphites tell Saul where David is hiding, so Saul sets out to look for him.]

⁶David spoke up and said to Ahimelek the Hittite and Abishai son of Zeruiah, Joab's brother, "Who will go down with me to Saul, into the camp?" Abishai said, "I'll go with you." ⁷So David and Abishai came to the company by night. There was Saul lying asleep within the encampment, with his spear stuck in the earth by his head, and Abner and the company lying around him. ⁸Abishai said to David, "God has surrendered your enemy into your hand today. Now let me strike him down with the spear, with one thrust into the earth. I won't [need to] do it twice." ⁹David said to Abishai, "Don't destroy him, because who can put out his hand against Yahweh's anointed and stay innocent?" ¹⁰David said, "As Yahweh lives, no, Yahweh will strike him, or his day will come and he will die, or he will go down to battle and perish. ¹¹Yahweh forbid that I should put out my hand against Yahweh's anointed. But do now take the spear at his head and the water jug, and let's get ourselves off." ¹²So David took the spear and the water jug from by Saul's head and they took themselves off, with no one seeing or knowing or waking up, because all of them were asleep, because a coma from Yahweh had fallen on them. ¹³David crossed over to the other side and stood on top of the mountain at a distance; the space between them was great. ¹⁴David called to the company and to Abner son of Ner, "Aren't you going to answer, Abner?" Abner answered, "Who are you calling to the king?" ¹⁵David said to Abner, "Aren't you a man? Who is like you in Israel? Why have you not kept watch over your lord the king? Because one of the company came to destroy your lord the king. ¹⁶This thing that you have done is not good. As Yahweh lives, you [all] deserve to die because you did not keep watch over your lord, Yahweh's anointed. Look now. Where is the king's spear and the water jug that were by his head?" ¹⁷Saul recognized David's voice and said, "Is this your voice, my son David?" David said, "[It is] my voice, my lord king." ¹⁸[David] said, "Why is my lord thus pursuing after his servant? . . . ²¹ Saul said, "I have done wrong. Come back, my son David, because I will not do wrong to you again, on account of the fact that my life has been valuable in your eyes this day. Yes, I have been stupid and have made very great mistakes. . . ." ²⁵ᵇBut David went on his way, and Saul returned to his home. ²⁷:¹David said to himself, "I shall be swept away now one day by the hand of Saul. There is no good [course] for me but to make a final escape to the country of the Philistines."

[First Samuel 27:1b–28:2 relates how David takes his company and his wives to Gath and becomes a vassal of King Achish, claiming then to live by raiding his fellow Israelites though actually raiding other peoples such as the Amalekites, but leaving no one alive there to tell the tale.]

This past weekend the U.S. Congress passed a bill designed to reform health care in the nation. By the time you read this we will know more about how it all works out. You may not approve of Congress's decision, but that will not affect one striking aspect of the process. Both Democrats and Republicans recognized that Democrats were putting their political futures on the line by taking this plan through Congress when very large numbers of people in the country opposed it. Both parties know that the electorate may make the Democrats pay a price during the midterm elections in a few months time. The president knows that it might cost him his second term. So why did they take this risk? Because they were convinced it was what was best for the nation. They placed their personal destinies and interests and jobs behind their perception of what was the right thing to do.

David here does so for the second time. The first story of this kind came in chapter 24, and it is an entertaining read; engaged in trying to capture David, Saul goes into a cave to relieve himself. It turns out to be the cave in which David and his men are hiding. They therefore have a chance to kill Saul, but David will only cut off the edge of Saul's coat while he is otherwise occupied. What David and Saul then say to each other is very similar to what they say in this story. It is tempting to infer that this is another example of 1 Samuel including two versions of the same story. Whether this is so or not, the inclusion of both stories shows the importance of the issues they raise.

Paradoxically, for all the fact that God has abandoned Saul, Saul is still king. He is still the person God anointed and is thus still marked out as God's servant. There is still a sense in which God is identified with him. The point is underlined in this version of the story by David's critique of the way Saul's men fail to protect him. He doesn't blame them for failing to check out the cave before Saul went in there (though the U.S. president's heavies would certainly do that). He does blame them for being asleep when some of them ought to be keeping watch over him. No matter that they are so deeply asleep that you could think there were in a coma that God had induced (it's the same word as is used when God puts Adam to sleep before borrowing one of his ribs).

The story thus neatly draws attention to the ambiguity in our attitude to rulers who seem to have forfeited God's approval and our loyalty. Other Old Testament stories presuppose that there are times when rebellion is right and God commissions a coup d'état. These stories underline how horrifying such an event is. One can infer another reason that David would be glad to have the story told twice. It will not be in his interest to encourage the idea that people are free to assassinate the king when they become convinced that God has abandoned him. Later, both when he is on the way to succeeding Saul as king and when he actually is king, there will be supporters of Saul who do not support David. We have noted that this is a theme underlying the account of the mutual **commitment** between Jonathan and David and David's ongoing support of Jonathan's family (see 1 Samuel 21). Saul's supporters could easily accuse David of always having been disloyal to Saul and always plotting his way to the throne. David's declining more than one opportunity to kill Saul would be another basis on which David and his supporters could confront the suggestion that he was somehow implicated in Saul's death.

It also draws our attention to the tension between our freedom or responsibility to take action and our freedom or responsibility to leave things to God. David knows that God intends to remove Saul, but he doesn't infer that therefore he can be the means of God's will being implemented, even when Abishai offers the tempting observation that God has delivered Saul into his hands (the equivalent to Saul's comment in chapter 23 that God has delivered David into his hands). It would be so simple for David to solve all his problems and even keep his hands clean (because Abishai will do it). No, says David, Nabal provides the model for us to remember. Maybe God will strike him down, or maybe he will die of natural causes, or maybe he will get killed in battle (as actually happens). Let

God's will be fulfilled in one of those ways. It's not David's job to fulfill it.

Neither is it David's job to be naïve. As Jesus will put it, he needs to be shrewd like a snake as well as innocent as a dove. When Saul says he sees the truth in David's words and speaks with remorse about his pursuit of David, David doesn't take his words at face value. He has heard all that before. After the exchange, when Saul goes back home, David doesn't go with him but goes deeper into **Philistine** territory and becomes a vassal of a Philistine city-king. That involves him and his men behaving more and more like an outlaw gang, playing one side against another and not worrying too much about the difference between truth and lies. The narrative doesn't comment on the rights and wrongs of all that. It doesn't offer any hint that we are supposed to disapprove of David's action. Maybe it simply accepts that sometimes this is how things are. Maybe it assumes that the obligation of truthfulness within the people of God (even between enemies within the people of God) is different from that obligation in relation to people whose own aim is to destroy the people of God.

1 SAMUEL 28:3–29:11

What Do You Do When You're Desperate?

³Now Samuel had died, and all Israel had lamented for him and had buried him at Ramah, his city; and Saul had removed the spirits and ghosts from the country. ⁴The Philistines gathered and came to Shunem and encamped; Saul gathered all Israel and encamped at Gilboa. ⁵Saul saw the Philistine forces and was afraid; his heart trembled violently. ⁶Saul inquired of Yahweh but Yahweh did not answer, either by dreams or by Urim or by prophets. ⁷So Saul said to his servants, "Seek out for me a woman who knows about spirits so that I can go and consult through her." His servants said to him, "Now. There is a woman who knows about spirits in En-dor." ⁸So Saul disguised himself and put on different clothes and went, he and two men with him, and came to the woman at night. He said, "Will you divine by means of a spirit for me, and bring up for me the one I shall tell you." ⁹The woman said to him, "Now. You know

what Saul has done, that he has cut off spirits and ghosts from the country. Why are you laying a trap for my life, to kill me?" [10]Saul swore to her by Yahweh: "As Yahweh lives, [punishment for] waywardness will not come upon you through this matter." [11]So the woman said, "Who shall I bring up for you?" He said, "Samuel. Bring him up for me." [12]When the woman saw Samuel, she cried out in a loud voice. The woman said to Saul, "Why have you deceived me? You're Saul." [13]The king said to her, "Don't be afraid. But what have you seen?" The woman said to Saul, "It's a divine being I have seen coming up from the earth." [14]He said to her, "What's he look like?" She said, "An old man is coming up. He is wearing a robe." Saul recognized that it was Samuel. He bent face down to the ground and bowed down. [15]Samuel said to Saul, "Why have you disturbed me and brought me up?" Saul said, "Things are very hard for me. The Philistines are fighting me. God has turned away from me. He has not answered me anymore either by means of prophets or by dreams. I called on you to enable me to know what I should do." [16]Samuel said, "So why do you inquire of me when Yahweh has turned away from you and become your enemy? [17]Yahweh has done to you as he declared by means of me. Yahweh tore the kingship from your hand and gave it to your fellow, to David, [18]when you did not listen to Yahweh's voice and did not perform his wrath on Amalek. That is why Yahweh has done this thing to you this day. [19]Yahweh will also give Israel with you into the hand of the Philistines. Tomorrow you and your sons will be with me. Yahweh will also give the Israelite forces into the hand of the Philistines."

[First Samuel 28:20–29:11 relates how Saul is overwhelmed by fear and how the woman and his servants get him to eat before they return. Meanwhile the Philistines insist that David not be allowed to join them in fighting against Israel because they do not trust his loyalty.]

This coming Sunday is the nine-month anniversary since my wife died. I think about her a lot and dream about her, sometimes in her wheelchair as she was for years but sometimes fit and able to live a normal life, as she once was. I picture her now asleep in a kind of cubicle in a dorm. I guess the image comes from the promise that there are plenty of places for people to stay in Jesus' Father's house (John 14:2). I wouldn't like to think of all these as single rooms; I like to picture angels walking around the dorm keeping an eye on everyone. I know she is "with Jesus," who is present throughout the dorm. It would also be biblical to picture her in Abraham's bosom, though that would seem a bit crowded, not to say a bit bizarre. I pray for her, for God to continue to keep an eye on her as she waits for resurrection day. She has never seemed to appear to me, as people who have been bereaved sometimes say has happened to them, and it doesn't occur to me to try to make contact with her, which makes me and most other Western people a bit odd. Most cultures have assumed that we can make contact with our dead family members and that one reason this is worth doing is that they likely have access to information we cannot access.

The last assumption underlies this story. The spirits or ghosts it refers to are the spirits of people who have died. In most cultures there have been people who were expert at making contact with spirits. No doubt some of them were charlatans, but the Bible does not say that making contact in this way is impossible; it simply says it is forbidden to Israel because Israel has other ways of discovering God's will and God's plans, but the ordinary instincts of the people of God commonly triumph over what the Bible says. The **effigies** that Saul's daughter and David's wife possessed (see 1 Samuel 19) would be used for making contact with dead family members. The most remarkable statement in the present story is that Saul has banished all the spirits and ghosts—that is, has banished the spiritists and mediums who were believed to be able to make contact with them. It is a notable expression of commitment to Yahweh, though evidently not enough to compensate for his failure in other ways to do exactly what Yahweh says. The **Torah** actually declares that spiritists and mediums are to be put to death, and the woman fears that practicing her craft may cost her her life, though there are many offenses for which the Torah prescribes the death penalty, and it seems not to mean it too literally.

It is the eve of the last great confrontation between Saul and the **Philistines**, and Saul needs God's guidance, but he cannot get it by dreams or **Urim and Thummim** or prophets, the means that Israel is supposed to use in place of ghosts and spirits. So he is driven to seek guidance by the very route he has forbidden. He promises that if anyone is to be punished for breaking the king's edict (!), if "waywardness comes upon" anyone, the punishment will not come on her as the person who made the contact but on him for persuading her to do so. When Samuel appears, something makes her realize who Saul actually is. She calls Samuel "a divine being"; it is the word usually translated *God* or *god* or *gods*, but it can refer to any being other than a regular earthly being. This ambiguity is not usually troublesome, as it is generally easy to see from the context which kind of being it refers to. Maybe using this word suggests that Samuel looked more impressive than your average spirit. Maybe there is something about his appearance that marks him as a prophet. Maybe the woman didn't really think someone as important as Samuel would actually appear for some ordinary person, and this is what makes her realize for certain who Saul is. A prophet's most important job was to guide the king. If Samuel was prepared to have his sleep interrupted, that suggested the visitor was someone important, though evidently Samuel doesn't like having his sleep interrupted. He is as brusque dead as he was alive, and also as tough with Saul.

Every time a prophet tells people that a terrible fate awaits them, they have the opportunity to turn around, and when they do so, God will relent (Jeremiah 18 is the great exposition of this principle, and Jonah 3 the great illustration), but most times they are too far gone, and the prophetic word functions to announce what actually will happen. Saul has been too far gone for a long time. As we have read his story, we have kept wanting to shout out to him, "Don't do it," "Turn around," "Let David have the stupid kingship." But he can't hear. We can't reach him. God can't reach him. I don't know whether to say, more tragically for him, that God doesn't want to reach him. Certainly God wants him out of the way. Further, the Philistines are about to get him out of the way and (ironically) to open the way for another leader who will sort them out.

Saul collapses in terror. He has not eaten all day or all night, and in a touching closing scene to the story the woman and his servants persuade him to let her make him the final meal of his life, after which he returns to his troops to meet his fate.

111

Saul had come to see the woman when the two armies were gathered in Israel's great central plain. It is another of the areas that are borderlands between country controlled by Israel and areas controlled by the Philistines. Once again Israel controls the mountains, here the northern part of the modern West Bank; the Philistines control the plain itself, with its great cities. In chapter 29 the story backtracks to when the Philistines had mustered their forces before marching to the central plain. They had mustered at Aphek, to the southwest, at another point on the border between the West Bank and the plain, near where the Israelites and the Philistines fought once before. David has succeeded in deceiving Achish, one of the Philistine city-kings, into believing that David really has gone over to the Philistine side, but the other Philistine city-kings are not so gullible. Like any decent double agent, David keeps a bold face and looks Achish in the eye, protesting his loyalty, though maybe Achish is also not shrewd enough to notice an ambiguity in his protest. "I want to go and fight the enemies of my lord the king," he says. He intends Achish to assume he means Achish as king. Does David rather mean Saul as king? Does he intend to change sides in the middle of the battle? Actually the question will not arise.

1 SAMUEL 30:1–31:13

A Last Act of Loyalty to Saul

[Chapter 30 relates how David, having been dismissed by the Philistines, finds that the Amalekites have attacked his base at Ziklag and captured the women and children, and he goes to rescue them.]

¹When the Philistines did battle with Israel, the Israelites fled from before the Philistines and fell slain on Mount Gilboa, ²and the Philistines caught up with Saul and his sons. The Philistines struck down Saul's sons, Jonathan, Abinadab, and Malchishua. ³The battle was hard against Saul, and the archers (the bowmen) located him. He was badly wounded by the archers. ⁴Saul said to his arms bearer, "Draw your sword and run me through so that these uncircumcised men don't come and run

me through and torment me." But his arms bearer was not willing because he was very fearful, so Saul took his sword and fell on it. ⁵When his arms bearer saw that Saul was dead, he also fell on his sword and died with him. ⁶So Saul died, and his three sons, and his arms bearer, as well as all his men, altogether on that day. ⁷When the Israelites the other side of the plain and the other side of the Jordan saw that the Israelites had fled and that Saul and his sons were dead, they abandoned their cities and fled, and the Philistines came and settled in them. ⁸Next day the Philistines came to strip the slain and found Saul and his three sons fallen on Mount Gilboa. ⁹They cut off his head and stripped off his arms and sent them around the country of the Philistines to bring the news to the house of their idols and to the people. ¹⁰They put his arms in the house of the Ashtorets. His body they fastened to the wall of Beth-shean, ¹¹but when the inhabitants of Jabesh-gilead heard about it (what the Philistines had done to Saul), ¹²they set off, every fit man, traveled all night, and took Saul's body and the bodies of his sons from the walls of Beth-shean. They came to Jabesh and burned them there, ¹³got their bones and buried them under the tamarisk at Jabesh, and fasted seven days.

When I first came to California, students would sometimes ask how long I would be here, thinking it might just be for sabbatical. At first I would reply, "I want to die here," which was a way of saying, "I am here permanently," but that made people look shocked, even made them recoil. I had mentioned death. You don't talk about death in California, where people like to think it's voluntary. The Bible likes talking about death. The last moments of Jacob or Joseph or Moses or Joshua or Eli or David (not to say Jesus, or Stephen) are important moments for everyone. They can be important teaching moments for the whole community.

But before coming to Saul's death, the narrative tells us what David was doing when he had been sidelined from the battle between the Israelites and the **Philistines**. Ziklag was in the Negev, in the region of Beersheba and Gath, another place in the borderlands between territory controlled by the Philistines and by the Israelites. It was far enough away from Gath for David to be able to get away with raids on people such as the Amalekites, without his boss, Achish, the city-king of Gath, being able to discover what was really going on when David said he was raiding nearby Israelite cities. Unfortunately, it was therefore near enough for the Amalekites to return the compliment. When he gets back from his job interview with Achish, he discovers that they have burned the city of Ziklag down, though not killed everyone as David would have done but captured them. David's men are not thrilled with David for allowing this to happen. David still has Abiathar with him and therefore gets him to bring the **ephod** so he can consult God about whether he can successfully pursue the Amalekites. It's difficult to see how he can avoid trying, but anyway, God says, "Yes." It's another sign that God is with him as God is not with Saul. On the way they come across a sick slave whom the Amalekites have abandoned but who is able to lead them in the right direction. So once again things work out through a combination of commitment, "luck," and divine guidance. Some of David's own men are apparently too weary to go on, but David insists on their subsequent sharing in the plunder gained from the battle; it again shows that David is a guy who does the right thing. He also sends a share to other Judahite cities; so he is also once again a shrewd guy, because that kind of action will pay off when election day comes.

I'm not sure Saul's death is a teaching moment like some others, except in a rather broader sense. It is the last act in a tragedy. The story doesn't deal with the question whether Saul's suicide was itself a sin; the Bible doesn't deal with that question in connection with any of the suicides it relates. Its focus is on the way it brings Saul's tragic story to its tragic close. This doesn't mean suicide is okay, but it points us in a different direction for thinking about it.

We now use the word "tragedy" in a rather broad sense, to refer to any awful event that causes great loss or grief, but more technically the word refers to the story of some significant person who goes from prestige and achievement to the loss of everything, often because of a character flaw. There's thus a certain logic or inevitability about a tragedy, but there can also be a sense that the person is the victim of considerations or factors that are external to him or her. Tragedies are thus frightening stories. They remind us of ways in which we can be our own worst enemies and ways in which we are responsible for our destinies while also not being in control of our destinies.

Saul's story is that kind of story. He was drafted to do a job that God didn't really want done. Saul knew he didn't have the gifts, and he didn't really want the job, but he didn't manage to evade it. God did show him that he could be enabled to do it, but he didn't give God the kind of obedience that God looked for, and God didn't make allowances for him in this connection. He wasn't the man after God's heart in the sense that David would be—not in the sense that David is noticeably more holy but in the sense that David happens to be the man in the right place at the right time, and Saul does not. God needed to make a point through Saul; having done so, God will make allowances for David that God never made for Saul. Saul cannot complain; his character flaws have been clear enough, and his tragedy issues from them.

You might think this all means that God is not fair, and that's a reasonable conclusion to draw. God is not very worried about fairness. Much later there will be another Saul to whom God appears, miraculously to shake him out of his opposition to Jesus and into being one of Jesus' most powerful preachers. That wasn't fair. Saul didn't deserve it. There were other opponents of Jesus who didn't get the kind of miracle Saul got to turn them around. That wasn't fair. In the stories of both Sauls, God is working at a bigger picture, and they get treated the way they do because of the bigger picture. All this has nothing to do with their eternal salvation; you are as likely to meet Saul on resurrection day as to meet David there. It has to do with the part they play in God's purpose. It also has nothing to do with their personal happiness or sense of fulfillment. When we come to the end of David's story, we will not exactly conclude, "Oh how lucky David was to have lived the life he lived." He too will end up in a mess. The more appropriate response on our part is gratitude for the fact that nearly all of us escape being cast into important roles in God's big picture.

Yet another appropriate response is another strange form of gratitude. In our own lives we are likely to experience our own unfairnesses. The fact that my wife, Ann, lived with multiple sclerosis for forty-three years and spent the last twelve years wheelchair-bound didn't issue from a character fault, and it wasn't fair for her; it wasn't much fun for me either. Yet God wove it into that divine big picture by giving Ann a ministry to other people that she was able to exercise only because of her disability. We usually can't see what makes things happen in our lives, as we can with Saul's life. We can know that God can weave them into that bigger picture.

We like our Hollywood movies to close with at least a tiny note of hope rather than with unremitting bleakness, and Saul's story does so, as Samson's did. On the crest of the huge tell at Beth-shean, the hill on which the successive cities had been built on top of one another long ago, there used to be a gnarled bare old tree. I used to imagine it as a tree on which Saul's body might have been hanged. There his body would end up as food for the vultures and as something that would bring impurity on the land, according to the **Torah**. But the men of Jabesh-gilead will not let that happen. At the end of Saul's story they thus remind us of his finest hour, the story told in chapter 11, and they remind us of the way many Israelites loved and appreciated Saul. Burning the bodies of Saul and his sons means the Philistines could not come and abuse them again. In a strange sense, Saul and his sons are free to rest. They do so under a tamarisk tree. There are only three tamarisk trees in the Bible, one that Abraham plants at Beersheba (Genesis 21), one that Saul himself sits under at Gibeah (1 Samuel 22), and one that he is buried under. They are big shady trees with pretty blossoms.

2 SAMUEL 1:1–2:31

How Are the Mighty Fallen

¹After Saul's death, and when David had come back from striking down the Amalekites and had stayed in Ziklag for two days, ²on the third day—there, a man came from the camp, from being with Saul. His clothes were torn and there was earth on

his head. When he came to David he fell to the ground and bowed low. ³David said to him, "Where were you coming from?" He said to him, "I escaped from the Israelite camp." David said to him, "What happened? Come on, tell me."

[In verses 4–16 the man describes what happened but says that he finished Saul off when Saul asked him to, and gives David Saul's crown and armband. David has him killed for striking down Yahweh's anointed.]

¹⁷David chanted this elegy over Saul and his son Jonathan, ¹⁸and said the Judahites were to be taught "The Bow" (written in the Book of Jashar):

¹⁹ The gazelle, Israel, is slain on your heights.
    How have the warriors fallen; ²⁰do not tell it in Gath,
    Do not announce the news in Ashkelon's streets
    Lest the daughters of the Philistines celebrate,
    Lest the daughters of the uncircumcised exult.
²¹ Mountains of Gilboa, may there be no dew,
    No rain on you or fields of offerings,
    Because there the shield of warriors was fouled,
    The shield of Saul, no more rubbed with oil.
²² From the blood of the slain, from the fat of warriors,
    The bow of Jonathan did not turn back,
    The sword of Saul did not return empty.
²³ Saul and Jonathan, loved and delightful,
    In their life and in their death they were not parted.
    They were swifter than eagles, they were stronger
         than lions.
²⁴ Daughters of Israel, weep over Saul,
    Who clothed you in scarlet and finery,
    Who put gold ornaments on your garments.
²⁵ How have the warriors fallen in the midst of the battle—
    Jonathan, slain on your heights, ²⁶it is hard for me because
         of you.
    My brother Jonathan, you were very delightful to me.
    Your love was wonderful to me, more than the love
         of women.
²⁷ How have the warriors fallen and the battle weapons
         perished!

[Chapter 2 relates how David took up residence in Hebron and was anointed as king there by the Judahites. He thanks the men of Jabesh-gilead for burying Saul. Abner, Saul's army commander, has Saul's son Ish-bosheth crowned as king over Ephraim. In a confrontation between Abner's forces and David's forces, Abner kills Asahel, one of David's senior men.]

The day before yesterday was Education and Sharing Day in the United States, a day established in honor of Rabbi Menachem Mendel Schneerson, who died in 1994. During his lifetime some of his followers believed him to be the messiah, and some continue in that belief after his death. This year as in other years, on this day that commemorates him, a newspaper advertisement urges people to accept his kingship as messiah. It includes the explanation that "a Jewish king cannot declare himself king; he can only become king through the acceptance of the people." It would be this acceptance that would lead to his resurrection and return as messiah. On a blog, someone commented, "Jewish kings don't need the backing of the people to be declared king; all it takes is a bit of oil, a stream, and a prophet."

David's story as a whole offers some support for both understandings of how someone becomes king of Israel. It involves both God's anointing and people's acceptance. Long ago, God sent Samuel to anoint David as the person who was to replace Saul. Henceforth you could perhaps say that in God's eyes David is king. But David becomes king in practice, in Israel's life, only when the people accept him. That will turn out to be a gradual, human, political, messy, conflictual process. Politically, David's position overlaps with that of the leader of an opposition group that has been seeking to overthrow the government. From the government's viewpoint and now from the viewpoint of Saul's supporters, he is a terrorist. Because his base lies in **Judah**, where he comes from, that is where he goes for his first human anointing. It is a humanly shrewd move, but it is also one he consults God about. He does not immediately show his hand or show his face in Saul's heartland, further north, and chapter 2's story about the clash between forces loyal to Saul and forces loyal to David shows the wisdom in his caution.

A theme running through the latter part of 1 Samuel was David's respect for and loyalty to the king. He has submitted to Saul in every way except by letting Saul kill him. He has committed what might be called acts of terrorism, but never against his own people. The story portrays David as Mr. Clean in this respect, though we can only guess whom it might be seeking to convince. They might be Saul's supporters when the succession is still an open question, or after it is formally settled. They might be subsequent malcontents tempted to assassinate David or a later king, to whom David is set forth as an example. This theme continues as we begin 2 Samuel. The repetition of the story of Saul's death reflects the way the first book runs into the second. As is often the case in Genesis to Kings, it is as if the first book represents one season of a TV series and the second book picks up the story in the subsequent fall, but the focus changes. The story of Saul's death at the end of 1 Samuel closes off the story of Saul's kingship. The story of Saul's death that begins 2 Samuel opens up the story of David's kingship. It does so in a way that continues to portray David as Mr. Clean.

Its opening contains more than one irony. While Saul was being defeated by the **Philistines** after failing to get any guidance from God except by unorthodox means that do him little good, with God's guidance David was defeating the Amalekites. Then the messenger who brings the news to David is—an Amalekite. This provokes a few questions. Given God's hostility to Amalek, how does Saul come to have Amalekites in his army? Given that Saul annihilated the Amalekites (see 1 Samuel 15), how does Saul come to have Amalekites in his army, and for that matter, how come there are enough Amalekites to capture Ziklag (1 Samuel 30)? It is another indication that we should not be too literal in understanding Old Testament statements about annihilating peoples. The story in 2 Samuel 1 offers a piece of information that may partly answer some such questions, because the Amalekite messenger explains to David that he is the son of a resident alien. Now, he has already lied to David about killing Saul in order to tell David a story he thought David would like to hear, so who knows whether he is lying about his status, but the lie is nevertheless an interesting one. It presupposes that Israelite immigration policy was an open-door one. Anyone can join Israel, even an Amalekite. He just has to become a "proper" Israelite; he has to live by the **Torah**. Further (David assumes) he has to honor the king, and on his own false profession he has failed to do so.

His story tells how David comes to possess Saul's crown and armband, which people sympathetic to Saul might find suspicious. The integrity of David's relationship with Saul and Jonathan, the son Saul had designated as his successor, finds further display in David's lament over them. The gazelle in its agility, speed, and grace stands for Saul or Jonathan or both. The Hebrew word for *gazelle* is the same as a word for beauty or gracefulness or honor, so Israelites could understand the word either way, but they liked to use animal images for people— hence the poem's later references to the lion and the eagle. In the past Saul and Jonathan have been effective warriors, but their demise is now summed up by the picture of Saul's shield stained in blood instead of cleaned up and ready for use next time. The elegy urges nature itself to mourn. David acknowledges that Jonathan's commitment to him had been a matter of life and death.

2 SAMUEL 3:1–4:12

The Struggle for Power

¹The war between Saul's household and David's household was long drawn out, but David was growing stronger and stronger, and Saul's household was growing weaker and weaker. ²Sons were born to David in Hebron. His firstborn was Amnon, by Ahinoam the Jezreelite. ³His second was Chileab, by Abigail, the wife of Nabal the Carmelite. The third was Absalom, the son of Maacah daughter of Talmai, king of Geshur. ⁴The fourth was Adonijah, the son of Haggith. The fifth was Shephatiah, the son of Abital. ⁵The sixth was Ithream, by David's wife Eglah. These were born to David in Hebron.

⁶As the war was continuing between David's household and Saul's household, Abner was gaining strength in Saul's household. ⁷Saul had a secondary wife whose name was Rizpah, daughter of Ayyah. [Ish-bosheth] said to Abner, "Why have you slept with my father's wife?" ⁸Abner was very angry at Ish-

bosheth's words. . . . [12]So Abner sent aides to David on his own behalf, saying, "To whom will the country belong?" [and] saying, "You should seal your covenant with me. There: my hand will be with you to turn all Israel over to you." [13][David] said, "Good. I myself will seal a covenant with you. Only, I ask one thing of you. You will not see my face unless beforehand you bring Saul's daughter Michal when you come to see my face." [14]And David sent aides to Saul's son Ish-bosheth, saying, "Give me my wife Michal whom I bethrothed to myself for a hundred Philistine foreskins." [15]So Ish-bosheth sent and got her from the husband, Paltiel son of Laish. [16]Her husband went with her, weeping as he followed her as far as Bahurim, but Abner said to him, "Go, go back," and he went back. . . .

[23b]They told Joab, "Abner son of Ner came to the king, and he sent him off; he went in peace. [24]Joab came to the king and said, "What have you done? Now. Abner came to you. Why did you send him off? He has gone right away. [25]You know Abner the son of Ner, that he would have come to deceive you and know you're coming and going and know everything you are doing." [26]Joab went out from being with David and sent aides after Abner, and they brought him back from the Sirah cistern. David didn't know. [27]When Abner came back to Hebron, Joab took him aside, inside the gateway, to speak with him in private, but stabbed him there in the stomach. He died for the blood of [Joab's] brother.

[The rest of chapters 3 and 4 relates how David rebuked Joab and had Abner mourned and buried. Two of Saul's army commanders then kill Ish-bosheth and take his head to David; David has them killed and buries Ish-bosheth's head with Abner.]

One of my colleagues holds a Bible study at his house for men he got to know through an organization that seeks to provide accommodation for homeless people in our city; they are typically people who have prison records and/or who have battled alcoholism or other addictions. Membership of the Bible study grows through word of mouth. The men had been reading John's Gospel and then for some reason started to read 2 Samuel, and some of them came alive when they read the stories about Abner's gang fighting Joab's gang and Abner killing Asahel and Joab killing Abner. As they read these stories, their eyes widened. If God could be involved with the kind of people who appear in 2 Samuel, maybe God could be involved with these men themselves, who have acted in comparable ways.

The stories are breathtakingly true to the way politics works. Just last week Britain expelled an Israeli diplomat for his country's use of forged British passports in conjunction with assassinating a Palestinian leader; it is a coincidence that this recent news item involves the modern state of Israel, and next week's story may involve action on the part of Britain, Palestine, or the United States. Both Old and New Testaments consistently portray God working through immoral political acts. They do not imply that God is involved in every assassination or act of deception, and they do not give us any basis for knowing every time whether God is involved in such an act, though sometimes a prophetic word or reflection after the event may suggest an answer. That is what happens here. Was it God's will that David came to the throne? Yes it was. Did God devise a clean way for that to happen? No, God did not.

As is often the case, there are two sets of convictions here about how to approach a political question and thus two sides involved in a political conflict. Both sides may believe they are right. Both sides may be concerned to pursue their own interests. Both sides are prepared to use violent means to bring about what they believe is right or to pursue their interests. Abner has put Saul's son on the throne of **Ephraim** and wants him to be king over **Judah** too, but one suspects that he intends him to be puppet king; it will be Abner who pulls the strings. The story tells us that Ish-bosheth was afraid of Abner. (First Chronicles 8 and 9 give Ish-bosheth's name as Esh-baal, which will be the "genuine" version. That name means something like "The Master is there" or "The Master gives." Because *baal* is an ordinary Hebrew word meaning "master," it was once the case that *baal* could be a word that referred to **Yahweh** as "the Master," just like "the Lord." But it became conventional to use the word *baal* only of the god whom the **Canaanites** called "the Master." Once that convention came about, the name Esh-baal would seem scandalous: an Israelite king seemed to be named after a Canaanite god. So the name was changed to Ish-bosheth, which means "man of shame.")

Individuals may pay with their own lives for the violence in which they get involved. They may also suffer for it in other ways. Chapter 2 has related how Joab, who was in effect Abner's equivalent in Judah, has had to watch Abner kill Joab's little brother Asahel as a result of his thinking he could get Abner. The women in the story suffer, too. Maybe Abner and Saul's **secondary wife** Rizpah loved each other, but more likely this was loveless sex imposed on a woman by someone with power. With some plausibility, Ish-bosheth likely assumes that sex with one of the former king's wives is designed to assert that there is indeed a sense in which Abner is taking Saul's place. What Rizpah thinks of all this is neither here nor there. Ish-bosheth's reaction apparently pushes Abner in another direction. He is a guy who can be hard-nosed about his own interests. We of course know how the conflict will turn out; we know David will win. When you are in the midst of it, you don't know. A canny calculator like Abner will not have supported Saul's son unless he had reason to think there was a fair chance of winning. But chapter 3 began by noting that in the ongoing conflict over who is going to be king of Israel, it is David's supporters who are winning. Abner knows which way the wind is blowing. So he changes sides. It looks like a good idea, but he pays for it with his life, even though he had done his best to avoid killing Joab's brother ("Don't make me do it . . .").

Michal continues her life as a political football passed from one man to another. Her sister had been due to marry David, and then her father had changed his mind. Michal had fallen for David and seemed to have won him because her father thought that might be a way of getting David killed. When this plan failed, her father again broke off the arrangement and gave her to Paltiel. This was likely possible because technically the marriage with David had not taken place. She was only "betrothed," a rather more cast-iron commitment than engagement in the West but one that remained one step removed from actual marriage (her status was like that of Mary when she gets pregnant and Joseph has to think in terms of divorcing her, not merely breaking an engagement). Now Michal has to come back to David; we know what Paltiel felt, but we don't know what Michal felt.

Like Abner, Ish-bosheth can see which way the wind is blowing, and he collaborates with David's demand for Michal. Abner
the political wheeler and dealer is not merely personally changing sides; he knows he can promise David that he will deliver the
support of the leadership in Benjamin that currently supports
Ish-bosheth. The trouble is that being a political wheeler and
dealer has its down side; Joab can plausibly claim that Abner
cannot be trusted and can make that the basis for implementing his own desire to kill Abner in redress for Abner's killing his
brother. Ish-bosheth will know that if his side loses, his own life
will be in danger, but his showing signs of his willingness not to
stand in David's way does not save him.

As was the case in previous chapters, these stories are told
in such a way as to keep projecting David as Mr. Clean. The
deaths of people such as Abner and Ish-bosheth are extremely
convenient for David, but he can claim to have had nothing
to do with bringing them about and to have honored the victims and/or brought the killers to justice. He is the man after
God's heart, the man God chose. God makes things work out
for David through the wrongdoing of the people around him.

2 SAMUEL 5:1–25

On Following Up Your Good Ideas but Not Taking Yourself
Too Seriously

[1]All the clans of Israel came to David at Hebron and said, "Here
are we; we are your flesh and blood. [2]Before now, when Saul was
king over us, you were the one who led Israel out and brought
Israel in. Yahweh said to you, 'You are the one who will shepherd my people Israel. You are the one who will be ruler over
Israel.'" [3]So all the elders of Israel came to the king at Hebron,
King David sealed a covenant to them in Hebron before Yahweh, and they anointed David as king over Israel. [4]David was
thirty when he became king; he reigned as king forty years:
[5]in Hebron he reigned as king over Judah seven years and six
months, and in Jerusalem he reigned as king thirty-three years
over all Israel and Judah. [6]The king and his men went to Jerusalem against the Jebusites, who were living in the region. David
was told, "You will not come in here. Actually, the blind and the

disabled could turn you back, saying [to themselves], "David will not come in here." ⁷But David captured the stronghold of Zion; it is the city of David. David said on that day, "Anyone attacking the Jebusites will reach to the conduit." ... ¹⁰David kept getting more powerful; Yahweh, God of Armies, was with him. ¹¹Hiram, the king of Tyre, sent aides to David with cedar wood, carpenters, and stonemasons. They built a house for David. ¹²David recognized that Yahweh had established him as king over Israel and that he had exalted his kingship for the sake of his people Israel. ¹³David took more secondary wives and wives from Jerusalem after he came from Hebron, and more sons and daughters were born to him.

[Verses 14–21 give the children's names, then describe a victory over the Philistines.]

²²The Philistines yet again came up and spread out in the Vale of Rephaim. ²³David inquired of Yahweh, but he said, "You shall not go up; turn around behind them and come at them in front of the baca trees. ²⁴When you hear the sound of marching in the tops of the baca trees, then take action, because Yahweh will have gone out ahead of you to attack the Philistine forces." ²⁵David did just as Yahweh commanded and struck down the Philistines from Geba to when you come to Gezer.

I am coming to the end of my fortieth year as a professor. On Sunday evening, the day before yet another new quarter started, a friend asked me a question that unintentionally made me feel rather chastised. After I've had so many "first days" of a quarter, she asked whether I have particular ways in which I pray or things that I hope for when I meet a new group of students. I felt chastised because I hadn't been praying about it and didn't have any expectations from God, though I didn't feel as chastised as the occasion on a Saturday evening previously when another friend asked me about my sermon for the next day, and I had to confess I didn't know what I was going to preach on. But the sermon went okay (at least, one or two people expressed appreciation); and the class went much better than I felt last quarter's classes did (which had been the background to the question). All this proves nothing; perhaps God was speaking through the sermon and working in the class for the sake of the congregation and the students while rolling eyes at my irresponsibility. Or perhaps it is okay for me to make use of the fact that I can usually get away with doing things quickly (as I am doing in writing this series on the Old Testament for Everyone, so you can decide) or with leaving things till the last minute and relying on my personality to get me through.

David could work both ways, sometimes looking to God, sometimes doing what seemed a good idea and being grateful afterward for God's involvement. He has made it to the throne without trying; his rivals and opponents have fallen by the wayside. Now, once again, human anointing supplements divine anointing. David has been king over **Judah** for seven years since Saul died, with Ish-bosheth king over the northern clans, "Israel" (that is, **Ephraim**). Now he is also anointed as king over those northern clans. The course of events points to the fragility of the unity between the clans and foreshadows the way they will fall back into being two peoples after Solomon.

Establishing Jerusalem as capital of the united nation relates to that fragility. As is the case with David's becoming king, it is difficult to think ourselves back into the situation when Jerusalem was not the capital. At the time, the idea of Jerusalem as the nation's capital was as revolutionary as the idea of Canberra being the capital of Australia as a compromise between Sydney and Melbourne. Jerusalem will later be described as the place God chose, but here it is simply the place David chose. Maybe David sought divine guidance over the question, but the narrative does not give that impression. Sometimes God takes an initiative in making a choice, and human action follows and goes along with it, as happened with David's being king; sometimes a human being takes an initiative in making a choice, and God goes along with it. (Of course sometimes human beings resist God's choice, as initially happened with the northern clans in relation to David; and sometimes God resists the human choice, as will initially happen with David's desire to build a temple.)

Hebron is the key city in the southern part of the territory David controls, while Gibeah is Saul's base. Jerusalem is merely an obscure Jebusite village in between, just off the mountain ridge, but that means it is in neutral territory, and the fact that the Jebusites still control it reflects the fact that it is in a very good defensive position, at the end of its own little ridge, with steep slopes on three sides that make it hard to capture. That is somehow the point about the comment about the blind and the disabled. You don't even need fit men to defend this city.

David's idea about the conduit was the key to proving the Jebusites wrong. Building a city involves a dilemma. You want it to be on top of a hill, to make it easier to defend; but there is no water supply on top of a hill. Typically, therefore, the Jebusites had to rely on a water supply some way down the hill, the Spring of Gihon, whose water flows into the later Pool of Siloam, and then they have to find a way of protecting this water supply when the city is under attack. There used to be a romantic theory about David's men climbing a shaft that led from the water source into the city and thereby surprising the overconfident Jebusites, but more likely David's comment means his men take control of the spring area itself, cut off the city's water supply, and wait it out until the city is forced to surrender.

So the city of the Jebusites becomes "the city of David" (in relation to Judah and Ephraim, it stays neutral; like Washington, it does not belong to one of the clans or states). This all happens because **Yahweh** (God of) **Armies** was with David, but it also happens because David was a shrewd politician as well as a shrewd warrior. Yet it happens in a way that enabled David to recognize that God had a hand in events. He could have complimented himself on what a great man he was. He could have started believing in his own publicity or believing what people said about him ("Saul has slain his thousands; David his ten thousands"). That is what happens to successful leaders. The story tells us that he didn't. He saw that God had exalted him for Israel's sake. The actual language of "servant leaders" isn't especially biblical (the Bible is more inclined to see leaders as the servants of God than as the servants of their people). But the idea is biblical. It is the people that matter, not the leader. The leader matters only for the sake of the people.

In tension with David's insight is the way he behaves in accumulating wives and children. In traditional societies, these are the marks of a leader, so David behaves like a leader. The story makes no overt negative comment, but events will unfold in a way suggesting that David's attitude to women and children is his downfall.

David's acting on his own initiative in relation to Jerusalem and marriage contrasts with his action in war, where he is more inclined to consult God. This is ironic, because the idea that God should be involved in war embarrasses modern people; maybe if we took the idea of consulting God more seriously, we would actually fight fewer wars. The **Philistines** realize they need to put David in his place before he becomes too big for them, and they march up toward Jerusalem and camp in the Rephaim Vale, to the southwest of the city. Not only does David ask God about whether to attack them; on the second occasion God issues him precise battle instructions. Given how the **ephod** worked, I imagine this meant David made suggestions and discovered whether God said yes or no. God also gives him promises. We don't know what kind of trees the baca trees were, but the rustling David will hear in the top of them will be the sound of the heavenly armies that are also involved in the conflict. It is indeed Yahweh the God of Armies who goes with David.

2 SAMUEL 6:1–23

Little Things Can Have Terrible Consequences and Foreshadow Tragedy

[1]David again assembled all the elite soldiers in Israel, thirty thousand of them. [2]David set off and went, he and the entire company with him, from Masters of Judah to bring up from there God's chest over which the name is proclaimed (the name of Yahweh Armies Who Sits [Enthroned] on the Cherubs). [3]They mounted the chest on a new wagon and carried it from Abinadab's house on the hill, with Abinadab's sons, Uzzah and Ahio, guiding the new wagon. [4]They carried it from Abinadab's house on the hill with God's chest and Ahio going in front of the chest, [5]and David and all the household of Israel celebrating before Yahweh with all cypress wood [instruments], guitars, banjos, tambourines, rattles, and cymbals. [6]When they came to Nakon's threshing floor, Uzzah reached out to God's chest and took hold of it because the cattle had let it slip. [7]Yahweh's anger

flared up at Uzzah, and God struck him down there because of the blunder. He died there by God's chest. [8]David flared up because Yahweh had burst out at Uzzah (that place is called "The Burst at Uzzah" until this day), [9]but David was afraid of Yahweh that day and said, "How can Yahweh's chest come to me?" [10]David was not willing to direct Yahweh's chest to him in the City of David. So David diverted it to the house of Obed-edom the Gittite.

[11]Yahweh's chest stayed at the house of Obed-edom the Gittite for three months, and Yahweh blessed Obed-edom and all his household. [12]King David was told, "Yahweh has blessed the household of Obed-edom and all that belongs to him because of God's chest," so David went and brought up God's chest from Obed-edom's house to the City of David with festivity. [13]When the people carrying Yahweh's chest had taken six steps he sacrificed a bull and a fatted calf. [14]David was dancing before Yahweh with all his might, and David was clad in a linen ephod [15]as David and all the household of Israel were bringing up Yahweh's chest with a shout and a blast on the horn, [16]but when Yahweh's chest came into the City of David, Saul's daughter Michal was watching through the window, and she saw King David jumping and dancing before Yahweh, and despised him inside. . . . [21]David said to Michal, "It was before Yahweh, who chose me rather than your father and all his household to appoint me ruler over Yahweh's people, over Israel. I will celebrate before Yahweh [22]and belittle myself yet more than this and be low in my own eyes, but with the servant girls that you speak of, with them I will find honor." [23]To Michal, Saul's daughter, no child was born to the day of her death.

I write this during Holy Week. In my Bible study group this week someone was expressing his unease with the way we speak of God's sending his Son to be crucified. Is God some sort of masochist? This person is a hospice chaplain and often expresses his agonizing about the grim experiences that come to the people he ministers to and to their families. Why doesn't God stop such things happening? Why does God even make them happen, in Jesus' case? In the Bible study we batted this question back and forth. This young man knows that one of the things I will say in such a discussion is that the problem of good is surely even greater than the problem of evil. As I write,

I look out on the sunshine and listen to a favorite CD and wrestle with obscure Hebrew words (I have strange passions) and look forward with enthusiasm to the arrival later today of my son and daughter-in-law and grandchildren who are coming to stay, even while also being aware of some sadness at the fact that my wife's death nine months last Sunday means she will not be among us as we celebrate Easter together. Why should there be so much good in life, but yes, why do such bad things also happen? Who knows?

In varying ways, David and Obed-edom are the recipients of God's blessing, and Uzzah and Michal have their lives taken away or spoiled, and none of them deserves it any more than most other people. David is God's chosen, he points out, but he's not so holy a person (indeed, maybe pointing out that he is God's chosen was itself not much of a sign of holiness). The reality of his humanness comes out with great clarity in this story. First Samuel 4–5 tells of how the **covenant chest** ended up for a while at Kiriath-Jearim, on the way from **Philistine** territory to Israel's heartland in the mountains. "Masters of **Judah**" is apparently another term for the same place, a rather worrying term given the connotations of the word Master, *baal* (see the comments on 3:1–4:12), which might explain why the name came to be changed. In contrast, the story emphasizes that "the name" is attached to the covenant chest; the name is **Yahweh Armies**, God Who Sits [Enthroned] on the **Cherubs**. The story doesn't tell us why David wanted to move the covenant chest to Jerusalem, but it seems a fair guess that his motives were mixed. He is honoring Yahweh, but it is also another canny political move, a way of giving Jerusalem some status in the eyes of Israel as a whole and encouraging the whole people to be committed to the city as their religious as well as political capital. When they get to the city, David distributes food to everyone, which also won't have done any harm to their enthusiasm for the event. Yet the celebration and festivity with which he personally leads the whole people expresses a heartfelt commitment to Yahweh on his part. When the accident happens, God gets angry, and David gets angry but also fearful. God is a real person with real emotions, and so is David, and they have an overlapping range of emotions. When the chest's journey resumes, offering sacrifice might be an expression of both thanksgiving and prayer.

Obed-edom just happens to be in the right place at the right time to find himself the recipient of God's blessing. Admittedly, I guess it would not initially have seemed to be the right place at the right time. After the calamity happens to Uzzah, Obed-edom is unlucky enough to be the guy who lives across the street and to have his house commandeered by the king. I guess his heart sinks, but he can't say, "Thanks, but no thanks." Maybe that is especially the case if you are a Gittite, a man from Gath, and therefore a Philistine, for goodness' sake! Whatever led to your living in Kiriath-jearim, you know you could easily lose your visa. You have no alternative but to say, "Yes, your majesty," with a sense of foreboding; and then you find your whole household blessed (your wife who seemed unable to have children gets pregnant, your crops grow really well . . .).

On the other hand, poor Uzzah makes one understandable mistake, with the best will in the world, and loses his life. The story reminds Israel once more that you have to be careful in the way you relate to the covenant chest. Israel will have assumed that Uzzah should have known better than to grab the chest, but maybe no one had told him to be careful in this fashion, or maybe he just reacted instinctively, in a way that might have been designed to honor the chest rather than treat it irreverently. At the end of the story there is Michal, who has been the political football between her father and two husbands and has now been taken away from the one who cared about her and given to the one who doesn't know what love means. She lets her feelings about him find expression, and she gets as good as she gives. Then the storyteller tells us how she never did have children. It doesn't connect the dots, but it suggests the grief that characterized her life as a whole.

It will soon be Good Friday. To a Brit it's odd that for several weeks U.S. Christians have been assuring themselves that Christ is risen. I wonder if we want to avoid thinking about Jesus' experience of abandonment and woe and unfairness and execution because we want to avoid thinking about those realities that run through human experience. Is that wise? The Bible is resolute about facing them.

2 SAMUEL 7:1–29

A House and a Household

¹When the king had settled in his house, after Yahweh had given him rest from all his enemies around, ²the king said to the prophet Nathan, "Do consider, I am living in a house of cedar, but God's chest is living in a tent." ³Nathan said to the king, "Go and do all that is in your mind, because Yahweh is with you." ⁴But that night a word from Yahweh came to Nathan, ⁵"Go and say to my servant David, 'Yahweh has said this: "Are you going to build me a house to live in? ⁶Because I have not lived in a house since the day I brought up the Israelites from Egypt to this day. I have been going about in a tent as a dwelling. ⁷Everywhere I went about with the Israelites did I speak a word with one of the Israelite clan leaders whom I appointed to shepherd my people Israel, saying, 'Why have you not built me a house of cedar?'?"' ⁸So now you are to say to my servant David, 'Yahweh Armies has said this: "I took you from the pasture, from following the flock, to be ruler over my people Israel, ⁹and I have been with you everywhere you have gone, and I have cut off your enemies from before you. I will make a great name for you, like the name of the great men on the earth. ¹⁰I will establish a place for my people Israel and I will plant them. They will dwell there and not tremble any more. Worthless people will not again afflict them as they did at the beginning, ¹¹from the day when I appointed leaders over my people Israel. I will give you rest from all your enemies. Yahweh hereby announces to you that Yahweh will make a house(hold) for you. ¹²When your days are complete and you lie down with your ancestors, I will raise up your offspring after you, who will come out from inside you, and I will establish his kingship. ¹³He will build a house for my name and I will establish his royal throne in perpetuity. ¹⁴I myself will be a father to him and he will be a son to me. When he does wrong, I will discipline him by means of the club of human beings, with the blow of human hands, ¹⁵but my commitment I will not remove from him as I removed it from Saul, whom I removed from before you. ¹⁶Your household and your kingship will be secure in perpetuity before you. Your throne will be secure in perpetuity."'"

[Verses 17–29 record David's response of astonishment, praise, and plea that this may indeed be so.]

132

One of my colleagues likes to remind people that Jesus never talks about our establishing God's kingdom or furthering it or building it or extending it. In the Gospels, the only things we do to God's kingdom are wait for it, see it, enter it, seek it, receive it, inherit it, and declare that it has come. In other words, we don't have an active relationship to it at all. In U.S. culture, this is an unpopular point to make, because people like to feel they can make a difference. They want to achieve. I enjoy watching students shift in their seats unhappily when I repeat my colleague's point. We don't like the fact that the gospel is about what God has done for us and not about what we do for God. (Yes, I know, we do have responsibility, and we are challenged to serve God and serve the world and so on, but we will not understand our role—and avoid disillusion—unless we see the point about the way Jesus talks.)

So David is our patron saint. Oddly (but like us), David started off as the person God simply selected. He did not become God's anointed because of what he had done. Indeed, for a long time he was rather good at not seeking to bring about the fulfillment of God's purpose and rather good at waiting for God to bring things about. Now he has seized history by the horns. He has determined on a capital city and moved the **covenant chest** there, and next he wants to build a proper house for it. He is amusingly embarrassed at the fact that he lives in a proper house, a rather splendid one at that, nicely roofed and/ or pillared and/or paneled with the cedar wood from Lebanon that was the gift of the king of Tyre (2 Samuel 5:11). God's sanctuary has always been portable, like a Bedouin tent. On the way to Canaan it moved around as Israel moved around, and it has moved around within the country since Israel arrived in Canaan, but now it can and surely should become a proper house, shouldn't it?

"Of course," says the prophet Nathan. Excuse me, who are you, we haven't heard of you, where did you come from? Nathan is not the first prophet who has been mentioned as advising David; a prophet called Gad has been doing so (see 1 Samuel 22:5). The best-known prophets, people such as Elijah, Isaiah, and Jeremiah, are pretty independent of the kings they are involved with, and that is a major reason for their existence.

133

They are there to stand up to the king. Like other Middle Eastern societies, however, Israel also had prophets who were on the king's staff, to provide him with the guidance he needs. The trouble is, once you are on the payroll, it's very hard to bite the hand that feeds you, especially when it may not merely bite you back but order your execution. You get sucked into the institution. This is why it is virtually impossible for a pastor to be a prophet (my students hate me for telling them that, too). Pastors therefore have to cultivate prophets who will stand up to them, and so do kings. I have just listened to an inaugural lecture by one of my colleagues in which he commented on how important it is to see people who disagree with you as a gift rather than a nuisance or threat. They are the people who help you find out that you are wrong. We will discover that Nathan developed that capacity, but on his first appearance he is just the king's yes-man. He takes God's name in vain, assuring David that God is with him without asking whether this is so.

Then, deliciously, God taps Nathan on the shoulder that night. Did Nathan have a nasty feeling he might have been a bit hasty in saying yes to David? Was he tossing and turning? "Err, excuse me, Nathan. You know this house. It's for me to live in, right? Do you think that perhaps I should be consulted about it? Actually I don't care so much for houses. I like being on the move, you see." God's problem with us is that we like to tie God down, keep God under control. We don't want God on the loose. God likes being on the loose.

God's other problem is the one from which we started. David is getting too fond of taking initiatives for God. He is reversing the relationship between people and God. He wants to build God a house; God counters that declaration by announcing the intention of building David a house. The Hebrew word for house, *beth* (as in Bethlehem or Bethel), means both a house made of brick or stone and a house made of people, a household, and God makes use of this double meaning in reversing David's plan. When God has reestablished who has the sovereignty in this relationship by starting to build David a household, in the sense that his son has succeeded him as king in the way Saul's son did not succeed him, then this son can fulfill David's plan and build God the house that God doesn't really want.

Thus when God agrees to the building of a temple, it has a similar significance to God's agreeing that Israel should have kings. God doesn't really want it, but God will let us have our way. Indeed, in both cases God goes much further than grudging agreement. The very **commitment** to the monarchy that God makes in this chapter shows how far God will go with us in connection with something that God doesn't really want. This is just as well, because the pattern that runs through 1 and 2 Samuel reappears in the church. The New Testament doesn't leave much room for the position of senior pastor or church buildings (our equivalents of king and temple), but the church soon invented them, and once again God shrugs shoulders and cooperates.

"I myself will be a father to him and he will be a son to me." God doesn't explicitly talk in terms of a covenantal relationship with David and his successors, though David will eventually do so (see 2 Samuel 23). Instead God talks in terms of adopting David's successor into a son-father relationship. The implication is that God can never cast him off. A friend of mine used to comment on the difference between motherhood and marriage. You can stop being a wife (and she did), but you can never stop being a mother. No matter what my sons do, she said, I could never stop being their mother. God here envisages the possibility of chastising his son, and God will do a fair amount of chastising in relation to David and his successors over the next four hundred years, but when you adopt someone as your son, God presupposes, he becomes a real son, just as if he was born to you. You can never un-son him in the way you can divorce your spouse. In our culture, there are occasions when birth mothers and adoptive fathers do so; God cannot imagine doing so. This was a fact that kept Israel going when it seemed that God had indeed cast off David's successors, given that after the year 587 no Davidic king ever sat on the throne of Jerusalem. It kept Israel hoping, and it kept Israel praying. Sometimes God encouraged it with the possibility that such a Davidic king would indeed reign again one day (see Jeremiah 23). Sometimes God encouraged it to see itself as the Davidic people and to see God's commitment fulfilled in the relationship all the people had with God (see Isaiah 55). God won't

go back on the commitment unless it is to swallow it up into
something better.

2 SAMUEL 8:1–10:19

The Peak of David's Achievement

*[Second Samuel 8:1–14a records David's victories over the Phil-
istines, Moabites, Edomites, Aramaeans, and the king of Zobah,
and his dedication of plunder to God.]*

[14b]So Yahweh delivered David wherever he went. [15]David
reigned as king over all Israel and David exercised authority in
accordance with what is right for all his people. . . . [9:1]David said,
"Is there anyone still left of Saul's household, so that I can show
commitment with him for the sake of Jonathan?" [2]There was
a servant belonging to Saul's household called Ziba, and they
summoned him to David. . . . [3b]Ziba said to the king, "There is
still a son of Jonathan; he is lame in both feet." [4]The king said
to him, "Where is he?" Ziba said to the king, "Well, he is in the
house of Machir son of Ammiel, in Lo-debar." [5]King David sent
and got him from the house of Machir son of Ammiel, from
Lo-debar. [6]When Mephibosheth son of Jonathan son of Saul
came to David, he fell on his face and bowed low. David said,
"Mephibosheth." He said, "Here is your servant." [7]David said to
him, "Don't be afraid, because I will definitely keep commitment with you for the sake of your father Jonathan. I will give
back to you all the land of your [grand]father Saul, and you
may eat at my table always."

*[Verses 8–13 relate how David entrusts oversight of Saul's land
to Ziba and his family on behalf of Mephibosheth and his family. Chapter 10 then recounts a conflict between Israel and the
Ammonites, into which the Ammonites also draw the Aramaeans. First Joab, David's military commander, and then David
himself rout the Aramaeans, and the Ammonites withdraw.]*

I've just started reading a social history of Britain since the end
of the 1939–1945 war. It thus begins with the celebration of
the allies' victory over Nazi Germany, personalized as Win-
ston Churchill's victory over Adolf Hitler (today someone was

contemporizing that conflict again in the upcoming World Cup soccer game between England and Germany). The war victory over Nazi Germany was Churchill's finest hour. Yet in the parliamentary election that soon followed, the British people forsook Churchill and elected Clement Atlee as prime minister. You could say that it illustrates how pride comes before a fall, as long as you mean this in the Old Testament sense, where pride isn't so much a sinful attitude as the fact of being in a position of majesty and honor. Even if they are not sinfully attached to their prestige and achievements, people in such positions often fall from them.

In these chapters of 2 Samuel, David reaches the height of his achievements, but he is about to fall. The chapters are the highpoint in his story with regard to his religious, military, economic, and political accomplishments. In 1 Samuel, a key factor in the people's desire for a monarchy was the pressure of the **Philistines** as the Israelites and the Philistines were vying for control of Canaan. David has brought that conflict to a successful conclusion. The Philistines do not cease to exist, but they become a minor people down on the Mediterranean coast who no longer have such ambitions and are not a particular threat to Israel. David likewise demonstrates to people such as the Moabites, Ammonites, and Edomites to the east and southeast, and the much more powerful Aramaeans to the northeast, that he is not someone they can mess with. In effect he becomes sovereign over a small empire, the only time Israel is an imperial power instead of a colony under the sovereignty of some other empire. You could see it as a sample fulfillment of God's purpose to be lord over all the earth through the agency of the king of Israel.

The chapters are a highpoint in another way. They speak of David's exercising **authority** in accordance with what is right for all his people. That is a longwinded translation of a two-word phrase that is impossible to render succinctly in English. Translations have expressions such as "what is just and right" or "justice and equity." The first word is a term for authority or leadership or the power to make decisions. The trouble is (as Samuel warned Israel when they asked for a king, in 1 Samuel 8) that kings and other leaders usually exercise authority in a way that is costly for their people. So Deuteronomy and the Prophets commonly link this word with one that denotes doing the right thing by people rather than taking advantage of them or being a burden to them or oppressing them; I usually translate it by the word *faithfulness*. In the Prophets, a standard critique of the kings is that they fail to exercise authority faithfully, in accordance with what is right for people. That can happen in the exercise of justice in the courts; it can happen in the imposition of taxes. Saying that David exercised authority in a way that did do right by his people is a great tribute to him. The comment is a brief one in the story, but its importance is out of all proportion to its brevity. If we are suspicious, we might say it has to be an exaggeration; somebody pays for the building of his palace and for all those wars. If, in effect, the cost is paid by the ordinary people of Moab, Edom, and so on, that doesn't make things so much better. Even if the comment does paint him a bit whiter than he deserves, it still sets the standard for his successors, especially if they want to be the beneficiaries of God's fatherly **commitments** described in 2 Samuel 7. Psalm 72 spells out further what is involved in the king's commitment to exercising authority in accordance with what is right for people, and it also associates this with his being recognized by other peoples in the way David was.

You could say that David acted in relation to Mephibosheth in a way that involved the exercise of authority in accordance with what is right for people to whom he has some covenant obligation. The sad story of how Mephibosheth became handicapped is told in 2 Samuel 4. It looks as if he was scared stiff when summoned by David, and he had good reason. We have noted that after a coup the new regime may well think it wise to dispose of people associated with the previous regime. Typically, David's action achieves the same end while doing the right thing by Jonathan's commitment to him. His action might win some grudging approval from people who still supported Saul and who had yearned to have someone from Saul's family as king. It also means that David has Mephibosheth under his eye and that it is not in Mephibosheth's interests to cooperate with anyone who does want to reinstall Saul's household on the

138

throne. There will be some footnotes to the story of Ziba and Mephibosheth in 2 Samuel 16, 19, and 21.

Alas, this is indeed the highpoint of David's story. Majesty comes before a fall. It's downhill from now on.

2 SAMUEL 11:1-27

But the Thing David Had Done Was Displeasing in Yahweh's Eyes

[1]At the turn of the year, the time when kings go out [to battle], David sent Joab and his servants with him, and all Israel, and they devastated the Ammonites and besieged Rabbah, while David stayed in Jerusalem. [2]One evening David got up from his bed and walked about on the roof of the palace, and from the roof saw a woman bathing. The woman was very good-looking. [3]So David sent and inquired about the woman. He was told, "This will be Bathsheba, daughter of Eliam, wife of Uriah the Hittite." [4]David sent aides, they got her, and she came to him. He slept with her while she was sanctifying herself from her taboo, and she went back home. [5]The woman got pregnant, and sent and told David, "I'm pregnant." [6]David sent to Joab, "Send Uriah the Hittite to me." Joab sent Uriah to David. [7]When Uriah came to him, David asked him about how well things were with Joab and with the company and with the battle. [8]Then David said to Uriah, "Go down to your house and bathe your feet." When Uriah went out from the palace, a present followed him. [9]But Uriah slept at the door of the palace with all the [other] servants of his master. He did not go down to his house.... [14]In the morning David wrote a message to Joab and sent it by means of Uriah. [15]He wrote in the message, "Place Uriah in the forefront of the fiercest battle and withdraw from him so that he may be struck down and die." ... [17]The men of the city came out and fought Joab, and of the company some of David's servants fell. Uriah the Hittite also died. [18]Joab sent and told David all the details of the battle.... [25]David said to the aide, "Say this to Joab: 'This thing is not to be amiss in your eyes, because the sword consumes one way and another way. Strengthen your fight against the city and destroy it.' Thus encourage him." [26]When Uriah's wife heard that her husband

Uriah was dead, she lamented over her master. ²⁷When the [time for] mourning had passed, David sent and fetched her to his house. She became his wife and bore him a son.

But the thing David had done was wrong in Yahweh's eyes.

There is a news item today about a state governor who had to resign because of a sex scandal a couple of years ago but is now trying to rehabilitate himself in the eye of the public. As governor, one of his strengths was that he had regarded all things as possible. He ignored the conventional wisdom that says, "You can't do that." In connection with his involvement in the sex scandal, a reporter asked whether there hadn't been a voice inside him that said, "You can't do that," and he agreed that apparently there wasn't. In other words, he also seemed to ignore that conventional wisdom in his private life, thinking he could get away with it. I know of no statistics suggesting that leaders are more prone to sexual wrongdoing than other people or that pastors are more prone than laypeople, but they don't seem to be less prone, and there are one or two ways in which this seems troublesome. We would like to think of our leaders as people of integrity, partly because we want them to lead with integrity, and it's not clear that they can lack integrity in their private lives and keep it in their public roles. Further, the risks our leaders take in their sexual lives seem stupid, and if they are stupid there, can we assume they will behave with wisdom in their public roles? It can seem as if they believe they can get away with things just because of their position, when (if anything) the opposite is the case.

Maybe David falls for this set of assumptions and reveals these flaws. Maybe it starts with the fact that he is at home in his palace, able to have his afternoon nap, when his army is out fighting a war. It is the time when kings go out to battle, and "all Israel" has done so, except David. East of the Jordan, Rabbah, the Ammonite capital (modern Amman, the capital of Jordan), is in an equivalent location to Jerusalem as the Israelite capital west of the Jordan. David's army is there to assert Israelite authority over the city and over the area as part of David's empire. To be fair, he was letting Joab be effective commander-in-chief in the previous chapter, so maybe it is fine for him to be a stay-at-home commander-in-chief now, like a U.S. president, but this would be a more impressive argument if he were staying home to focus on exercising authority in a way that does the right thing by his people, the commitment we considered in connection with chapter 8. He is doing no such thing, and in chapter 12 he will be only too willing to show up at Rabbah for the actual fall of the city so that the credit goes to him rather than to Joab, the man who does the donkey work.

You can't necessarily blame David for spotting Bathsheba bathing on the roof, nor Bathsheba for doing so. She was apparently undertaking the bath that the **Torah** required at the end of her period, and the roof is normally the place where people go when they want to be in private. Maybe the only residence that would overlook her roof would be the palace, which was located at the height of the city; only the sanctuary was located above the palace. While this implied the elevation of the king over his people, it also implied his responsibility. It suggests that literally and metaphorically he can keep an eye on the city. From there he can see what is going on and thus indeed exercise authority to ensure that right is prevailing in the city, but his instincts take him in another direction. While David is never said to love anyone, the number of children he procreates indicates that he has sex with various wives, yet (being a regular man) he is still capable of fancying another woman. A friend of mine was telling me the other day about a billionaire who was asked how much money was enough and who replied that it is always "a little more than you have." The same is true about sex.

David and his agents are the subject of a series of verbs that are chilling for Bathsheba—he saw, he sent, he inquired, he sent, they got, he slept with. She is then the subject of the verb that often excites a woman, but sometimes frightens her: she got pregnant. If it were the modern West, David would be arranging for her to have an abortion, and in traditional societies there are ways of seeking to do so, though they are either very dangerous for the woman or unlikely to succeed, but in any case the Old Testament's failure to mention abortion and the Torah's failure to prohibit it suggests it wasn't within the framework of thinking for Israelites even when pregnancies were totally unwelcome. David's first thought is to try to get

Uriah to sleep with Bathsheba so she can pass off the child as his, but Uriah won't cooperate.

It's horrible how one thing can lead to another. When he cast his eye over the city from his roof David could not have imagined that spotting a hot woman would lead to murder, and if he had imagined this possibility, one can also imagine he would hurry to look the other way, but one thing does lead to another. He has Uriah killed. It was when he discovered that Bathsheba was married to someone who was ethnically a Hittite (presumably not a Hittite recently arrived from Turkey but someone from the tribe that lived in the Hebron area in Abraham's day), a foreigner, that David decided to send for her. Did that make it easier? After all, she is married to a Hittite. Does the same consideration make it easier to have him killed? After all, he is only a Hittite. Yet he is evidently a worshiper of **Yahweh** (his name means "Yahweh is my light"). Indeed, when he declined to go and sleep with his wife, maybe he smelled a rat, but what he actually said was that he couldn't possibly go home like that when the rest of the army was engaged in a war. It is just the kind of thought that should surely have been in David's head.

Instead, David is now thinking of murder. He turns the man himself into the messenger who carries the instructions for his own death. In the next engagement, some of Israel's crack troops are killed, and Joab makes sure Uriah is with them. The story doesn't quite say that the deaths result from the need to get Uriah killed, though that need seems to dictate Joab's strategy. Joab does fear that David may decide that Joab took unwise risks in the engagement, but he knows David won't mind the sacrifice of those warriors if Uriah is among them. David's response is as cynical as Joab's instructions to his aide about how to break the news to David.

Problem solved. Bathsheba can fulfill the proper mourning for her husband; then David can send for her again. Once more she is the object of verbs; at no point is there any suggestion that she has any say in what happens. He is the king, after all. You don't say no to the king (or the professor or the pastor or the governor or the president) whether it concerns a one-night stand or a marriage.

"But the thing David had done was wrong in Yahweh's eyes."

2 SAMUEL 12:1–15a

The Man Who Has Learned How to Be a Prophet

[1]So Yahweh sent Nathan to David. He came to him and said to him, "There were two men in a certain city, one rich, one poor. [2]The rich man had very large flocks and herds. [3]The poor man didn't have anything except one small ewe lamb that he had acquired. He had raised it and it had grown up with him and his children, all together. It used to eat from his serving, drink from his cup, and sleep in his arms. It was like a daughter to him. [4]A man on a journey came to the rich man, but he spared taking something from his own flocks or herds to make dinner for the traveler who had come to him, and took the poor man's ewe lamb and made dinner for the man who had come to him." [5]David's anger flared right up at the man. He said to Nathan, "As Yahweh lives, the man who did this should die. [6]He should pay fourfold for the ewe lamb because he did this thing, and since he did not spare [him]." [7]Nathan said to David, "You're the man. Yahweh the God of Israel has said this: 'I myself anointed you as king over Israel. I myself rescued you from Saul's hand. [8]I gave you your master's household and your master's wives into your arms. I gave you the household of Israel and Judah. If that was [too] little, I would have added to you as much again. [9]Why did you despise Yahweh's word by doing what is wrong in my eyes? Uriah the Hittite you struck down with the sword, and his wife you took as your wife. Him you slew with the sword of the Ammonites. [10]So now the sword will not depart from your household, ever, because you despised me and took Uriah the Hittite's wife to be your wife.' [11]Yahweh has said this: 'Right. I am going to raise up trouble for you from your household. I will take your wives before your eyes and give them to someone else. He will sleep with your wives in broad daylight. [12]Because you yourself acted in secret, but I shall do this thing before all Israel and in broad daylight.'"

[13]David said to Nathan, "I have acted wrongly against Yahweh." Nathan said to David, "Yes. But Yahweh has removed your wrongdoing. You will not die. [14]Nevertheless, because you have shown total contempt for [the enemies of] Yahweh by this act, yes, the child born to you will definitely die." [15]And Nathan went home.

A pastor once came to talk to me because he had had an affair. He had actually "got away with it." He thinks his wife never realized, but he knew he had behaved in a way that was both wrong and stupid, and he knew he needed to talk through what happened in order not to get into the same mess again. One thing that struck me was the gradual nature of the way things happened. The woman had come to him for counseling because she felt there was a sadness that permeated her life. She was attractive, and it soon became apparent that her marriage was unhappy. The pastor had some problems in his own marriage. All this ought to have rung alarm bells, and in a way it did—at least he took steps to involve one of his female colleagues in the counseling. After a while they all decided they had done what they could do, but the woman asked if she could come to see him one more time just for coffee, and that ended up with a farewell hug that turned into a kiss and. . . .

One thing led to another. That was how it had been for David. But he didn't go to see his pastor, and his pastor would have reason to be hesitant about going to see him. Prophets who take it upon themselves to confront kings risk their lives, and they sometimes lose them. The first striking feature of this story is thus the contrast between Nathan in chapter 7 and Nathan in chapter 12. There, he was David's yes-man. Here, he confronts David. He does so in a way that shows how a prophet may need shrewdness as well as guts. When he realizes he has to go and see David, I like to imagine him reacting the way Ananias will react when told to go and see Saul of Tarsus (see Acts 9), which (roughly paraphrased) amounts to saying, "Lord, are you insane?" Then either God gives Nathan his parable or Nathan dreams it up, and it is the means of breaking through David's defenses.

David can hardly complain when his comment on what ought to happen to the rich man anticipates what will happen to David himself. There looks to be an illogic about it (death *and* fourfold restitution?), but it corresponds to the implications of the **Torah**. The man should die, David says; therefore he will pay fourfold for his meanness. We noted in connection with the story of Saul and the medium at En-dor that many of the Torah's rules prescribe the death penalty for

144

an offense (including murder or adultery; David is guilty of both), but that in practice Israel does not exact that penalty. By saying that the guilty person should die, it marks how serious the offense is, but by not exacting the penalty it perhaps recognizes that execution raises as many problems as it solves, and the reference to restitution comes nearer to stating what should actually happen.

Outside the parable, the punishment that God announces is thus not execution, as one might expect, but a calamity that arises from within David's own household. God will bring this calamity about, but there will be nothing supranatural about it. You could say it will be the natural outworking of the way David has behaved; certainly the punishment will fit the crime. David has let violence and sexual immorality loose in his household and in Uriah's; but when you have let these loose, you may not be able to get them back into their cage.

Both David and God act and speak in jaw-droppingly mysterious ways in this story. The first enigma is articulated in God's question to David. David has so much. Why on earth did he do what he did? The second question is raised by his reaction to Nathan: "I have done wrong against Yahweh." As Western readers with our stress on emotions, we think David should say how deeply sorry he is, and we wonder if this acknowledgment is enough. Yet when public figures caught guilty of some wrongdoing go in for public hand-wringing, it makes us squirm. To an Israelite way of thinking, too, confession primarily means facing and acknowledging the facts. It is impossible to tell what is actually going on in David, but the spare, bald acknowledgment contrasts with the impression of grief that will shortly be conveyed by his response to his son's illness.

It's also difficult to know what to make of God's response. God has "removed" David's wrongdoing. What does that mean? Has God forgiven it, and if so, in what sense? God doesn't cancel the sentence that Nathan has declared, and over the coming chapters, what Nathan said would happen, does happen. Perhaps that is not surprising. In Western culture, when a person guilty of a crime repents, we don't usually decide that therefore they needn't pay their penalty. Indeed, God imposes an extra punishment; Bathsheba's baby will die.

Nathan declares that David has despised God's word. There are two senses in which that is so. He has despised the kind of word that appears in the Ten Commandments, where God proscribes acts such as adultery and murder. While leaders in any society can think they can do what they like, in Israel the Torah places particular constraints around the king. David has ignored these. Yet his story has made more reference to another kind of word, God's word of promise to him, which came in Nathan's previous message to him. God's *word* came to Nathan, and David urged God to establish the *word* spoken to him (2 Samuel 7:4, 25). Reference here to God's word reminds David of the great things God has done for him, which were a fulfillment of that word of promise, and of the further great things God intended for him, which were designed to be a further fulfillment of that promise. He has despised that word, that promise. One might think he has imperiled it, but that same word of promise gave God no escape from a commitment to David. God can chastise David but not abandon him.

In turn, that fact suggests the possibility that God's removing David's wrongdoing means refusing to let it be an obstacle to the fulfillment of God's purpose with Israel through David, even though the wrongdoing will have other terrible consequences. It also raises the possibility that God's removing the wrongdoing wasn't a response to David's confession at all. It doesn't make a difference whether that confession indicated real sorrow or just remorse and a regret at being found out. God's refusing to put David to death or abandon him emerges from God, from God's grace and God's commitment. God doesn't have mercy on us because we deserve it. God has mercy on us because that is God's nature.

There is one further, strange and paradoxical reason why David will not simply be let off. He has shown total contempt for Yahweh's enemies. I put the phrase about the enemies in brackets because it might be a later addition to the **text**—you will see that modern translations leave it out. But it's part of the text, and it suggests an insight. David's job was to rule over Yahweh's enemies and be the means whereby they came to acknowledge Yahweh. His action has shown him to be someone whom Yahweh's enemies could reasonably despise. How can he now be the means of their coming to acknowledge Yahweh? By his act he has undermined the fulfillment of his vocation.

2 SAMUEL 12:15b–13:14

The Price the Family Begins to Pay

[15b]Yahweh struck the child that Uriah's wife bore to David. When it became sick, [16]David sought God for the boy. David fasted and came and spent the night lying on the ground. [17]The elders in his household stood over him to stand him up from the ground but he was not willing and he did not eat food with them. [18]On the seventh day the child died. David's servants were afraid to tell him that the child had died, because [they said], "Now. When the child was alive, we spoke to him and he did not listen to our voice. How can we say to him, 'The child is dead'? He may do something bad." [19]David saw that his servants were whispering to each other, and David perceived that the child was dead. David said to his servants, "Is the child dead?" They said, "He is dead." [20]David stood up from the ground, bathed, put on his oils, and changed his clothes. He came to Yahweh's house and bowed low. Then he went to his house and asked and they presented him with food and he ate. [21]His servants said to him, "What is this thing that you have done? When the child was alive, you fasted and wept. Now that the child is dead, you stood up and ate food." [22]He said, "While the child was still alive, I fasted and wept because I said, 'Who knows? Yahweh may be gracious to me. The child may live.' [23]But now that he is dead, why should I fast? Am I able to bring him back again? I am going to him, but he will not come back to me."

[24]David comforted his wife Bathsheba and had sex with her. He slept with her and she had a son and called him Solomon. Because Yahweh cared about him, [25]he sent by means of the prophet Nathan and called him "Beloved by Yah," on account of Yahweh.

[Verses 26–31 relate how David took part in the capture of Rabbah, tying off the story in chapter 11.]

[13:1]This happened subsequently. David's son Absalom had a beautiful sister named Tamar, and David's son Amnon loved her. [2]It was so stressful for Amnon that he became sick because of his sister Tamar, because she was a young girl, but it seemed impossible in Amnon's eyes to do anything about her. ³But Amnon had a friend named Jonadab, the son of David's brother Shimah, a very clever man. . . . ⁵Jonadab said to him, "Lie down on your bed and act sick. Your father will come to see you and you can say to him, "May my sister Tamar come and give me something to eat. . . ." ⁸So Tamar went to her brother Amnon's house; he was lying down. She got dough and kneaded it and made pancakes in front of him, and cooked the pancakes. ⁹But when she got the pan and poured them out in front of him, he refused to eat them. Amnon said, "Send everyone out from me," and everyone went out from him. ¹⁰Then Amnon said to Tamar, "Bring the food into the room so I can eat from your hand. . . ." ¹¹When she offered it to him to eat, he took hold of her and said to her, "Come to bed with me, sister." ¹²She said to him, "Don't, brother. Don't violate me, because such a thing is not done in Israel. Don't do this stupidity. ¹³What about me? Where would I take my disgrace? And you, you will be just one of the stupid men in Israel. So now, won't you speak to the king, because he would not withhold you from me." ¹⁴But he would not listen to her voice. He took hold of her and violated her and bedded her.

At a concert last night a singer was telling us the background to a song about her grandfather. He was French-Canadian, spoke mostly in French, and died when she was a child. For both reasons she feels she never really got to know him, and she often looks at a 1920s photograph of his marriage to her grandmother, in which she imagines she can see a mischievous look in his eye, and in her grandmother's eye a look that says, "What have I let myself in for?" The song imagines how her grandfather was thinking on that day, but it is imagination; she has no way of knowing if she gets him right.

In this story, I continue to be uncertain whether it is David or God who is harder to fathom. What is God doing, striking this child? Like many people, I am horrified at the idea that someone could abort a baby on the basis of not wanting to have a baby at the moment, let alone that someone could kill a baby. God's action takes no notice of any idea that this individual baby has a right to life. A child's life is always bound up in the web of life with its parents; we know how the sins of the parents are visited on the children. In this story, the feelings of its mother are also totally ignored. The child's death is simply a declaration of divine judgment on its father. Once again it reflects the fact that the stakes are very high when you are born into the family through which God's purpose is being put into effect. We may breathe another sigh of relief that we are just ordinary people and that God may not relate to us the way God relates to David and to people close to him.

That God's action is a judgment on David is reflected in the way the story goes on to describe David's reaction to the boy's sickness (again, there is no mention of his wife's reaction). How can God be so stonyhearted as to refuse to respond to David's fasting and prayer? "With difficulty," I guess is the answer. (How will God be able to sit there in heaven and watch Jesus be executed?) Often the Old Testament portrays God showing mercy when people do not deserve it. Indeed, this story is an example; David deserves to die for what he has done, and his continuing to live (and continuing to reign as king) issues from God's grace. Why didn't God simply let David die and let the child live? Perhaps God has already ruled out that option by the commitment expressed in 2 Samuel 7. So God is compromising between treating David as he deserves and letting him get away with his wrongdoing.

It is also a mystery why David should be so upset about the boy's illness. He has many children, and he has not shown any sign of caring about anyone in the story so far, and the conceiving of this child was (after all) a disastrous accident. David's staff find the depth of his concern mystifying, and they then understandably find his reaction to the child's actual death also mystifying. There is a strange ruthless logic about it. Okay, that's over. He goes to the sanctuary to bow down to God in acknowledgment that God is sovereign over whether prayers get answered, and he resumes his normal life. He will join the boy in **Sheol**. The boy will never join him again on earth.

I hope David didn't think he could comfort Bathsheba by taking her to bed again, though the story may hint at this assumption, or at least hint that conceiving another child can compensate for the loss of one child. It does not do so. But once again the story is more concerned with God's wider purpose than with the feelings of David or Bathsheba. Bathsheba's conceiving is a sign that God has not abandoned David and his line. At this point, David and Bathsheba do not know, but the readers of the story know, that the child she conceives is the person who actually will succeed David and in whom those promises in 2 Samuel 7 will be fulfilled (though he will get himself in a mess that is in its own way just as bad as his father's). God's love for this child relates not to him as an individual but to the fact that he is the son who will eventually succeed David. The name he is given is not a correction of the name Bathsheba gave him or a change in the name by which he actually will be known; it is more like names that occur in Isaiah, such as "A Wonderful Counselor is the Mighty God; the Everlasting Father is a Prince of Peace" (Isaiah 9:6), which is not exactly a name in the sense of the way other people speak of the person. The new name is a kind of courtesy name.

This story may seem even more astonishing when one relates it to Psalm 51, whose heading invites readers to make a connection with these events. If David prayed the way Psalm 51 does, it seems that God did not grant his prayer. Perhaps God would have thought it a fine prayer, but not one that David really meant. Or perhaps it was in some ways the kind of prayer that David ought to have prayed. Or perhaps it was a fine prayer in principle, but not one that was fitting on David's lips. After all, if David did say to God, "Against you alone have I sinned" (Psalm 51:4), it would seem that he has a thing or two to learn about what he has done.

The story of Tamar begins immediately to show that David has not sinned merely against God and against Uriah and against Bathsheba and against the child who died and against the Israelite troops at Rabbah and against Israel as a whole. He has sinned against his daughter Tamar (and for that matter against his son Amnon) because the kind of person he was issues in the kind of behavior that appears in his family and because he brings down God's judgment on his own household as a judgment on David himself. The story presupposes that David's grown-up sons have their own homes, and Amnon's rape of Tamar does not involve incest in the strictest sense,

150

as they will have two different mothers. Tamar can therefore raise the possibility that David would be willing for Amnon to marry Tamar, though she may simply be trying any means to avoid the rape that in fact happens.

2 SAMUEL 13:15–14:24

The Grief of a Sister and the Strife between Brothers

[15]Amnon then felt a very great revulsion for [Tamar], in that the revulsion he felt for her was greater than the love he had felt for her. Amnon said to her, "Get up; go." [16]She said to him, "No! This wrong in sending me away is greater than the other that you did with me." But he would not listen to her. . . . [17]He called the boy who attended on him and said, "Will you people send this woman off, out from my presence, and bolt the door after her?" [18]She had a long-sleeved gown on, because the king's young daughters used to dress in such robes. [19]Tamar put dirt on her head and tore the long-sleeved gown that she had on and put her hand on her head and went her way, crying out as she went.

[20]Her brother Absalom said to her, "Sister, was it your brother Amnon who was with you? Now, sister, quieten down. He is your brother. Don't give your mind to this thing." So Tamar stayed, a desolate woman, in her brother Absalom's house. [21]King David himself heard about all this and was very angry. [22]Absalom did not speak with Amnon anything good or bad, because Absalom refused to have anything to do with Amnon because of the fact that he had violated his sister Tamar. [23]Two years later Absalom's sheep shearers were at Master-of-Hazor, which is near Ephraim, and Absalom invited all the king's sons. . . . [28]Absalom ordered his boys, "Will you watch when Amnon is in a good mood because of the wine, and I will say to you, 'Strike Amnon down, kill him, don't be afraid. After all, I myself am the one who has given you the order. Be resolute. Be strong.'" [29]Absalom's boys did to Amnon as Absalom ordered. . . . [37]Absalom fled and went to Talmai, son of Ammihud, king of Geshur, and [David] mourned over his son all the time. [38]When Absalom had fled and gone to Geshur, he was there for three years, [39]but King David stopped going out [to fight] against Absalom because he had gotten over Amnon, that he was dead.

14:1Joab son of Zeruiah recognized that the king's mind was on Absalom. 2Joab sent to Tekoa and got a clever woman from there. He said to her, "Will you act as someone mourning and dress yourself in mourning clothes? Don't put on oils, be like a woman who has been mourning for a long time over someone who has died. 3Come to the king and speak to him in this way" (Joab put the words into her mouth). 4So the woman from Tekoa came to the king, fell on her face to the ground, bowed low, and said, "Help, your majesty!" 5The king said to her, "What is your need?" She said, "Actually I am a widow; my husband died. 6Your servant had two sons. The two of them fought in the fields and there was no one to separate them. One of them struck the other down and killed him. 7And there: the whole kin group has risen up against your servant and said, 'Give us the one who struck down his brother and we will kill him for the life of his brother whom he slew. We will dispose of the heir, too.' So they will quench the last ember that remains to me, and not give my husband a name or a remnant on the face of the ground." 8The king said to the woman, "Go home and I will give an order concerning you."

[In verses 9–24 the woman explains that she has really been talking about David's attitude to Absalom, and David agrees to fetch Absalom from exile, though he is to go home and not come before David.]

I once knew someone who was sexually abused on an ongoing basis by a family member when she was a young girl. She never told me the details of what happened, and to be honest I never wanted her to do so, but I knew that twenty years later she was still dealing with issues that this experience raised. What makes me think about her now is the way she also spoke of the pressure that family members put on her to keep quiet about it when she was grown up and when she wanted to talk about it, partly because she was concerned about other people who might be this man's victims. In a similar way the British television dramatist Dennis Potter, sexually abused by his uncle who lived with his family, spoke of the way he couldn't talk about this business because it felt as if it would have been like throwing a bomb into the middle of everything that made him feel secure.

It may be hard to imagine Tamar's hurt and shame. To this end, the best thing to do is to go back more than once to read her story and to keep listening to her words. In many cultures the mere fact of its becoming known that a young woman has had premarital sexual experience is inclined to bring great shame on her. She becomes used goods. The chances of her parents being able to find someone to marry her are low—hence the **Torah's** requirement that the man himself be willing to marry her if she wishes, specifically so in a case of rape. To put it another way, in such cultures having sex is virtually tantamount to consummating a marriage. Related to this is the fact that Amnon talks about sending Tamar off and that she protests at this action; "send off" is also a verb that denotes "divorce." She is thrown out of what by rights should now become her house, and the door is bolted. Whereas she arrived with food for her sick brother, she has been overwhelmed by a nightmare: bedded against her will, divorced, and shamed. Her life is over. Putting dirt on your head, **crying out**, holding your head in your hands, and tearing your clothes are regular signs of mourning; one point about such gestures is that you don't care what you look like. To continue to look good would be a contradiction of how things are. She had come dressed in the way a teenage princess would be dressed; we aren't sure about the meaning of the word translated "long-sleeved" (it's the word used to describe Joseph's dream coat), but evidently it is a form of dress that marks your position in the family or community. Tearing this dress is especially telling.

Her father is angry at what happens, but he DOES NOTHING ABOUT IT. Once again the enigmatic mystery of David's character surfaces. In political and military contexts he can be decisive, but in family matters he is inexplicably, bafflingly paralyzed. The ancient Greek translation of the **text** adds that David's problem was Amnon's being his firstborn son, which is a plausible insight, though it also makes David's inaction more serious. This is the son who could be expected to succeed David, and he is behaving the way his father had behaved; "I am the present king/the future king and I can do what I like." Perhaps Amnon's being his eldest son is why David is so strangely inactive. He sees himself in Amnon.

Absalom's reaction is initially enigmatic in another way. He is the one who bids Tamar keep things quiet. The dirty linen of the family shouldn't be washed in public, especially the dirty linen of the royal family. Yet it looks as if the event gnaws away at Absalom. Each day over breakfast he meets the sister whom he has invited to live with him, her eyes dark with weeping, her princess clothes never restored, apparently having no choice about staying unattached all her life. Eventually he formulates a plot that involves inviting his father and his brothers to the celebration that often happened at sheep-shearing time. It seems that David smells a rat; indeed, his staff says Absalom has been plotting Amnon's murder ever since the rape. Later chapters will tell us about Absalom's attempt to take over from his father as king, and it may be that his plot relates as much to intentions he is already formulating in that direction. David declines to come to Absalom's party and won't give permission for Absalom to invite Amnon (the heir apparent to his throne), but Absalom does so anyway, and Amnon fails to smell a rat.

Perhaps Amnon has been living for the two years with the moral burden of his action and is subconsciously willing to face his destiny. Yet over many of these matters the text is silent. It tells us little about people's feelings and motivation but leaves us to reflect on them. It does the same in making no moral judgment on what went on, not because it doesn't realize that it has told a story about morally horrifying events but because it assumes we can work out that this is what they are. In both connections (the psychological and the moral) leaving things unsaid draws us into making judgments and thus involves us in a way we might not be personally involved if it explicitly provided the answers.

It looks as if Absalom is right in thinking that his life is now in danger so that it is wise for him to take refuge with Talmai, his maternal grandfather. David then gets paralyzed in his relationship with Absalom, and this time it is Joab who has to take the decisive action, though this decisive action contributes to the fact that Absalom can organize his subsequent coup and to the way God's judgment is worked out in all these events. Once again David is the victim or the beneficiary of a parable. The woman's story is totally fictional, like Nathan's parable.

Once again it gets beneath David's skin. For the purposes of the story, David has just two sons, Amnon and Absalom; the others are ignored. One has killed the other, and David's colluding with Absalom's self-banishment means Absalom is dead to David and to Israel. He agrees that if he would pardon the woman's nonexistent murderer son, he should restore his own actual murderer son, though he does so in rather half-way fashion. This might seem reasonable, but it may be another aspect of the background to the further trouble that will follow.

2 SAMUEL 14:25–16:23

Absalom's Coup

²⁵Compared with Absalom, there was no one in all Israel to be so admired as handsome. From the sole of his foot to the crown of his head there was no shortcoming in him. ²⁶When he shaved his head (at the end of each year he would shave, because it was too heavy for him, so he would shave), he would weigh the hair on his head, two hundred shekels by the royal weight. ²⁷There were born to Absalom three sons and one daughter, named Tamar; she became a fine-looking woman. ²⁸Absalom lived in Jerusalem for two years but did not go into the king's presence. ²⁹Then Absalom sent to Joab in order to send him to the king, but [Joab] would not come to him.

[In verses 30–32 Absalom sets Joab's barley field on fire to persuade him.]

³³So Joab came to the king . . . and he summoned Absalom. He came to the king and bowed low to him, with his face to the ground, and the king hugged Absalom.
¹⁵:¹Some time later, Absalom got ready for himself a chariot and horses and fifty men running ahead of him. ²Absalom would get up early and stand by the side of the road to the gate, and when anyone had a case that was to come to the king for a decision, Absalom called to him, "What city are you from?" and the person said, "Your servant is from one of the Israelite clans," ³Absalom said to him, "Look, your statements are good and honest, but there is no one to listen to you on the king's behalf." ⁴Absalom said, "If only someone would make me an

authority in the country so anyone who had a case for decision could come to me and I would see he got his rights." ⁵When someone approached to bow down to him, he would extend his hand and take hold of him and hug him. ⁶Absalom acted in this way to all Israel who would come to the king for a decision. So Absalom stole the heart of the Israelites.

[Second Samuel 15:7–16:23 relates how Absalom gets himself made king in Hebron. David flees with some troops loyal to him and with his household. He leaves behind ten secondary wives to mind the palace, Zadok and Abiathar the priests with the covenant chest, and an ally called Hushai to pretend to be loyal to Absalom. Mephibosheth also stays in Jerusalem, thinking the conflict may make it possible for him to gain Saul's throne, so David gives his property to Mephibosheth's minder, Ziba. Another supporter of Saul, Shimei, hurls insults at David as he passes, but David will not have him killed. Meanwhile Absalom arrives in Jerusalem from Hebron.]

When I was an assistant pastor, a leading political figure in the Church of England came to speak at a conference at our church, and talked about policies for which he was working in the Church of England. It was clear that the man was a skilled political operator; he knew how to get things done. During his address, my rector whispered to me, "It's just as well that man is a Christian, he would be a rogue if he were not." Actually, it's hard to be someone devoted to God and also someone who is good at getting things done. It's easier to be someone who is devoted to God but doesn't know how to get things done, or to be a Christian who seems just as ruthless as the rest of the world.

Despite the fact that David's moral faults are huge, he becomes a standard against which to evaluate a king in comments on whether he did "what was upright in the eyes of Yahweh his God, like his ancestor David" (2 Kings 16:2). We have noted that this favorable evaluation becomes more explicable when we take into account the basis for critiquing those later kings. It is their inclination to tolerate or even encourage the kind of worship that Yahweh in no way approves (in that case, sacrificing a son to Yahweh), or to tolerate or even encourage worship of other gods. For all David's faults and for all the cluelessness about the way he relates to Yahweh and the way he lives his life, he is resolute in his commitment to Yahweh. That fact comes through in the story of Absalom's coup. At one level the coup issues from God's judgment on David for killing Uriah and taking Bathsheba, but at another level it issues from David's incompetence as a father. Likewise his response to the coup contrasts with the decisiveness of his reactions in other political contexts. It deepens the mystery of who David is. There may be a positive point about telling the story in a way that suggests David has lost his groove. It parallels another strand in the earlier stages in David's story. He trusts God and leaves the outcome of things to God.

With some irony, Absalom is now the clever political operator. He is made in the image of his father in being such a hunk. He is also made in the image of his father in the way he can get people to follow him. The shrewdness of the way he disposed of Amnon reappears in the audacity of the way he gets Joab's attention. He was in Joab's debt for manipulating David into letting him come back from exile, but he makes clear to Joab that Joab cannot assume he is therefore Joab's underling. Joab had better take him seriously. So he is able to get back into public life in Jerusalem, and then after a discrete interval build up a power base in the city and "steal the heart of the Israelites"— that is, win over their commitment to him instead of to David. In his doing so, he implies David has lost his groove in another way. Absalom's offer to people is an offer to do the thing David used to do, seeing that decisions were taken in accordance with what was right (2 Samuel 8:15). Absalom could hardly win support by making such an offer if David was still fulfilling that aspect of a king's responsibilities.

Absalom also wins over his father's adviser Ahitophel, whom the story describes as offering the kind of counsel that was as reliable as an oracle from a prophet. (Ironically, Ahitophel's name seems to mean "My Brother is Folly"; presumably this is a bowdlerized form of his real name, which might have been something like Ahipelet, "My Brother is Deliverance," or Ahibaal, "My Brother is the Master"—which would sound like a homage to Baal.) He makes up a story to explain a need to visit Hebron to fulfill a promise he had made when he was in exile if God ever made it possible for him to return (a story that involves taking God's name in vain), and with further audacity gets himself crowned in Hebron as David once had.

Even as David flees, he demonstrates his trust in God. It is as if he can afford not to fight, because God is the basis of his position. When Zadok the priest brings the **covenant chest** to accompany the king, David sends him back: "If I find favor in Yahweh's eyes, he will bring me back and let me see it and its abode. But if he says, 'I do not want you,' here I am; he can do to me as it is good in his eyes" (2 Samuel 15:26). Admittedly, sending Zadok back to Jerusalem will also mean he has a useful ally there. When he hears that Ahitophel is among the conspirators, his reaction is to pray, "Do make Ahitophel's advice seem like nonsense, Yahweh!" When Shimei hurls insults at him and one of his lieutenants wants to cut Shimei's head off, David's reaction is to suggest that God sent Shimei with his insults and that it is God's business to recompense Shimei for his insults, not David's.

The chapter closes with Absalom seeking Ahitophel's advice about what he should do next. Ahitophel advises him to have sex with his father's secondary wives, which will be a way of claiming them and underlining the fact that he has taken over as king. Absalom does this on the palace roof, further fulfilling the declaration God had made about the trouble that would issue from David's killing of Uriah and his taking of Bathsheba. Indeed, David's own behavior and words as he abandons the city suggest an attitude of penitence. Once again, what the women think of this is irrelevant.

2 SAMUEL 17:1–19:40

Wise Advice Treated as Folly

[1]Ahitophel said to Absalom, "I should pick twelve thousand men and set out to pursue David tonight [2]so that I come upon him when he is weary and weak. I'll make him panic and the entire company with him will flee. I'll strike down the king alone [3]and bring back the entire company to you. When everyone has come back [except] the man you are seeking, all the people will be at peace." [4]The words seemed sound in the

eyes of Absalom and all the Israelite elders, [5]but Absalom said, "Will you summon Hushai the Archite so we can also hear what he says?" [6]So Hushai came to Absalom and Absalom said to him, "This is the way Ahitophel spoke. Shall we act in accordance with what he says? If not, you speak." [7]Hushai said to Absalom, "The advice Ahitophel has given is not good this time." [8]Hushai said, "You yourself know your father and his men, that they are warriors. They are as fierce-spirited as a bear in the wild that has lost its cubs. And your father is a man of war: he will not spend the night with the company. [9]Yes, he will now have hidden in one of the pits or in some [other] place. And when some of [Absalom's] men fall early on, someone who hears will hear and say, "Disaster has come on the company following Absalom!" [10]That person, even if he is a strong man whose spirit is like the spirit of a lion, will totally faint, because all Israel knows that your father is a warrior, as are the strong men with him. [11]Therefore I advise that all Israel from Dan to Beersheba (like the sand on the seashore in numbers) gather to join you, with you personally going in the midst. [12]Then we will come against him in some place where he may be found and descend on him as the dew falls on the ground. None will be left of him and of all the men with him, not even one. . . ." [14]Absalom and all the Israelite men with him said, "The advice of Hushai the Archite is better than the advice of Ahitophel." Yahweh had ordered the frustrating of Ahitophel's good advice so that Yahweh might bring trouble on Absalom. . . . [23]When Ahitophel saw that his advice was not acted on, he saddled his donkey, set off, and went home to his city. He gave orders concerning his household, and hanged himself. He died and was buried in his father's tomb.

[Chapters 17, 18, and 19 also relate how Hushai gets information to David about Absalom's plan, which gives David time to cross the Jordan. David's company defeats Absalom's there and against David's orders kills Absalom himself. When David is overcome by grief, Joab rebukes him for not caring about the way his men have given themselves for him. The people as a whole agree to ask David to return to Jerusalem as king.]

In the 1990s there was a political crisis in the state of Israel over King David's good name. The Foreign Minister had been accused of slandering David in a parliamentary debate, and his words prompted three motions of no confidence against the coalition government. Although the ruling party made it through this particular crisis, they were anxious that the affair might have an effect on an upcoming general election since it might unite the whole religious community against the party. The chairman of the coalition called on the Foreign Minister to make a public apology, but he was unwilling to do so, though he had said that he did not intend to denigrate King David by remarks he had made about his relationship with Bathsheba. His actual words were, "Not everything that King David did, on the ground, on the rooftops, is acceptable to a Jew or is something I like."

We have noted that David is consistently a mysterious, enigmatic character. There are many sides to him, and many sides to the Old Testament portrait of him. It is thus possible to be selective in one's assessment of him; indeed, it is almost inevitable. He can come across as a great hero, as a great man of God, as a Machiavellian schemer, as a consummate leader and warrior, or as an incompetent ditherer. In a way, the dilemmas and the choices that people make as they read his story parallel the choices and dilemmas that his subjects and his staff had to make.

Perhaps Absalom epitomizes this. While he may have been governed purely by self-interest and ambition, he was given some excuses for his action by David's dithering over Amnon and Tamar and over his attitude to Absalom himself, and by his (possible) neglect to see that **authority** was exercised in a fair way for people. Ahitophel also epitomizes it. Perhaps he, too, can see no future for David the ditherer and has a sense of affront at David's failure to rule properly.

If this is so, it transpires they have nevertheless made the wrong choice for reasons that they might or might not have been able to take account of. Ahitophel's strategy was dead right; it is imperative to pursue and kill David now before he has a chance to regroup and reprovision. Absalom's strategy in also seeking the advice of Hushai was also dead right; the more advice you have, the more likely you are to make a good decision. Hushai's advice was plausible, too, plausible enough to mislead Absalom. Ahitophel's and Absalom's problem was that God was not on their side. God has made a commitment to David that God could not go back on, even though David was a ditherer and an incompetent father, even though David was a seducer and a murderer. No doubt the success of Hushai's advice could be explained by its plausibility; one does not need to hypothesize that God manipulated Absalom into accepting it (though in other contexts God is prepared to act thus). It sounded like good advice, but it was actually the opposite. Its success also links with that commitment of God's to David. God was not bringing trouble on Absalom because Absalom was a wicked person but because Absalom was seeking to dispose of the man God had put on the throne; or one could say that this was what his wickedness consisted of. Why did Ahitophel commit suicide? Because of a sense of failure to bring about what needed to happen? Because he knew his number was up when David returned? Because he realized he had been opposing God?

The delay duly does give David the chance to cross the Jordan, get supplies from allies there, and organize his troops. He yields to pressure from his troops not to take part in the battle himself but to stay safe in Mahanaim, where in effect he sets up a government in exile. As the troops leave for the battle, his last order is that they are to deal gently with his son. Everybody knows it. David's troops take on the much more numerous Israelite forces in wooded country, which might be more favorable to them than open country; as the story puts it, "the forest devoured more of the company than the sword." With some irony, Absalom's magnificent head of hair gets tangled in the branches of a tree he passes under. His donkey races on, and Absalom takes refuge in the tree, but some of David's men see him and tell their commander, Joab. Notwithstanding David's orders, Joab and some of his men kill Absalom. That brings the battle to an end; Absalom's army flees. Joab sends runners to tell David the good news, but he is distraught when he hears that Absalom is dead: "Absalom, my son, Absalom, my son, my son! If only I myself had died instead of you, Absalom, my son, my son!"

Hard-headed Joab points out that David's preoccupation with his son risks once again surrendering the support of his men as he makes them ashamed of their victory instead of being proud of it. He cares about his enemies (which might seem okay), but he acts with enmity toward the people who care about him (which is at best unwise). He is behaving as if he would be glad if Absalom were alive and his own supporters all dead. A leader cannot allow family considerations thus to dominate his life. So David gets his act together and receives his troops, and the people as a whole remind themselves of the reasons they were once glad to have him as king. David is thus able to encourage them to welcome him back. He resists any temptation or pressure to take redress from people who had rejected him but rewards people who supported him.

2 SAMUEL 19:41–21:22

Leaderly Calculation and Mother Love

[Second Samuel 19:41–20:26 relates further conflicts between the northern clans and Judah over the reinstalling of David and describes a further rebellion against David led by a man called Shebna, which David puts down.]

[1]There was a famine in the days of David for three years, year after year. So David sought an audience with Yahweh, and Yahweh said, "It is in connection with Saul and the blood-stained household, because he killed the Gibeonites." [2]So the king summoned the Gibeonites and spoke to them. (The Gibeonites were not Israelites but rather part of what was left of the Amorites, and the Israelites had sworn an oath to them, but Saul had tried to strike them down in his zeal for the Israelites and Judah.) [3]So David said to the Gibeonites, "What shall I do for you? How shall I make expiation, so you can bless Yahweh's own people?" [4]The Gibeonites said to him, "We have no [rights to] silver or gold with Saul and his household and we have no [rights to] put a man to death in Israel." So he said, "Whatever you are going to say, I will do for you." [5]They said to the king, "The man who finished us off and thought we could be exterminated so we would not keep a place in any Israelite territory: [6]seven of the men from among his sons are to be given to us and we will impale them before Yahweh in Gibeah of Saul, Yahweh's chosen one." The king said, "I myself will give them. . . ." [10]Then Rizpah

daughter of Aiah got some sack and spread it out on a rock for herself from the beginning of the harvest until water poured on them from the heavens. She did not let the birds of the heavens descend on them by day or the beasts of the wild by night.

[Second Samuel 21:11–22 relates how David then gave proper burial to the men's remains, and to those of Saul and Jonathan, after which God responded to prayer for the country. It also tells of several further battles against the Philistines.]

We care about what happens to the bodies of our loved ones. My wife and I long ago agreed that we would be cremated and then have our ashes scattered in the valley where we had spent the first night of our honeymoon. Now that she has died, it will be a place with which I especially associate her and a place I shall visit and where I shall think of her. I'm glad to know when I die that my sons will scatter my ashes there so that I shall join her. Admittedly, during the months after she died I sometimes worried about having her burnt up like that, even though I also knew that cremation only hastens the process of dissolution that also happens when we bury someone. Further, I don't know how to fit together the dissolution of her body and the scattering of her ashes with the fact that in some other sense, as a person she is not in that valley but is asleep until resurrection day, when God will recreate us. Nor do I know how God will bring about that resurrection. I do know that there will need to be some relationship between the bodies we have had and the resurrection bodies we will acquire (otherwise they will not be *our* bodies). What happens to our bodies therefore does matter.

Rizpah's story reflects that fact, even though she doesn't know about resurrection; it is going to be a neat surprise for her and her sons and the other men that David put to death. Once again David's action raises our eyebrows. The Old Testament recognizes that trouble such as a failure of the harvest (like personal disasters or sickness) is often "just one of those things" but that it can be God's chastisement for some wrongdoing. Either way it means you turn to God, but in doing so you do have to ask the question whether some wrongdoing is the explanation for the calamity. In this case, it is when the famine goes on year after year that David realizes the need to ask that question. "Seeking an audience with Yahweh" (literally, "seeking Yahweh's face") suggests going to the meeting tent, as Moses used to do, though doing so would not exclude also asking questions of his staff (including his prophets) about possible explanations for what had happened, and/or utilizing **Urim and Thummim**.

One way or another, it emerges that Israel had failed to keep its commitment to the Gibeonites. As the story notes, the Gibeonites were not Israelites. They had deceived Joshua about their identity and had manipulated Joshua into making a **covenant** with them (see Joshua 9), and Joshua had explicitly recognized that wrath would come on Israel if Israel failed to keep their oath. Evidently Saul had broken this covenant and had tried to eliminate the Gibeonites, and evidently no statute of limitations applies to this wrongdoing. As people in the United States or Britain still have to accept some responsibility for the actions of their forebears in relation to African Americans or people in British colonies, so David's generation has to accept some responsibility for this action of their forebears. So David asks the Gibeonites what he needs to do to put things right with them. The **Torah** includes rules to answer this kind of question in connection with personal wrongdoing. One can imagine, for instance, that a person who destroyed someone else's crops would have to make up for this act; even more solemnly, if a man killed the head of another family, he would have to take some responsibility for that family.

Ironically, whereas Joshua had declared that the Gibeonites were cursed to be servants of the Israelites as a result of their deception, they have now brought a curse on the Israelites; perhaps they had deliberately done so. David thus wants to get them to be willing to bless Israel instead—to pray positive not negative prayers for the Israelites. The Gibeonites' reply is enigmatic. Perhaps they are frankly acknowledging that they have no legal rights in the situation. Perhaps they are just being polite, like the Hittites with whom Abraham has to negotiate in Genesis 23. Either way, they are putting the ball back into David's court. What kind of offer does he want to make? He turns the question back to them. Their response is then chilling.

Yet it might have served David rather well. One might even wonder whether this abbreviated version of the negotiation omits an offer by David along the lines that are eventually agreed on. The death of seven more people from Saul's descendants eliminates seven more potential rivals for the throne. Second Samuel 20 closes off the various attempts to remove David from the throne, and the book's last chapters are a series of appendices to the story. There need be no assumption that they come in chronological order. This story would make sense in the context of the early years of David's reign, when he still needed to consolidate his position against possible rivals. This action helps him do so. Maybe the Gibeonites themselves devised the terms that would satisfy them, and David jumped at the chance to take action that suited him rather well. He then didn't worry too much about asking what the Torah would think of it (answer: not very much, because it doesn't believe in people being punished for other people's wrongdoing, and specifically in children being punished for their parents' wrongdoing).

The Old Testament mentions only one full wife of Saul's, Ahinoam, and one **secondary wife**, Rizpah. A price Rizpah earlier paid for her marriage to Saul was Abner's sexual attention (2 Samuel 3:7). The price she now pays is the death of her sons, along with five of Saul's grandsons. The Old Testament is generally accepting of the fact that after people die, they go to join their ancestors. Being buried in his family tomb even provided a postscript to Ahitophel's suicide, a postscript that took the edge off the tragedy that was his life and death. But if the vultures and the coyotes eat your body, there is hardly enough of you to bury; the price you pay in dying is augmented by the price you pay afterward. Rizpah will not let that happen, and perhaps her action brings David's conscience to life so that he then sees to the proper burial of the remains not only of these seven but also of Saul and Jonathan. This action would also do no harm to his need to associate himself positively with Saul's family rather than encourage anyone to think that he was a betrayer of Saul who ought not to be accepted as Saul's successor. At the same time, it was a proper act of reverence. It was after this act (not the execution) that God responded to prayers that the famine should end. Who knows David's motivation? The ambiguity of the story again functions to remind us to be realistic about the mixed nature of our own motives and in particular about the mixture of motives that affects people in leadership.

2 SAMUEL 22:1–20

The God of the Storm

¹David spoke the words of this song to Yahweh on the day Yahweh rescued him from the hand of all his enemies and from the hand of Saul.

² "Yahweh, my crag, my fortress, my rescuer, ³God who is my
   rock in whom I take refuge!
  My shield, the horn that delivers me; my stronghold, my
   refuge, my deliverer: you deliver me from violence.
⁴ I call on Yahweh, one who is to be praised, and from my
   enemies I find deliverance.
⁵ For death's waves overwhelmed me, torrents of destruction
   engulfed me,
⁶ Sheol's ropes encircled me, death's snares confronted me.
⁷ In my vulnerability I called on Yahweh, to my God I called.
  He listened to my voice from his palace, my cry for help
   being in his ears.
⁸ Then the earth trembled and rocked, the foundations of the
   heavens shook, they trembled because he was furious.
⁹ Smoke went up from his nostrils, consuming fire from his
   mouth; coals blazed from it.
¹⁰ He spread the heavens and came down, with thundercloud
   beneath his feet.
¹¹ He mounted a cherub and flew, he appeared on the wings
   of the wind.
¹² He made darkness around him his screen—a mass of water,
   clouds of mist.
¹³ From the brightness before him, fiery coals blazed.
¹⁴ Yahweh thundered from the heavens, the Most High gave
   out his voice.
¹⁵ He shot arrows and spread them about, [shot] lightning
   and rumbled.

¹⁶ The channels of the sea became visible, the foundations of
   the world came into sight.
¹⁷ He sent from on high and took me, drew me out of
   mighty waters.
¹⁸ He rescued me from my enemy, the strong one, from my
   foes because they were too mighty for me.
¹⁹ They confronted me on the day of my calamity, but Yahweh
   became my support.
²⁰ He brought me out into a roomy place; he rescued me
   because he delighted in me."

The song says, "It never rains in Southern California," but it
goes on to say that they never warn you that it does sometimes
pour. I myself never needed galoshes in Britain, where we usually have only gentle rain, though we have it rather often. In
Los Angeles I was once caught for three minutes in a down-
pour, and I was as wet as if I had lain in the bath in my clothes.
Yet nothing here has compared with a storm we once drove
through in southern France, when at midday the sky became
as dark as midnight except at the moments from time to time
when vast sheets of lightning briefly illumined the whole sky,
rain fell as if we were in a waterfall, and the earth shook.

This "song" of David's presupposes that the songwriter
knew about that kind of storm. The fact that David is said to
have "spoken" the song need not imply that he wrote it; like
presidents, kings presumably did not write their own speeches
or songs. Yet evidently David and/or the author of 2 Samuel
thought it was a song that fit his lips.

One can see this is so in the way the song begins. It piles
up images to glorify God as the great protector. That was the
way God had proven to be God for David in those years when
he was on the run from Saul. God was a rock he could climb
on, a shield he could protect himself behind, a refuge he could
hide in. God was a horn—that is, God acted with the strength
and aggressiveness of a bull with its horns. God could therefore
fend off anyone who made violent attacks on David, as Saul did
a number of times. On those occasions it was as if death were
about to overwhelm him, as if **Sheol** were about to take him
before his time. Those were the circumstances in which David

resisted any temptation to act with violence toward his king. He relied on God to protect him, and God did so. In those circumstances, instead of acting, he cried out to his King.

When David became king in Jerusalem, he lived in a palace at the top of the city. In connection with the Bathsheba story, we noted that this enabled him as king to keep an eye on events in the city below. That provides Israel with a way of envisaging God's relationship with the world. God lives in a palace in the heavens from which it is possible to look down and keep an eye on things in the world (no doubt some Israelites realized this was a metaphor and others were rather literalistic about it). Further, a citizen can show up at the palace and urge the king to check things out and intervene when another citizen is doing wrong; any human being can also appeal to the heavenly King to do so.

What is it like when the heavenly King acts? The realities of earth, the heavens, and the space in between again provide a way of picturing what happens. The kind of storm I once experienced in the Alps gives the songwriter a way of picturing God's coming from the heavens and having an effect on the earth. God rides in a chariot that is carried by **cherubs** and propelled by the wind. The thunderclouds are the screen that protects humanity from seeing God and thus being blinded. The thunder is Yahweh's roar. The flashes of lightning are the fiery arrows God shoots. Even the seas are parted in such a way as to expose the water reservoirs beneath.

The significance of this result appears in some of the lines that precede and follow in the song. David has often been in danger of death, in a situation where death was staring him in the face. It was as if Death or Sheol had ropes with which it was snaring him in the way a hunter snares a wild animal, or as if death or Sheol were a flood of waters that was about to sweep him away, or as if he were already dead and buried beneath the earth. In such a situation, God comes down to rescue us from this enemy hunter, or divides the sea to reach down into those floods, or reaches down into the realm beneath the earthly world to where death has almost taken us. The fact that this song appears as Psalm 18 in the book of Psalms in a slightly different version, with a link to this story, indicates that it's for people like us to use in our prayer and praise; it isn't just for David.

The implication of the song's language is not that God's action actually involves a tumultuous thunderstorm—at least, when the Old Testament pictures God acting in the world, it is not in the habit of referring to a thunderstorm. The song is a piece of poetry; the thunderstorm provides a way of describing the dramatic results of God's acting in the world. The overlap between the metaphorical and the literal appears in verse 18, where it speaks first of a strong enemy (which sounds like Death personified) but then speaks of mighty foes (plural). The attacks of *the* enemy come in the form of the attacks of these foes; the attacks of these foes are the means whereby Death seeks to take one before one's time. The arrival of God and God's acting against Death to bring **deliverance** takes the form of an escape from enemies that the person under attack experiences, in a way that seems miraculous. Before that happens, the individual was under constraint (the Hebrew word for *vulnerability* suggests being confined into a narrow place); when it happens, he or she is brought into a place of freedom, into "a roomy place."

2 SAMUEL 22:21–51

I Have Kept Yahweh's Ways?

21 "He repaid me in accordance with my faithfulness; in accordance with the purity of my hands he recompensed me.
22 For I have kept Yahweh's ways and not been faithless to my God.
23 For all his rules are before me; his laws—I have not departed from them.
24 I was a person of integrity with him, and I have kept myself from waywardness that I might have done.
25 So Yahweh has recompensed me in accordance with my faithfulness, in accordance with my purity before his eyes.
26 With the committed person you show yourself committed, with the warrior of integrity you show integrity.

27 With the pure you show purity, but with the crooked you
   show yourself refractory.

28 A lowly people you deliver, but you avert your eyes from
   important people.

29 Because you, Yahweh, are my lamp; it is Yahweh who
   illumines my darkness.

30 Because with you I can rush a barricade, with my God I
   can scale a wall.

31 God: his way has integrity, Yahweh's word is proven; he is
   a shield to all who take refuge in him.

32 Because who is God apart from Yahweh, who is a crag apart
   from our God?

33 God is my stronghold, [my] strength; he released one who
   was upright in his way.

34 He is one who makes my legs like a deer, enables me to
   stand on the heights.

35 He is one who trains my hands for battle; my arms can
   bend a bronze bow.

36 You have given me your shield that delivered; your
   response made me great.

37 You gave room to my steps beneath me; my ankles did
   not give way.

38 I pursued my enemies and annihilated them; I did not turn
   back until I had finished them off.

39 I consumed them, shattered them, they could not rise; they
   fell beneath my feet.

40 You girded me with strength for battle; you put down my
   adversaries beneath me.

41 My enemies you made turn tail for me, my opponents—
   and I wiped them out.

42 They looked, but there was no deliverer, [looked] to
   Yahweh, but he did not answer.

43 I pounded them like the dust of the earth; like the dirt in
   the streets I crushed them, beat them out.

44 You rescued me from the conflicts of my people; you kept
   me as head of the nations, a people I did not
   acknowledge serve me.

45 Foreigners cowered before me; on hearing with their ear,
   they heeded me.

46 Foreigners wilted; they came trembling out of
   their strongholds.

^{47} Yahweh lives! May my crag be praised! God, the crag, my deliverance, is to be exalted,
^{48} God who gives me redress, subjects peoples under me,
^{49} Who rescues me from my enemies, exalts me above my adversaries, saves me from violent men.
^{50} Therefore I will confess you, Yahweh, among the nations, and make music to your name.
^{51} A tower bringing deliverance to his king, showing commitment to his anointed, to David and his seed forever."

Last night I was talking to one of our students who served in the U.S. forces in Iraq as an antiterrorism operative. Like many soldiers, he came home with trauma that he has subsequently had to try to talk through over a period of years. There is a grittiness about him that is a strength, yet it also manifests itself as a clumsiness in relationships and some incoherence in the way he tries to articulate things. Although I can't compare him with the way he was before he went on these missions, I can't help but assume that he has come back wounded in spirit though not in body. I am particularly struck by the fact that he is not the only such student who has turned from being a soldier to being a pacifist. Sometimes it seems that the Christian world is divided into people who are gung ho about war and people who are pacifists; perhaps the nature of modern warfare has made it harder to maintain a position in between these two extremes.

Our awareness of the trauma that war brings to the military makes one wonder how David was affected by his life of warfare. Reading between the lines of his story as a whole makes one reflect on whether this experience relates in some way to the enigma of who he is. Yet the strange thing about this psalm is that it implies no reflection on that question. That people can move from being committed fighters to being pacifists reflects the ambiguity (at best) about being involved in war. The song recognizes no such ambiguity.

Its previous section (vv. 1–20) closed with a declaration that God gave David victory because God "delighted" in him. Why did God delight in David? You can't explain why God chooses someone, and you may not be able to explain why God delights in someone. Delight can't always be explained. In this context, however, the song believes it is quite possible to see the basis for God's delight. It lies in the person's **faithfulness, commitment**, integrity, purity of hands, walking in God's ways, living by God's rules, and avoiding faithlessness and waywardness.

Such claims are inclined to worry Christian readers as a matter of principle because they sound like self-righteousness. Yet both Testaments imply the conviction that there is something strange if people who are supposed to be committed to God cannot make claims of this kind (in the New Testament, see, for instance, 2 Timothy 3:10–4:9). Such claims do not imply sinlessness; they do imply that one's life is oriented in one direction and not another.

So in principle a song that makes such claims isn't odd. What is odd is seeing such claims on David's lips. There are several considerations that have surfaced earlier in David's story that might lie behind them. We have noted that the Old Testament's recurrent declarations about David's faithfulness do make sense if we relate them to his commitment to Yahweh rather than to other gods and to forms of worship that Yahweh approves rather than to forms Yahweh forbids, such as worship by means of images or human sacrifice (though chapter 21 may have compromised that claim). On David's lips, this song constitutes a great recognition by a fabulously successful warrior and king of his dependence on God and of God's being the one who lies behind his success, even though he himself is the one who does the rushing and the scaling and the pursuing and the shattering.

Another consideration is suggested by ambiguity about the preamble to the song, which speaks of his **deliverance** from Saul. It would be surprising for David at the end of his life to be still rejoicing in that particular deliverance rather than in other ones that have followed. Yet we have noted that the last chapters of 2 Samuel are a series of footnotes to the main story, and that chapter 21 related to events in the time of Saul. So maybe this song has in mind the earlier part of David's story. The beginning of his reign, when his deliverance from Saul was quite recent, would have been a more plausible time for David to have claimed to have been faithful to God on a broader front than he could claim at the end of his reign. Placing the song here thus reminds us once more of the ambiguity of David's life. He was once a person of integrity, but he did not remain such.

There is a related, third consideration. Was David himself ever capable of reflecting on his life? Did he ever think about its ambiguity? Did he ever think about the tension between his loyalty to God and trust in God and his failure as a husband and father and the way this affected other people and even affected his exercise of power? We can't answer that question with regard to David; it is between him and God. We have to answer it in regard to ourselves.

David's enemies, he says, looked for a deliverer and did not find one. They looked to God, but God did not answer. David himself knows that experience; God did not answer him when he prayed for his sick baby. Perhaps there is a way of looking to God to which God responds and a way of looking that God ignores. Yet we have to be wary of thinking that we have our minds round the basis on which God sometimes answers and sometimes does not. When Job looked to God, there was nothing in Job that made God decline to respond (unless, paradoxically, it was the fact that he was such a committed person and God was allowing that commitment to be tested). Once again, God's choice of someone and the grace God shows to someone and God's nonresponsiveness to someone else may reflect something about God's bigger purpose and not something about the individuals or communities involved.

2 SAMUEL 23:1–38

The Last Words of David

¹These are David's last words.

"An utterance of David son of Jesse, an utterance of the
 man exalted by the Most High,
The anointed of the God of Jacob, the delight of
 Israel's compositions.

² Yahweh's spirit spoke through me, his message was on
  my tongue.
³ The God of Israel said, the Crag of Israel spoke to me,
  'When the one who rules over people is faithful, when he
    rules in reverence for Yahweh,
⁴ He is like the morning light when the sun rises, a morning
    with no clouds;
  Because of brightness, because of rain, there is growth
    from the earth.'
⁵ Is my household not stable with God, because he made a
    lasting covenant for me, laid out in every respect
    and secured?
  Will he not bring to accomplishment all my deliverance
    and all my desire?
⁶ But the evil are like thistles, thrown away, all of them,
    because people do not take them in the hand.
⁷ The person who touches them equips himself with iron or
    the wood of a spear, and they are totally burnt up where
    they lie."

*[The chapter goes on to give a list of David's warriors and some
of their achievements.]*

Even when one makes allowance for the way it can pour, living
in Southern California of course spoils you. My son and his
family from England have just stayed with us for a week, and
they laughed when I apologized that it wasn't so warm. Indeed,
this April it has rained several times. Last night a friend commented, "I know we are supposed to be glad when it rains, but
I want to say, 'Enough already!'" At the same time, the day after
a rain the air is always clear, with the smog all washed away and
the mountains looking pure, and in the spring we marvel at
the green of the mountains and the wildflowers. You can't have
it both ways. (Well, you could have it both ways. God could
make it rain only at night. Indeed, I was just reading that in
Costa Rica the sun shines all morning, then it rains after lunch,
then the sun comes out again later in the afternoon. But the
fact that this is not so everywhere shows—as God points out
in Job 38–39—that the world is not actually organized just for
our benefit.)

David's "last words" recognize the importance of both sun and rain. We don't know in what sense they are his last words; what they do offer is another look at his significance. The poem in chapter 22 was like a psalm. This poem is more distinctive. It is called an *utterance*, which usually denotes a message from God and thus suggests a kind of prophecy, though not one about the future. The point is confirmed by David's describing it as a message that was on his tongue because God's spirit was speaking through him. In case we haven't got the point, David adds that it is something that God said, that God spoke. It is thereby marked as something David and/or God thinks is really important.

Initially the poem is an objective, general statement. It's not about anyone in particular; it simply declares how leadership is supposed to work, with a ruler being **faithful** and ruling in reverence for God. In the Old Testament those are two key ideas. Once more there's some ambiguity or potential irony in the use of the word *faithful*. David could claim to have been faithful to God in that he had not served other gods or encouraged forms of worship that God does not welcome; in this sense faithfulness and reverence for God are not so different from each other. Translations often have "fear of God" instead of "reverence for God," but that's misleading. While there are contexts in which it's appropriate to be afraid of God (for instance, when you have done something seriously wrong or when God has been manifest in awesome power), more often the Hebrew words denote a positive attitude of worship and obedience.

In Hebrew poetry, it's common for the two halves of a line to say similar things in different words. This, too, means that following a reference to faithfulness by a reference to reverence for God could imply that faithfulness simply denotes the way David related to God. Yet the Old Testament's allusions to faithfulness commonly concern relationships with human beings as well as with God, and this concern lost priority in David's personal life and in his leadership as years went by. Perhaps, then, the comment about faithfulness has to operate with a narrowed-down understanding of what faithfulness means (David could claim to have lived this way in relation to God but not in relation to other people). Or perhaps the comment can apply only to the early years of his reign. Or perhaps, more solemnly, the poem's generic definition of leadership condemns David, apparently without his recognizing it. He knows that leadership involves faithfulness; he has not faced the fact that he has failed in this connection. Further, if we should assume that faithfulness applies to human relationships as well as relationships with God, failure regarding faithfulness raises the question whether he can really claim to have lived in reverence for God, because reverence for God also implies doing what God says in our relationships with other people, and David has not lived that way.

Supposing a leader does fulfill God's vision by ruling in faithfulness and in reverence for God. That's when the sun and rain image comes in. In nature, growth depends on both sun and rain. The Hebrew references to brightness and rain are actually a bit obscure, but there is no doubt that David refers to both, and there's no doubt that growth in nature requires both rain and sun. In Southern California (as in Israel) we can take sun for granted, and we would have to worry about rain if we didn't siphon it off from farther north. In Britain we can take rain for granted, and we have to worry about sun. A decent harvest requires both. When you have both, then things flourish. In a parallel way (David knows), when you have leadership that makes a priority out of faithfulness and reverence for God, the society flourishes.

I just answered an e-mail from a student about a paper she has to write. She wants to consider the kingship of Saul, David, and Solomon in light of the way Ezekiel 34 talks about good and bad "shepherds"—that is, kings; and she wants then to think about this topic in light of the way we think about leadership in the church, taking the New Testament into account. I thought this was a great idea, but I said I hoped that in reflecting on the implications of the Old Testament for today, she wouldn't confine herself to thinking about leadership in the church. Saul, David, and Solomon were kings, and the image of shepherds in the Old Testament is an image for kings. So the significance of her study relates to our understanding of and our vision for politics and government as well as for leadership in the church. That's true of David's vision here, whether or not he fulfilled it.

176

David continues to be ambiguous when he goes on to speak of the stability of his household. Is he claiming that he and his household have been stable in the way they relate to God? That is not the picture the story has been giving us. Or does he mean that they are stable in the sense that God will keep them secure on the throne? This could not be taken for granted, as the preceding chapters have shown. So it is significant that David links his household's stability with the **covenant** God made with him. Given that David and his household are not very stable in their faithfulness and reverence for God, it is just as well that this covenant is more like God's covenant with Noah or Abraham than the covenant at Sinai or the covenant in Deuteronomy. That is, it's a commitment that God just decides to make; it's not a response God makes because David deserves it, as the covenants with the world after the flood and the covenant with Abraham were not based on anyone's deserving them. God's promises to David in 2 Samuel 7 made that explicit. God exalted David; God anointed David. David became the person Israel loved to tell stories about and sing songs about. God took the risk of giving up the option to be free to withdraw commitment to David. God's covenant commitment to David is one that his successors and his people as a whole will always be able to appeal to. Yes, his household will be stable. God will keep them on the throne.

The ambiguity and irony continues into the last two lines of the poem. Sun and rain make good things grow; they also make thistles grow. These are not only useless but harmful. The first time we went to Israel, I will never forget the way my young son and I got lots of little splinters in our hands from prickly pear cacti, which we had never seen before. So you don't touch them, David notes. You just use something to gather them and burn them (the prickly parts, at least). That's what happens to people who manifest godless evil rather than faithfulness and reverence for God. The fact that God's covenant with David emerges from God's will rather than from David's attitudes and actions doesn't mean David's attitudes and actions have no significance. God's covenantal commitment does require a response. You can't trust in God's graciousness in a way that suggests your response doesn't matter.

2 SAMUEL 24:1–16a

I Would Rather Fall into God's Hands than into Human Hands

[1]Yahweh's anger flared up against Israel again, and he incited David against them, saying, "Go and count Israel and Judah." [2]So the king said to Joab, the army commander with him, "Go around all the Israelite clans from Dan to Beersheba and appraise the company, so I may know the company's numbers." [3]Joab said to the king, "May Yahweh your God indeed add to your company a hundred times over compared with what they are now, while the eyes of my lord the king watch, but why does my lord the king desire this?" [4]But the king's word was firm toward Joab and over the army officers. So Joab and the army officers left the king's presence to appraise the company, Israel. [5]They crossed the Jordan and camped in Aroer, to the right of the city, which is in the middle of the Gad wash, and [went on] to Jazer. [6]They came to Gilead and to the country of Tahtim-hodshi and came to Dan-jaan and around to Sidon. [7]They came to the fortress of Tyre and all the cities of the Hivites and the Canaanites and went on to the Negev of Judah (Beersheba). [8]They went about the whole country and at the end of nine months and twenty days came to Jerusalem. [9]Joab gave the king the numbers from the company's appraisal: Israel came to 800,000 soldiers drawing the sword, and the men of Judah came to 500,000.

[10]David's conscience attacked him after he had counted the company. David said to Yahweh, "I have acted very wrongly in what I have done. But now, Yahweh, will you remove your servant's waywardness, because I have been very stupid." [11]When David got up in the morning, Yahweh's word came to the prophet Gad, David's seer: [12]"Go and speak to David, 'Yahweh has said this: I am holding out three things over you. Choose one of them for yourself, and I will do it to you.'" [13]So Gad came to David and told him. He said to him, "Is a seven-year famine to come to you in the country, or are you to have a three-month flight before your foes as they pursue you, or is there to be a three-day epidemic in your country? Now recognize and see what reply I shall give to the one who sent me." [14]David said to Gad, "I am very vulnerable. Do let us fall into the hands of Yahweh, because his compassion is great. I will not fall into human hands." [15]So Yahweh sent an epidemic on Israel from morning

until the set time, and there died of the company, from Dan to Beersheba, seventy thousand men. [16a]The aide stretched out his hand over Jerusalem to destroy it, but Yahweh relented of the calamity and said to the aide who was destroying the company, "That's plenty! Now lower your hand!"

By a nice coincidence, it's census month in the United States. Many an advertisement is urging us to make sure we fill in forms; even the announcements in church repeat the exhortation, and the government hires hundreds of people to go around to the homes of the one-third of the population who don't return their forms. "We can't move forward until you give your answers back," says the census motto. The census will decide how many seats a state has in the House of Representatives. It will provide a basis for deciding on expenditure on services and infrastructure. People who oppose the census do so on the basis of its being an invasion of privacy and a suspicious poking of the government into our lives.

David's census and God's disapproval of it have a different background. In itself, there was nothing wrong with a census. God commissioned one after the Israelites left Egypt, and another when they were about to enter the promised land (see Numbers 1 and 26). In part, this related to needs similar to ones underlying a modern census. The land was to be distributed in an appropriate way among the Israelite clans, and their respective numbers were significant in this connection; that was the reason for omitting the Levites from the census, as they were not to receive an allocation of land. David's census has a different concern. When he bids Joab undertake the census, some translations have him counting the people as a whole. But there have been many stories in 1 and 2 Samuel where the Hebrew word for "people" has denoted the army—I have used the word *company* because that is also both an everyday word and a military term. Here the census is undertaken by the military, and the account of its results refers to the number of men drawing the sword in **Ephraim** and **Judah**. David is indeed checking on the size of his military.

Therein lies at least part of the problem. The implication is that the size of the military is of key importance to the survival and flourishing of the nation. You could say that David is only being a responsible leader in discovering what forces are available to him, but stories such as Gideon's in Judges 7 reminded Israel that when God is involved, the size of the army isn't the crucial factor—or even a significant factor—in the working out of God's purpose. David has forgotten a consideration of key importance to a leader of the people of God.

The carrying out of David's decision reveals another aspect of the problem. The army officers go around the whole country, with the account describing the boundaries of the area they take into consideration. It starts with Israelite territory across the Jordan, which is fair enough, and then works north and west, but before working its way south to the Negev it finds itself in Phoenicia, in the area of modern Lebanon, an area occupied by Hivites and **Canaanites**. Politically they are part of the little empire that David controls, but isn't there something questionable about their counting as in some sense part of Israel and part of Israel's military forces? Paradoxically, even Joab and the other army officers recognize that David's census is a questionable idea, though they do not say why they are uneasy. Perhaps they share the unease about counting that is felt in other traditional societies. Counting is unlucky, and people or animals that are counted may die, partly because it can be an expression of or an encouragement to pride.

The story begins by giving us another astonishing explanation of why David undertook the census. Whereas in due course it seems that God is angry with David for taking the census, the story begins by telling us that God was angry with David before the census. The very idea of the census came from God as an expression of God's anger. Why God was angry the story doesn't tell us; maybe it was irrelevant to the story, since it's what follows that counts. Maybe the narrator simply didn't know why God was angry. Maybe the only possible explanation for David's undertaking this crazy action was that God was angry with him. Speaking of God's inciting David to do it doesn't imply God somehow forced him. The language parallels talk of God's hardening people's hearts or stiffening their resolve. The experience parallels occasions when someone suggests an idea to us and we accept it freely but with hindsight recognize it was a bad idea. The story knows that there is some sense in which God is behind all that happens, especially all that involves a servant of God like David, whose actions are so important to the people.

The aftermath of David's action reminds us of the story of David, Bathsheba, and Uriah. One solemn side to this fact is the way it confirms our impression that nothing much goes right for David after that series of events. Once again David does the wrong thing. Once again he realizes it too late. Once again God sends one of David's own prophets to him, though this time not to bring David to a realization of his wrongdoing (it seems that David somehow gets there on his own) but in connection with determining what happens next. Once again David says, "I have acted wrongly," though here he underlines the admission more than he does in the story of Bathsheba and Uriah. Once again the story raises the question of "removing" David's wrongdoing. And once again his action has terrible implications for other people who pay the price for his wrongdoing, as people often do when we do wrong (especially when leaders do wrong).

David's perceptiveness in his response to people astonishes us; the man is a bewildering combination of stupidity and insight. "It's better to fall into Yahweh's hands than into human hands," he says, "because we know Yahweh is compassionate." The judgment that follows proves his point. Admittedly, the people pay a terrible price. The account recalls the story of the exodus, where God's destroyer wreaks judgment on the people of Egypt. Everything has thus been turned upside down here if the destroying angel is wreaking judgment on Israel itself. As God can have Israel destroyed in the way God had the Canaanites destroyed, so God can treat Israel as God treated Egypt. Israel cannot trust in its position of privilege. Yet at the last moment God cannot bring himself to let Jerusalem itself be destroyed. For people reading this story later, it is a poignant statement. Much later, God will summon up the determination and hard-heartedness to have Jerusalem destroyed. In the meantime, the story encourages people to remember that Yahweh is the compassionate God. Even when you have done wrong, it is always worth urging God to relent of imposing the punishment we deserve. We can perhaps see the truth of this in our lives as nations, which continue despite what we deserve.

2 SAMUEL 24:16b–25

I Will Not Offer Worship That Costs Me Nothing

[16b]So Yahweh's aide was by the threshing floor of Araunah the Jebusite. [17]David said to Yahweh when he saw the aide striking the company down—he said, "Now. I am the one who acted wrongly. I am the one who went astray. These sheep, what did they do? Your hand should be against me and against my father's household." [18]Gad came to David that day and said to him, "Go up, erect an altar for Yahweh at the threshing floor of Araunah the Jebusite." [19]So David went up in accordance with Gad's word, as Yahweh commanded. [20]Araunah looked down and saw the king and his servants coming across to him. Araunah went out and bowed low to the king, his face to the ground. [21]Araunah said, "Why has my lord the king come to his servant?" David said, "To acquire the threshing floor from you, to build an altar for Yahweh, and so that the epidemic may hold back from the people." [22]Araunah said to David, "My lord may take it and offer up what is good in his eyes. See the oxen for a burnt offering and the threshing sledges and the oxen's equipment for wood. [23]All this Araunah gives to the king, your majesty." Araunah said to the king, "May Yahweh your God accept you." [24]The king said to Araunah, "No, because I will definitely acquire them from you for a price. I will not offer up to Yahweh my God burnt offerings that cost me nothing." So David acquired the threshing floor and the oxen for fifty silver shekels. [25]David built an altar there for Yahweh and offered up burnt offerings and fellowship sacrifices, and Yahweh responded to intercessions for the country. The epidemic held back from Israel.

As we left a concert last night, one of my friends commented that he always emerges from live music with renewed energy. I am the same. It reminded me of how I felt after a terrific, animated, dynamic worship service the other week. We were all singing enthusiastically. We were all clapping rhythmically. (Actually I wasn't, because my hands are rhythmically challenged, but I was stamping enthusiastically; my feet are rhythmic.) The worship band (especially the lead guitarist) was in fine form. The three lead singers were encouraging us with fervency. I left the service with renewed energy as I left the concert with renewed energy. So for whose benefit was I worshiping?

Second Samuel has kept giving us surprises, and it raises our eyebrows to the very end as David's sinful act that issues in terrible judgment leads into David's building the **altar** around which Solomon will build the temple. Perhaps part of the reason that the story in 2 Samuel 24 is a bit puzzling (for instance, in not telling us what had made God angry) relates to the fact that its real concern is with the way this event led to the building of this altar, which was so important to every later generation of Israelites. They might well find it puzzling and a little worrying that the great King David didn't build the temple, and the story shows some concern with making clear that David lies behind its building. The story in 2 Samuel 7 makes that clear in one way; this story does so in another way. (First Chronicles in turn retells the story of David with more emphasis on David's role in preparing for the building of the temple and also offers an alternative take on the background to David's undertaking the census. First Chronicles 21 attributes this to "an adversary" rather than directly to God. English translations have "Satan" rather than "an adversary," which is a bit misleading; Chronicles has in mind one of God's underlings in heaven, through whom God sometimes works. But it does offer a take on the puzzling issues raised by the beginning of this story, which apparently troubled Israelites as it troubles us.)

Farmers locate the family's or community's threshing floor high up where the wind can catch the grain as the farmer throws it up after crushing it. The chaff is lighter, and the wind blows it away, but the grain itself is heavier and falls back to the ground. The actual city of Jerusalem in David's day is in a secure position at the end of a little ridge, while Araunah's threshing floor is higher up the ridge above the city, and the supernatural destroyer is standing there. David had conquered the city from the Jebusites but evidently had not cleansed it of its previous occupants. Araunah the Jebusite, at least, had come to acknowledge Yahweh as had people such as Uriah the Hittite.

The story's importance in connection with the history of the building of the temple may also explain the jumpiness of the way it is told. It looks as if more than one version is combined in 2 Samuel 24, and it's hard to be clear about the sequence of events. At first we get the impression that the altar was built on Araunah's land to commemorate the fact that this was where the supernatural **aide** was when the epidemic stopped, but the way the story unfolds suggests rather that building the altar and offering the sacrifices while the aide stood there was what led to the cessation of the epidemic. So the account of God's limiting the effects of the epidemic (v. 16a) summarizes the results of the story that then unfolds (vv. 16b–25).

With the typical boldness of his relationship with God, David challenges God about the epidemic, like Moses challenging God about the punishment God brings to the people on Sinai after Aaron makes the gold calf. Like us, David is offended at the way the people have to suffer for his wrongdoing. He too does not recognize how bad leadership can bring terrible trouble to a people, as good leadership can bring them great blessing. Like Moses, he seeks to identify with his people and doesn't wish that he himself (and his successors) should be excused from punishment, though unlike Moses he has to accept that he is to blame for what has happened. Like Moses he shows that boldness in prayer can produce great results even when you are not in the right.

He has already spoken of God's compassion, and it is this compassion that limits the toll the epidemic takes. God does not wish to take up David's offer by turning to punish David and his successors. Rather David's prophet Gad advises him on how to elicit God's compassion. He is to build an altar where the aide stands as he is apparently in the midst of bringing about the three-day epidemic of which Gad had spoken. Whenever a divine aide appears in the Old Testament, he does so representing God and virtually mediating God's own presence. Building the altar in God's honor thus matches the way other Old Testament figures such as Gideon build an altar when a divine aide appears to them. Building an altar is also something people do when there is a crisis and they need to call on God, as Saul did in 1 Samuel 14. While it is possible simply to pray in those circumstances, building an altar and making offerings enhances the prayer. It indeed means that your worship costs something. It's not just words. Thus burnt offerings and prayer often accompany one another.

Offerings always cost you. That is especially clear with the offerings that David makes, because they involve burning up a whole animal so that it goes up in smoke to God in its entirety. David also offers fellowship sacrifices, which God and offerers share—that is, some goes up in smoke and some the offerers eat in a fellowship meal with God. So even these offerings cost you. On this occasion David also has to pay good money for the land on which to build the altar. In his negotiation with David, Araunah may mean what he says when he speaks of simply giving up the land for this purpose, or he may be being polite—in other words, he may be expecting David to make him an offer (the conversation recalls Abraham's negotiation with the Hittites over somewhere to bury Sarah, reported in Genesis 23). Either way, it gives David the opportunity to declare that he does not want to undertake this action on the cheap.

With God's responding to David's prayer and the cessation of the epidemic, 2 Samuel ends. It is not the end of a story. The last scenes in David's life appear at the beginning of 1 Kings. As usual, these narrative books stop rather than finish. We will have to read on.

GLOSSARY

aide

A supernatural agent through whom God appears and works in the world. Standard English translations call them "angels," but this rather suggests ethereal figures with wings, wearing diaphanous white dresses. Aides are humanlike figures; hence it is possible to give them hospitality without realizing that this is who they are (Hebrews 13). They have no wings; hence their need of a stairway or ramp between heaven and earth (Genesis 28). They appear in order to act or speak on God's behalf and represent God so fully that they can speak as if they are God (Judges 6). They thus bring the reality of God's presence, action, and voice without bringing such a real presence that it would electrocute mere mortals or shatter their hearing. That can be a reassurance when Israel is rebellious and God's presence might indeed be a threat (Exodus 32–33), but they can themselves be means of implementing God's punishment as well as God's blessing (Exodus 12; 2 Samuel 24).

altar

A structure for offering a sacrifice (the word comes from the word for sacrifice), made of earth or stone. An altar might be relatively small, like a table, and the person making the offering would stand in front of it. Or it might be higher and larger, like a platform, and the person making the offering would climb onto it.

Apocrypha

The contents of the main Christian Old Testament are the same as those of the Jewish Scriptures, though there they come in a different order, as the Torah, the Prophets, and the Writings. Their precise bounds as Scripture came to be accepted some time in the years before or after Christ; we don't know exactly when or how. For centuries, most Christian churches used a broader collection of Jewish writings, including books such as Maccabees and Ecclesiasticus, which for

Jews were not part of the Bible. These other books came to be called the "Apocrypha," the books that were "hidden away"—which came to imply "spurious." They are now often known as the "deuterocanonical writings," which is more cumbersome but less pejorative; it simply indicates that these books have less authority than the Torah, the Prophets, and the Writings. The precise list of them varies between different churches.

Assyria, Assyrians

The first great Middle Eastern superpower, the Assyrians spread their empire westward into Syria-Palestine in the eighth century, the time of Amos and Isaiah, and first made **Ephraim** part of their empire. When Ephraim kept trying to assert independence, they invaded in 722, destroyed Ephraim's capital at Samaria, transported many of its people, and settled people from other parts of their empire in their place. They also invaded **Judah** and devastated much of the country but did not take Jerusalem. Prophets such as Amos and Isaiah describe how God was thus using Assyria as a means of disciplining Israel.

authority

People such as Eli, Samuel, Samuel's sons, and the kings "exercise authority" over Israel and for Israel. The Hebrew word for someone who exercises such authority, *shopet*, is traditionally translated *judge*, but such leadership is wider than this. In the book called Judges, these leaders are people who have no official position like the later kings but who arise and exercise initiative in a way that brings the people **deliverance** from the trouble they get into. It is a king's job to exercise authority in accordance with **faithfulness** to God and people.

Babylon, Babylonians

A minor power in the context of Israel's early history, in Jeremiah's time they succeeded Assyria as superpower and remained that for nearly a century until conquered by **Persia**. Prophets such as Jeremiah describe how God was using them as a means of disciplining **Judah**. They took Jerusalem and transported many of its people in 587. Their creation stories, law codes, and more philosophical writings help us understand aspects of the Old Testament's equivalent writings, while their astrological religion forms background to aspects of polemic in the Prophets.

Canaan, Canaanites

As the biblical terms for the country of Israel as a whole and for its indigenous peoples, Canaanites is not so much the name for a particular ethnic group as a shorthand term for all the peoples native to the country.

cherubs

These are not baby angelic figures (as that word may suggest in modern usage) but awesome winged creatures that transport Yahweh, who sits on a throne above them. There were statues of them in the temple standing guard over the **covenant chest**; they thus pointed to the presence of Yahweh there, enthroned invisibly above them.

chest

The "covenant chest" is a box a bit more than a yard long and half a yard wide and high. The King James Bible refers to it as an "ark," but the word simply means a box, though it is only occasionally used to refer to chests used for other purposes. It is the **covenant** chest because it contains the stone tablets inscribed with the Ten Commandments, key expectations God laid down in connection with establishing the Sinai covenant. It is kept in the sanctuary, but because there is a sense in which it symbolizes God's presence (given that Israel has no images to do so), the Israelites sometimes carry it with them as a symbol of God's presence with them. It is sometimes referred to as the "declaration chest," with the same meaning: the tablets declare God's covenant expectations.

commitment

The word corresponds to the Hebrew word *hesed,* which translations render by means of expressions such as steadfast love or lovingkindness or goodness. It is the Old Testament equivalent to the special word for love in the New Testament, the word *agapē.* The Old Testament uses the word *commitment* when it refers to an extraordinary act whereby someone pledges himself or herself to someone else in some act of generosity or allegiance or grace when there is no prior relationship between them and therefore no reason that he or she should do so. This is the nature of Jonathan's commitment to David (1 Samuel 20). It can also refer to a similar extraordinary act that takes place when there is a relationship between people but one party has let the other party down and therefore has no right to expect any faithfulness from the other party. If the party that has been let down continues being faithful, it is showing this kind of commitment. God's promises such commitment to David (2 Samuel 7).

covenant

The Hebrew word *berit* covers covenants, treaties, and contracts, but these are all ways in which people make a formal commitment about something, and I have used the word *covenant* for all three. Where you have a legal system that people can appeal to, contracts assume a system for resolving disputes and administering justice that can be utilized if people do not keep their commitments. In contrast, a covenantal relationship does not presuppose an enforceable legal framework of that kind, but a covenant does involve some formal procedure that confirms the seriousness of the solemn commitment one party makes to another. Thus the Old Testament often speaks of *sealing* a covenant, literally of *cutting* it (the background lies in the kind of formal procedure described in Genesis 15 and Jeremiah 34:18–20, though such an actual procedure would hardly be required every time someone made a covenantal commitment). People make covenants sometimes *to* other people and sometimes *with* other people. One implies something more one-sided; the other, something more mutual.

cry, cry out

In describing the Israelites' response when they are defeated by their enemies, 1 and 2 Samuel use the word that the Old Testament uses to describe Abel's blood crying out to God, the outcry of the people of Sodom under their oppression, and the Israelites' crying out in Egypt. It denotes an urgent cry that presses God for **deliverance**, a cry that God can be relied on to hear even when people deserve to have the experience that is assailing them.

deliver, deliverer, deliverance

In the Old Testament, translations often use the words *save*, *savior*, and *salvation*, but this gives a misleading impression. In Christian usage, these words commonly refer to our personal relationship with God and to the enjoyment of heaven. The Old Testament does speak of our personal relationship with God but does not use these words in that connection. They refer rather to God's practical intervention to get Israel or the individual out of a mess of some kind, such as false accusations by individuals within the community or invasion by enemies.

devote, devotion

Devoting something to God means giving it over to God irrevocably. Translations use words such as "annihilated" or "destroyed," and that is often the implication, but it does not convey the word's distinctive significance. You could devote land, or an animal such as a donkey, and in effect Hannah will devote Samuel; the donkey or the human being then belongs to God and is committed to God's service. In effect the Israelites devoted many Canaanites to God's service in this way; they became people who chopped wood and drew water for the **altar**, its offerings, and the rites of the sanctuary. Devoting people to God by killing them as a kind of sacrifice was a practice known from other peoples, which Israel takes over on its own initiative, but which God eventually validates. Israel knows this is how war works in its world, and it assumes it is to operate the same way, and God goes along with that.

effigies

The Hebrew word for these is *teraphim*. First Samuel 15:33 presupposes a link between the *teraphim* and divination, which involves techniques (like those of astrology) for trying to discover things about the future so that we can make sensible decisions or safeguard against trouble that might come. One form of divination involves consulting the dead. The effigies would be images of family members who had passed (a little like family photographs), whom people would seek to consult on the assumption that they might now know things that their relatives who were still alive could not know. Israel was not supposed to be involved in such procedures because it was expected to rely more directly on God for guidance.

ephod

In some passages the Old Testament implies that an ephod is a kind of vest worn by a priest, but in some passages it at least incorporated something that contained the **Urim and Thummim**.

Ephraim, Ephraimites

After Saul's death, the Israelite clans split into two groups for a while, then did so more permanently after Solomon's death. Politically, the bigger of the two groups, comprising the northern and eastern clans, kept the name **Israel**, with the much smaller southern group being called **Judah**. This is confusing because Israel is still also the name of the people as a whole as the people of God. So the name Israel can be used in both these connections. The northern state can, however, also be referred to by the name of Ephraim, one of its central clans, so I use this term to refer to the northern clans in the time of David and in that later context, to try to reduce the confusion.

exile

At the end of the seventh century **Babylon** became the major power in **Judah's** world, but Judah was inclined to resist its authority. As part of a successful campaign to get Judah to submit to it, in 597 and in 587 BC the Babylonians transported many people from Jerusalem to Babylon, particularly people in leadership positions such as members of the royal family and the court, priests, and prophets. These people were compelled to live in Babylonia for the next fifty years or so. Through this period, people back in Judah were also under Babylonian authority, so they were not physically in exile but were living in the exile as a period of time.

faithfulness

In English Bibles the Hebrew words *sedaqah* or *sedeq* are often translated "righteousness," but they denote a particular slant on righteousness. They suggest doing the right thing by the people with whom one is in a relationship, such as the members of one's community or God. Thus they are closer to "faithfulness" or even "salvation" than "righteousness." In later Hebrew *sedaqah* can refer to almsgiving. It suggests something close to generosity or grace.

Greece

In 336 BC Greek forces under Alexander the Great took control of the **Persian** Empire, but after Alexander's death in 333 his empire split up. The largest part, to the north and east of Palestine, was ruled by one of his generals, Seleucus, and his successors. Judah was under its control for much of the next two centuries, though it was at the extreme southwestern border of this empire, and it sometimes came under the control of the Ptolemaic Empire in Egypt, ruled by successors of another of Alexander's officers.

Israel

Originally, Israel was the new name God gave Abraham's grandson, Jacob. His twelve sons were then forefathers of the twelve clans that comprise the people Israel. In the time of Saul, David, and Solomon these twelve clans became more of a political entity; Israel was both the people of God and a nation or state like other nations or states. After Solomon's day, this one state split into two, **Ephraim** and **Judah**. Ephraim was far bigger and often continued to be referred to as Israel. So if one is thinking of the people of God, Judah is part of Israel. If one is thinking politically, Judah is not part of Israel, but once Ephraim has gone out of existence, for practical purposes Judah *is* Israel, as the people of God.

Judah, Judahites

One of the twelve sons of Jacob, then the clan that traces its ancestry to him, then the dominant clan in the southern of the two states after the time of Solomon. Later, as a Persian province or colony, it was known as Yehud.

peace

The word *shalom* can suggest peace after there has been conflict, but it often points to a richer notion, of fullness of life. The KJV sometimes translates it "welfare," and modern translations use words such as "well-being" or "prosperity." It suggests that everything is going well for you.

Philistia, Philistines

The Philistines were people who came from across the Mediterranean to settle in Canaan at the same time as the Israelites were establishing themselves in Canaan, so that the two peoples formed an accidental pincer movement on the country's inhabitants and became each other's rivals for control of the area.

secondary wife

Translations use the word *concubine* to describe people such as Rizpah and some of David's wives, but the Hebrew term does not suggest they were not properly married. Being a secondary wife rather means that a woman has a different status from other wives. It perhaps implies that her sons had fewer or no inheritance rights. It may be that a wealthy

or powerful man could have several wives with full rights and several
secondary wives, or just one of each, or just the former, or even just a
secondary wife.

Sheol

One of the Hebrew names for the place where we go when we die; it is
also referred to as the Pit. In the New Testament it is called Hades. It
is not a place of punishment or suffering but simply a resting place for
everyone, a kind of nonphysical analogue to the tomb as the resting
place for our bodies.

spirit

The Hebrew word for spirit is also the word for breath and for wind,
and the Old Testament sometimes implies a link between these. Spirit
suggests dynamic power; God's spirit suggests God's dynamic power.
The wind in its forcefulness with its capacity to fell mighty trees is an
embodiment of the powerful spirit of God. Breath is essential to life;
where there is no breath, there is no life. And life comes from God. So
human breath and even animal breath is an offshoot of God's breath.
God's spirit came on Saul as it came on people in the book of Judges
to inspire them in undertaking things that look humanly impossible.

text

There is an odd aspect of studying 1 and 2 Samuel; appreciating it
requires an understanding of some general background. The basic
Hebrew text of the Old Testament lying behind English translations
goes back to Jewish scholars called the Masoretes who did their work in
the millennium beginning in New Testament times. Their name comes
from the Hebrew word for "tradition," and they made it their responsibility to preserve the tradition of what the text of the Old Testament
said and how it should be read. Despite all the care and commitment
of their work, it would not be surprising if for one reason or another
they sometimes preserved not the original tradition but a form of the
text that had got slightly changed over time. One indication of this
is that sometimes there are oddities in the text that make one think,
"Can that really be right?" For reasons we don't know, 1 and 2 Samuel
raise that question particularly frequently. For instance, in the Masoretes' text Hannah takes three bulls to sacrifice at Shiloh in 1 Samuel
1:24, which sounds rather a lot, but in the next verse she sacrifices only

one bull. Among the Qumran Scrolls, manuscripts found by the Dead Sea in the middle of the last century, there is a manuscript of these two books that has Hannah taking only one bull, which makes better sense. Another version of the Old Testament text appears in a translation of the Old Testament into Greek, called the Septuagint, which was made at about the same time as the Qumran scrolls were being copied; it too sometimes seems to make better sense. It might be that the Qumran and Greek texts have "corrected" the original version because (like us) they didn't think it made sense. Or it might be that they have the original version. There is example after example in 1 and 2 Samuel of differences of this kind between the Masoretes' Hebrew text and the Qumran and/or Greek texts. Generally I have stuck with the Masoretes' text, but occasionally I have followed the Qumran and/or Greek text.

Torah

The Hebrew word for the first five books of the Bible. They are often referred to as the "Law," but this title gives a misleading impression. Genesis itself is nothing like "law," and even Exodus to Deuteronomy are not "legalistic" books. The word "torah" itself means "teaching," which gives a clearer impression of the nature of the Torah. Often the Torah gives us more than one account of an event (such as God's commission of Moses), as Samuel-Kings and Chronicles give us two versions of the story from Saul to the **exile,** but whereas the Old Testament keeps these latter two versions separate (as will happen with the four versions of the Jesus story in the Gospels), in the Torah the versions were combined.

Urim and Thummim

The Old Testament never describes the nature of these, but they were somehow means of God's guiding Israel. It seems they were something like two rocks that had marks on either side signifying yes and no. You could ask God a question, and if you got two yes's or two no's, God's answer was clear; if you got a mixed message, that meant God was not answering.

Yahweh

In most English Bibles, the word "LORD" often comes in all capitals, as sometimes does the word "GOD" in a similar format. These represent the name of God, Yahweh. In later Old Testament times, Israelites stopped using the name Yahweh and started to refer to Yahweh as "the Lord." There may be two reasons. They wanted other people to recognize that Yahweh was the one true God, but this strange foreign-sounding name could give the impression that Yahweh was just Israel's tribal god, and "the Lord" was a term anyone could recognize. In addition, they did not want to fall foul of the warning in the Ten Commandments about misusing Yahweh's name. Translations into other languages then followed suit in substituting an expression such as "the Lord" for the name Yahweh. The downsides are that this ignores God's wish to be known by name (see Exodus 3), that often the text is referring to Yahweh and not some other (so-called) god or lord, and that it gives the impression that God is much more "lordly" and patriarchal than actually God is. (The form "Jehovah" is not a real word but a mixture of the consonants of Yahweh and the vowels of the word for "Lord," to remind people in reading Scripture that they should say "the Lord" not the actual name.)

Yahweh Armies

This title for God usually appears in English Bibles as "the LORD of Hosts," but it is a more puzzling expression than that implies. The word for Lord is actually the name of God, **Yahweh**, and the word for Hosts is the regular Hebrew word for armies; it is the word that appears on the back of an Israeli military truck. So more literally the expression means "Yahweh [of] Armies," which is just as odd in Hebrew as "Goldingay of Armies" would be. Yet in general terms its likely implication is clear; it suggests that Yahweh is the embodiment of or controller of all war-making power, in heaven or on earth.

9 780664 233792